Sculpting New Creativities in Primary Education

This book introduces the new term 'creativities' with cutting-edge examples of creativities research that has influenced the thinking and work of teachers and school leaders in their practice. Co-edited by one of the leading international experts in creativity and the arts, this book is packed with imaginative ideas and practical classroom suggestions underpinned by theory and research to help teachers become research-informed and research-generating.

Sculpting New Creativities in Primary Education will inspire us, invite us to think, and share ways in which research is informing and enabling a role for new and creative practices in primary education. Each chapter is collaboratively written by an academic and a practicing teacher covering areas such as: creative spaces, intercultural and interdisciplinary creativity, art, wellbeing, mathematics, STEM and leadership creativities. It importantly highlights the need to inspire, shape, and unfold change-making practices that (re-)invigorate, (re-)empower and (re-)position primary education practice.

Drawing from projects originally conducted both in the UK and beyond, this revolutionary book invites teachers, teaching assistants and school leaders to co-create ways to unlock research together as mutually informative ways of authoring change.

Pamela Burnard is Professor of Arts, Creativities and Educations at the Faculty of Education, University of Cambridge. She chairs the University of Cambridge Arts and Creativities Research Group and is co-editor-in-chief of the international journal *Thinking Skills and Creativity*.

Michelle Loughrey is a successful teacher and education leader with over two decades' experience working in education, leading schools most recently as Headteacher. As an educational consultant she provides skilled coaching and strategic support to individuals, teams, schools and trusts.

Unlocking Research
Series Editors: James Biddulph and Julia Flutter

Unlocking Research offers support and ideas for students and practising teachers, enriching their knowledge of research and its application in primary school contexts. Packed with imaginative ideas and practical suggestions, the series aims to empower teachers, teaching assistants and school leaders to take research-informed and principled approaches to making necessary changes in schools so that teaching and learning ignites the social imagination for 21st century educators and learners.

Sculpting New Creativities in Primary Education
Edited by Pamela Burnard and Michelle Loughrey

Reimagining Professional Development in Schools
Edited by Eleanore Hargreaves and Luke Rolls

Inspiring Primary Curriculum Design
Edited by James Biddulph and Julia Flutter

For more information about this series, please visit:
https://www.routledge.com/Unlocking-Research/book-series/URS

Sculpting New Creativities in Primary Education

Edited by Pamela Burnard
and Michelle Loughrey

LONDON AND NEW YORK

First published 2022
by Routledge
2 Park Square, Milton Park, Abingdon, Oxon OX14 4RN

and by Routledge
605 Third Avenue, New York, NY 10158

Routledge is an imprint of the Taylor & Francis Group, an informa business

© 2022 selection and editorial matter, Pamela Burnard and Michelle Loughrey; individual chapters, the contributors

The right of Pamela Burnard and Michelle Loughrey to be identified as the authors of the editorial material, and of the authors for their individual chapters, has been asserted in accordance with sections 77 and 78 of the Copyright, Designs and Patents Act 1988.

All rights reserved. No part of this book may be reprinted or reproduced or utilised in any form or by any electronic, mechanical, or other means, now known or hereafter invented, including photocopying and recording, or in any information storage or retrieval system, without permission in writing from the publishers.

Trademark notice: Product or corporate names may be trademarks or registered trademarks, and are used only for identification and explanation without intent to infringe.

British Library Cataloguing-in-Publication Data
A catalogue record for this book is available from the British Library

Library of Congress Cataloging-in-Publication Data
Names: Burnard, Pamela, editor. | Loughrey, Michelle, editor.
Title: Sculpting new creativities in primary education / edited by Pam Burnard and Michelle Loughrey.
Description: Abingdon, Oxon ; New York, NY : Routledge, 2022. | Series: Unlocking research | Includes bibliographical references.
Identifiers: LCCN 2021014145 | ISBN 9780367654962 (hardback) | ISBN 9780367654979 (paperback) | ISBN 9781003129714 (ebook)
Subjects: LCSH: Creative teaching. | Creative thinking—Study and teaching (Primary) | Creative ability—Study and teaching (Primary) | Education, Primary—Activity programs.
Classification: LCC LB1025.3 .S397 2022 | DDC 371.102—dc23
LC record available at https://lccn.loc.gov/2021014145

ISBN: 978-0-367-65496-2 (hbk)
ISBN: 978-0-367-65497-9 (pbk)
ISBN: 978-1-003-12971-4 (ebk)

DOI: 10.4324/9781003129714

Typeset in Bembo and Helvetica
by Apex CoVantage, LLC

Contents

Acknowledgements vii
List of contributors ix

Part 1 Sculpting primary school change 1

  1 Creativities of change in primary education 3
     Pamela Burnard and Michelle Loughrey

  2 Using school corridors to support learning: spatial creativity driving primary education 26
     Thomas Bellfield, Emma Dyer, Karolina Szynalska McAleavey and Ben Erskine

  3 Storying the journey to new spaces of intercultural creative learning 45
     James Biddulph and Pamela Burnard

  4 Animating primary schools, inside and out: enlivening learning through meaningful memory-making 62
     Elsa Lee and Sarah Stepney

  5 Posthumanist creative ecologies in primary education 76
     Anne Harris

Part 2 Sculpting primary curriculum change 89

  6 Innovating change through creativities curricula 91
     Michelle Loughrey and Richard Gerver

7 The creative pedagogue: enacting affective pathways for
interdisciplinary embodied creativity in primary education 107
Anna Hickey-Moody, Peter J. Cook and Nathan Portelli

8 Activating creativities by emphasising health and wellbeing:
a holistic pedagogical practice from Finland 123
*Kristóf Fenyvesi, Christopher S. Brownell, Jukka Sinnemäki
and Zsolt Lavicza*

9 Cultivating primary creativities in STEAM gardens 146
Donald Gray and Laura Colucci-Gray with Louise Robertson

Part 3 Sculpting 'change' differently in primary education 163

10 Unlocking creative leadership in the primary school 165
Megan Crawford, Deborah Outhwaite and Matthew Crawford

11 Learning at a snail's pace: *what if* and *what else* is happening in a
South African primary classroom? 182
Karin Murris, Joanne Peers and Nadia Woodward

12 'What can be otherwise': embodying a collective *phronesis*
(or practical wisdom) for sculpting new creativities in primary
education and beyond 203
Julia Flutter

Afterword: sculpting new creativities in primary education 221
Alison Peacock

Index 224

Acknowledgements

James Biddulph and Julia Flutter, Series Editors, for the opportunity to contribute to this unique series.

Fiona Elden, Book Administrator, for her great support in enabling us to stay on track and communicate effectively with our community of authors.

Federico Baca, artist, for his generosity in creating a work of art which captures the metaphorical message running through this book.

The learning communities voiced with/in these chapters whose new creativities are transforming primary education, building muscles of response unlocked through research that sheds light upon crucial educational matters.

This book was written and edited during the 2020-2021 international coronavirus pandemic. The editors wish to give unbounded gratitude to this remarkable community of contributing authors who showed passion, resilience, and commitment to the ecology of energetic co-authorings during a time of unprecedented challenges.

> *'Teaching for openings will always be fraught with risks, yet only by daring to seek such openings can we hope to survive – and perhaps even transform – an uncertain world'.*
> *From The Passionate Mind of Maxine Green: 'I am . . . not yet'.*
> (1998: 87)

Acknowledgements

Illustration by Federico Baca (federicobaca.com)

Creativities
spreading dandelion seeds
bringing hopeful change

This haiku was written by Michelle during an online event called '(Academic) Writing Through/ In Performance'. This event was organised by the Arts and Creativities Research Group which is chaired by Pamela Burnard. During the event, arts-science writer and children's author Isabel Thomas introduced attendees to The Sciku Project, whilst Professor Elizabeth Mackinlay, University of Queensland, Australia led a collective performance from the DRAW (Departing Radically in Academic Writing) community. Following these presentations, participants were invited to write their own/communal haikus to capture a current project.

Contributors

Thomas Bellfield
Tom is a Part II Architectural Assistant at SCABAL, an architecture practice specialising in School Design. Before joining full-time, he completed his PhD at the University of Cambridge, funded by the AHRC and within a collaboration between Dr Catherine Burke and Dominic Cullinan. Previously, Tom studied architecture at Sheffield University and has worked in architectural practice on a variety of educational, residential and healthcare projects, including alterations and repairs to listed buildings. Interested in the potential of participatory design practices, he has been involved in a variety of projects that sought to engage with different groups of people through both design and construction in primary and secondary education as well as the third sector.

James Biddulph
Following a degree in English and Music from Durham University, James won a travel scholarship and volunteered in two schools in Nepal. After this, his passion for education evolved and in 2001 he started his career following a PGCE at the Faculty of Education, University of Cambridge. In 2002, his creative approach to teaching gained him Advanced Skills Teachers (AST) status in Music and in 2003 he was awarded Outstanding New Teacher of the Year for London. Having transformed two failing schools in East London as Deputy headteacher, he was the inaugural headteacher of Avanti Court Primary School, one of the first new Hindu-based primary schools in the UK. He is now the first headteacher of the University of Cambridge Primary School, the first primary University Training School in the UK, which was recently graded as Outstanding by Ofsted.

Christopher S. Brownell
Christopher S. Brownell, (BA, MA, PhD) is an Associate Professor of Mathematics & STEM Education at Fresno Pacific University in Fresno, California. His research

interests include the role of creativity in teaching and learning, the teaching of data science, humanistic mathematics, and its impact on joyful learning. He is a Fellow of the International Society of Design and Development in Education and an author of *Math Recess Playful Learning in an Age of Disruption* (2019).

Pamela Burnard
Pamela Burnard is Professor of Arts, Creativities and Educations at the Faculty of Education, University of Cambridge (www.educ.cam.ac.uk/people/staff/Burnard/). She has published widely with 20 books and over 100 articles which advance and expand the conceptualisation and plural expression of creativities across education sectors including early years, primary, secondary, further and higher education, through to creative and cultural industries. She is co-editor of the journal *Thinking Skills and Creativity*.

Laura Colucci-Gray
Laura Colucci-Gray is Senior Lecturer in Science and Sustainability Education at Moray House School of Education and Sport, University of Edinburgh. Laura has recently co-edited 'Why Science and Art Creativities Matter. (Re)configuring STEAM for future-making education', published by Brill-i-Sense.

Peter J. Cook
Peter J. Cook is Associate Deputy Vice Chancellor (Students) for Southern Cross University and a Lecturer in Arts in the School of Education. He has the institutional responsibility for the Transitions program, which provides an evidentiary base for initiatives that enhance the student experience as they move toward, into, through and beyond the university journey. His fields of interest are in arts-based educational research with significant expertise in dance and online pedagogy. He is also publishing in the areas of student engagement and experience and transitions to higher education. Peter is an award-winning teacher and educational leader in all school sectors as well as in tertiary education.

Matthew Crawford
Matthew Crawford is the Trust Leader of Embark Federation which has grown from two schools in January 2017 to 12 schools as of July 2020. Previously head teacher at Richardson Endowed since September 2011, Matthew was designated as a National Leader of Education (an NLE) in February 2017. Matthew believes that schools should be at the heart of their communities and give their children the best possible education. The Embark Federation have an exciting curriculum which is accompanied by a rich diet of wider opportunities in music, sport, science and particularly the arts, with West End visits and links.

Megan Crawford
Megan has extensive experience of higher education, research, teaching and administration, and has worked at several universities including Cambridge, the Institute of

Education, Plymouth, and the Open University. She worked as a leadership trainer for the Work Foundation, and is very involved in governing schools, currently as the Chair of the Kingsbridge Educational Trust in Milton Keynes. She has worked on, or led, over 12 funded research projects in leadership. Her research and publications are concerned with emotion and leadership, with particular focus on leadership planning and succession, as well as policy enactment. Megan works regularly with schools.

Emma Dyer
Emma Dyer is a teacher and educational advisor who currently works across three local authorities to the west of London, supporting looked-after and previously looked-after children's education, and leading a research project about the design of therapeutic spaces in schools.

Emma began her working life as a researcher for BBC World Service radio. Her love of reading and interest in addressing disadvantage led her to teaching and she worked for several years as a primary and Reading Recovery teacher in London. Emma's doctorate in Architecture and Education (Cantab. 2018) investigated how reading spaces for beginner readers could be improved in primary schools.

Ben Erskine
Ben Erskine is Principal at Fulbridge Academy in Peterborough and Executive Principal for the Four Cs MAT. He started his career working in a Pupil Referral Unit. He has led on maths and assessment for the school and undertaken the roles of Team Leader, Assistant Principal and Vice Principal. Ben has been a leading maths teacher and an SLE (Specialist Leader of Education) for maths, assessment and leadership. He has delivered talks on curriculum for Whole Education, Cambridge Primary Review Trust, plus other education companies. Ben wrote an Assessment Beyond Levels course for Pearson and delivered CPD in schools on assessment.

Kristóf Fenyvesi
Kristóf Fenyvesi, PhD (b. 1979) – is a researcher of STEAM (Science, Technology, Engineering, Arts, and Mathematics), Trans- and Multidisciplinary Learning and Contemporary Cultural Studies in Finland, at the Finnish Institute for Educational Research, University of Jyväskylä. He is a member of the Research Group for Innovative Learning Environments and Research Group for Education, Assessment & Learning. Fenyvesi's articles have appeared on fora, such as The Notices of the American Mathematical Society, MAA Focus – Newsmagazine of the Mathematical Association of America, Nexus Network Journal, The Mathematical Intelligencer and Comparative Philosophy.

Julia Flutter
Julia Flutter has worked in education research for over 20 years as a Research Associate at the Faculty of Education, University of Cambridge, where she focused on collaborative approaches for improving classroom teaching. She was a director of the Cambridge Primary Review Trust, a not-for-profit organisation promoting

excellence in primary education and a contributing author to the Cambridge Primary Review final report, *Children, Their World, Their Education* (edited by Robin Alexander and published by Routledge, 2010). More recently, she has worked for The Chartered College of Teaching as the Research Partnerships and Networks Manager and she is currently carrying out a professional doctorate research project on phronesis and teacher professionalism.

Richard Gerver

Richard began his career in education, most notably as headteacher of the failing Grange Primary School. He famously transformed the school into one of the most acclaimed learning environments in the world and was celebrated by UNESCO and the UK Government for its incredible turnaround. Richard has since transitioned to the global stage where he delivers passionate, provocative and authentic speeches. He draws upon the first-hand experiences and unique insights garnered from frontline education to explore the links between great leadership, human potential, change and innovation. Having successfully transitioned from teacher to thought leader, Richard has had the opportunity to regularly advise governments and major corporations globally.

Donald Gray

Donald Gray is Professor of Science and Outdoor Learning at University of Aberdeen, School of Education. He has written around science education futures, outdoor learning, and children's experiences of nature.

Anne Harris

Anne M Harris is an international expert in creativity education and creative methodologies through a heuristic of creative ecologies. Anne is the series creator and editor of *Creativity, Education and the Arts* (Palgrave Macmillan), has authored over 100 articles/book chapters and 17 books on creativity-related topics, in addition to public productions of plays, films and spoken word performances, and has won over $2 million in competitive research funding since 2010. Anne is currently an Australian Research Council Future Fellow, and RMIT Vice Chancellor's Senior Research Fellow, and the Director of Creative Agency research lab: www.creativeresearchhub.com

Anna Hickey-Moody

Anna Hickey-Moody is Professor of Media and Communication at RMIT University. She is an expert in arts-based approaches to researching with children. She is interested in generating new stories about experiences of marginalisation in ways that do not re-inscribe disadvantage. Anna is known for her methodological expertise with arts practice, or practice research, which has links to contemporary debates on methodological invention. Recently she has been developing a concept of little public spheres, which theorises disadvantaged young people's creative practices as forms of civic participation. Anna also researches and publishes on masculinity and is interested in the politics and aesthetics of masculinity as embodied critique of institutionalised patterns of hegemony.

Zsolt Lavicza

Zsolt Lavicza is Professor in STEM Education Research Methods at Johannes Kepler University's Linz School of Education. From JKU he is working on numerous research projects worldwide related to technology integration into schools; leading the doctoral programme in STEAM Education at JKU; teaching educational research methods worldwide; and coordinates research projects within the International GeoGebra Institute.

Elsa Lee

Elsa Lee is an educationalist with an interdisciplinary approach centered on environmental sustainability education and place-based learning. She spent 10 years teaching science at secondary schools in the UK and Mexico before returning to university for further study. Since completing her doctorate at the University of Bath in 2013, she has worked alongside anthropologists and sociologists on a number of United Kingdom research council-funded research projects seeking to understand human relationships with/in the natural world and their behaviour towards the environment and how this intersects with education and society. Elsa has used ethnographic research techniques widely in her work in Global North and South contexts, including walking interviews and arts-based research methods.

Michelle Loughrey

Michelle is a successful teacher and education leader with over two decades' experience working in education, leading schools, including most recently as Headteacher. As an education consultant she provides skilled coaching and strategic support to individuals, teams, schools and trusts; her particular interest and specialism is in leadership development, values-led culture, and organisational change. Michelle is a trustee of the national children's charity School-Home Support.

Karin Murris

Karin Murris is Professor of Early Childhood Education at the University of Oulu (Finland) and Emerita Professor of Pedagogy and Philosophy, University of Cape Town (South Africa). She is a teacher educator and grounded in academic philosophy and a post-qualitative research paradigm, her main interests are in childhood studies and democratic post-developmental pedagogies. She was principal investigator of the Learning through Digital Play (2019-2020) and the Decolonising Early Childhood Discourses: Critical Posthumanism in Higher Education (2016-2019) projects in South Africa.

Deborah Outhwaite

Deborah Outhwaite has worked in education for more than 25 years: an 11-18 teacher for 12 years, training teachers, then spending a decade in higher education teaching undergrad and postgrad. She is the Director of the Derby Teaching Schools Alliance (DTSA), specialising in school to school support; an EdD supervisor and Internal Examiner at the University of Liverpool; and the External Examiner for the MA Ed at the University of Worcester. She is Vice-Chair of a rural Derbyshire Multi-Academy Trust, and holds a range of national roles, including being BELMAS Vice-Chair, 2020-2023. Deborah is involved in mentoring and supporting women leaders in education into senior roles in education.

Dame Alison Peacock
Dame Alison Peacock is the Chief Executive of the Chartered College of Teaching. Prior to joining the Chartered College, Dame Alison was the Executive Headteacher of The Wroxham School in Hertfordshire. Her career to date has spanned primary, secondary and advisory roles. She is an Honorary Fellow of Queens' College Cambridge, member of the Royal Society's Education Committee, a trustee of Teach First and a Visiting Professor of both the University of Hertfordshire and Glyndŵr University. Her research is published in a series of books about 'Learning Without Limits', offering an alternative approach to inclusive school improvement.

Joanne Peers
Joanne Peers is a lecturer and teaching practice convener in the BEd Foundation Phase degree programme at The Centre for Creative Education and a methods lecturer in the PGCE for early years education at The University of Cape Town in South Africa. Her unique position of working in Higher Education and fulfilling the role as collaborator with resourced and under-resourced schools in Cape Town allows an extensive amount of practice, mentoring, and relationship building. Recently her role as a researcher of the Learning through Digital Play presented another line in the network of education with children, teachers, families and communities.

Nathan Portelli
Nathan Portelli is a primary educator currently employed at Kororo Public School, on the Coffs Coast of New South Wales, Australia. On graduating from Southern Cross University in 2016, Nathan was offered this sought-after position as a targeted graduate. While studying, Nathan worked full time as a teacher's aide in special education and out-of-hours school care. Nathan was also contracted with the Gold Coast Titans as a semi-professional rugby league player. Nathan has worked across stage 1, 2 and 3 (5-12-year-olds) and coordinated whole school wellbeing, social skills and technology programme using LEGO robotics. He led his school team to receive second place at a national event. As a result of providing high-level practical placement opportunities, Nathan received a certificate for excellence in mentoring. Nathan is working towards becoming accredited as a highly accomplished teacher.

Louise Robertson
Louise Robertson is a former primary school headteacher and artist with experience of setting up and developing gardens in her primary schools.

Jukka Sinnemäki

Jukka Sinnemäki, (b.1975) is a class teacher at the Jyväskylä Christian School in Finland. He was among the top 50 finalists at the Global Teacher Prize in 2018 in Dubai. In 2019, he won the Global Teacher Award in New Delhi, India. In late 2019, Sinnemäki was selected by RoundGlass as one of the 75 world's most progressive thinkers and doers in the field of learning and from key disciplines that centre on wellbeing. Jukka has 20 years of experience in education as class teacher, subject teacher and principal. He is the founder of the KnowNow-key educational enterprise and cycle-model teaching. Sinnemäki's motto is 'learning happens when you see the unseen in every child'.

Sarah Stepney

Sarah came in to teaching 12 years ago having completed an Open University degree and a PGCE at Homerton College, Cambridge. She had an eclectic range of jobs prior to teaching, from publishing to waitressing, law, to cake making, and these employment experiences support her outlook on both life and education. Sarah joined Mayfield Primary School in 2015 and became co-headteacher in 2019. During this time she has led the implementation of 'Spirals of Enquiry', an enquiry-based approach to learning. Alongside this, Sarah and her co-headteacher have introduced outdoor learning, recognising that children benefit enormously from being outside and connecting with their environment, and that successful learning can happen in a range of ways and in a range of places.

Karolina Szynalska McAleavey

Karolina is a Senior Lecturer at the Lincoln School of Architecture and the Built Environment, University of Lincoln. She recently completed her doctorate at the University of Cambridge. Her multidisciplinary research explored how the design of secondary schools affects pupils' motivation and promotes innovative pedagogical practices. Previously, she completed an MA in Architectural History at UCL and worked as a lecturer and undergraduate course leader at the Hull School of Architecture. As a practitioner, she worked for Stem Architects on several award-winning buildings for the University of Lincoln, and has ran her own architectural practice, Karaolides Szynalska Architects, focusing on community projects.

Nadia Woodward

Nadia Woodward is a Grade 1 educator at iThemba Primary School in Cape Town, South Africa. She joined the iThemba team at the opening of the school in 2018 after having graduated with a PGCE from UCT in 2017. The school is a young school situated in Capricorn, an informal township serving children from low-income households in the area. Prior to completing her degree in education, Nadia had worked in the theatre industry for 7 years as a director and performer. While working as a performer and facilitator with Clowns Without Borders South Africa and ASSITEJ (an NPO dedicated to bringing theatre to young children), Nadia developed an interest and passion for education in South Africa. During her years working with the two organisations she spent a lot of time in rural and township schools across the country.

PART

Sculpting primary school change

This chapter explores the possibilities arising from the application of change-making practices when research is unlocked and enables a role for new and diverse creativities (diverse forms of authoring) for moving from linear, technocratic conceptions of education as 'preparation for the future' to future-making education.

CHAPTER 1

Creativities of change in primary education

Pamela Burnard and Michelle Loughrey

Introduction: creativities + hope = sowing seeds for co-authoring change

Being a primary educator in the twenty-first century is an inspiring journey, but one which has become increasingly complex. Educating children to be positive, healthy, engaged, active global citizens who are prepared for uncertainty has become even more relevant because of the complex societal challenges of global health crises, climate change, disruptive geopolitical matters and increased inequalities. Meeting the challenge of educating children necessitates new practices, new spaces and new forms of leadership. Primary education can help to create new societies where educational encounters are sculpted by new creativities to inspire change. But how are these seeds of change sown?

Primary educators are being called to make greater use of research to inspire change and to co-create ways to unlock research together to co-author change. These iterative unfoldings and seeded meshings of innovative research-informed change-making practices demand at least a radical break – and at best an accelerated change – in ways of thinking about our primary schools. This requires more than 'tinkering' with our professional practices but rather rethinking and transforming our primary education systems.

At the centre of this chapter – as (dandelion) seeds sown across its parts – are the planks of an argument and catalyst for unlocking research. In many childhood memories, blowing a seeded dandelion flower involves making a wish. Using this as a metaphor for this chapter, if you blow the seeds from a dandelion plant and make a wish, what comes true is *new creativities, each of which activates the seeds, moving in the winds of change*. Each creativities seed is a performed enactment of hope, which, we suggest, can be ground-breaking and sustainable. Brazilian educator and philosopher Paulo Freire (1995) identified hope as a foundational element that renders education possible; how hope, as a human experience, is constructed in and through social institutions such as education. How might hope be explored and mobilised? The seeds sown across all parts of this chapter (and all other chapters in this book) are intended to inspire, shape and unfold change-making practices that (re-)invigorate, (re-)empower and (re-)position primary education practice. How can this come about? By *diversifying creativities* with specific purposes in particular contexts, which helps re-balance, improve and support changes, and which generate new meaning and significance in the lives of children and educators. Here, our invitation and challenge to the reader is to perform new forms of relating, thinking, and communicating, to inspire new acts of peer group inquiry, to co-author new partnerships, and to catalyse and operationalise a multiplicity of creativities. These will inspire ways of re-imagining and shifting away from the stubborn remnants of outmoded primary education systems (in particular the dominant discourses that block innovation in pedagogic practice, school curricula and leadership roles).

How does this type of seeding-change work? In the past, creativity was seen as a clearly defined concept. As Biddulph and Burnard (Chapter 3) explain, it was largely monocultural or culturally blind. In diversifying and pluralising creativities, the whole panoply of what we usually see in primary education practices is displaced. Fostering multiple creativities should play a central role in any commitment to future-making education because a future-making education is a widening-out of possibilities for appraising and attending to our presence and our purpose in the world. This calls for different kinds of creativity, however, wholly different from the kind coveted in earlier centuries. Pre-Enlightenment associations with the concept of 'creativity' referred to 'god' or the god principle, divine aspect, god as creator, a god impulse. Throughout the Renaissance, 'creativity' became a characteristic of 'great men', not as conduits for the divine, but as 'geniuses' themselves. The origins of creativity scholarship, emerging from philosophy, psychology, aesthetics and other fields, carried a humanist focus until after the Renaissance, as it slowly turned toward the multiple nexus of creativity-aesthetics-imagination (Craft, 2015). More recently, a focus on creativity's value-creating factors has moved the rhetoric of creativity from leading economies and social good, to secure democratic and political capital in the Imagination Age, and from the source of the romantic lone genius to an era defined by constant innovation which is technologically more-than-human (Burnard & Colucci-Gray, 2020). While the ability to think and act creatively is recognised as an educational imperative, it is also one of the core competencies recognised – in and through research – by proponents of twenty-first-century (future-making) education (Harris, 2016). This is producing educators who think differently and more critically about education systems and movement makers who initiate change and are preparing to educate the next generation. This remaking and reseeing requires an openness to the multiplicity of new creativities in motion, so that we might materialise the possibilities for future-making primary education.

Long-standing creativity research provides evidence of the many different pathways needed to mitigate and manage the economic, social, and cultural contingencies that continue to make teachers feel constrained, such as the culture of accountability in primary education. This is *where* these different creativities matter as seeded sets of points and positions for realising transformational change. This is *how* new creativities open us up and set in motion the possibilities for co-authorship and co-design. This is *why* co-creating ways to unlock research together is inspiring and inspires change by mutually connecting with what children, families, and their communities need to flourish in their lives, along with what educators need to thrive in their profession. Thus, this chapter offers ways for thinking through and framing new ways in which educating for diverse creativities – for both children and teachers – offers hope for a bold new agenda of change in and through primary education.

The idea of 'multiple creativities' is not new. Howard Gardner (1983) proposed a theory of multiple intelligences which has been applied to creativities which can be bounded by subject disciplines, but also engenders different practices in and across the interrelationships between sciences and the arts. For example, where creatives often relied on different intelligences to manifest their creativity, where for example, Jane Austen, Virginia Woolf, Maya Angelou and T. S. Eliot made their reputation through linguistic intelligence and language creativity, they also opened new paths that intersected with literary creativity. Ada Lovelace, Katherine Johnson and Albert Einstein developed processes of reciprocal capture in mathematical creativity through logical-mathematical intelligence. Similarly, Hildegard von Bingen, Amy Beach, Clara Schumann and Igor Stravinsky became famous through the combination and fusing of their musical intelligence and musical creativity (Gardner, 1983).

Reconfiguring the concept and theory of multiple 'creativities', as a core element of primary education found in the moments of always becoming creative, allows us to re-think one of the most significant concepts in society, and therefore future-making primary education. From this premise, the conception of a plurality of creativities (rather than the outmoded singular notion of creativity) addresses a performative space (rather than a representational space) and acknowledges different and diverse enactments. These are both emerging and continuously re-made through material enactments, which are authored together (co-authored) by teachers and children. This authoring of diverse creativities arises in and permeates everything at the level of classroom practice. For, of course, it is teachers, not politicians, who determine the nature and quality of children's learning and it is teachers who define and shape which creativities are encouraged and become commonplace in primary schools. The research evidence reported in the UK and beyond shows the significant positive impact that diverse (posthumanising) creativities can have on motivation, engagement and achievement (Craft, 2015). The evidence of multiple creativities can offer differentiations specific to language, mathematics, science, music and art that are interdisciplinary, transdisciplinary, collaborative, communal, digital, everyday, spatial, environmental and pedagogical (Burnard & Colucci-Gray, 2020; Burnard et al., 2017).

Pamela Burnard and Michelle Loughrey

Creativities we live by: co-authoring hope

Whether a child, a headteacher, a classroom teacher, a teaching assistant, part of the support staff team or a parent/carer, being a member of a primary school learning community which is bravely building community means authoring the performative uses of diverse creativities. By this we refer to a plural conception of creativities, where language creativity (or the artful use of language) and science creativity, mathematics creativity and other types of creativity for specific purposes in particular contexts generate meaning and significance, and inspire and transform the lives of children and teachers in diverse communities. From this starting point, the advancement of multiple creativities can enable us to work differently as learning communities, to engage with children in classrooms differently. Acknowledging multiple and diverse creativities is key to opening more *hopeful possibilities for change*.

Throughout this book, you will find examples where enacting diverse creativities has brought about new or reimagined possibilities for primary education such as the learning environment, pedagogical approaches, leadership, and community building. Performing creativities are both emerging and continuously re-made through material enactments, which are authored in material relationships that are complex, dynamic, and situated. This can be seen as authoring and performing change at strategic, policy, or system levels, and seeing how this permeates everything else at the classroom practice level. In so doing, developing and sustaining the capacity to (co-)author, co-create, make, co-design, experiment, and open up to new practices and new possibilities will enable us to create together what might, to others, seem impossible or barely possible. Herein lies the potency and potential of shared action and ideas which open space for *performing* the indefinite and uncertain. In this pluralisation and multiplicity of creativities is the foundation for hope and for bringing about *hopeful communities*. In this unification lies the promise of primary education turned around by sculpting new creativities. Such education, rather than teaching children about the world, allows children to be taught by it and enables their co-creation of ways through it.

In this chapter, we invite you to ask yourself where, how and when you have authored (and/or co-authored); that is, come up with new ideas, actions, ways of doing, thinking, and being as primary educators and performed change (individually and/or collaboratively) through designing, experimenting and doing new pedagogic practices. Here we invite readers to consider what new creativities look like and how they might inspire ways of co-authoring change through storying examples of spatial creativity, intercultural creativity, interdisciplinary creativity, curricula creativity, everyday creativity, STEAM garden creativity, leadership creativity, child-centred creativity, posthuman creativity and phronesis creativity. In Figure 1.1 we have illustrated the diverse creativities found in this book as seeds, each of which has endless possibilities for bringing about transformational change.

We are learning to advance changes rapidly. Through a pivotal juncture of climate change and global health crises, the generative flux of challenges to normative

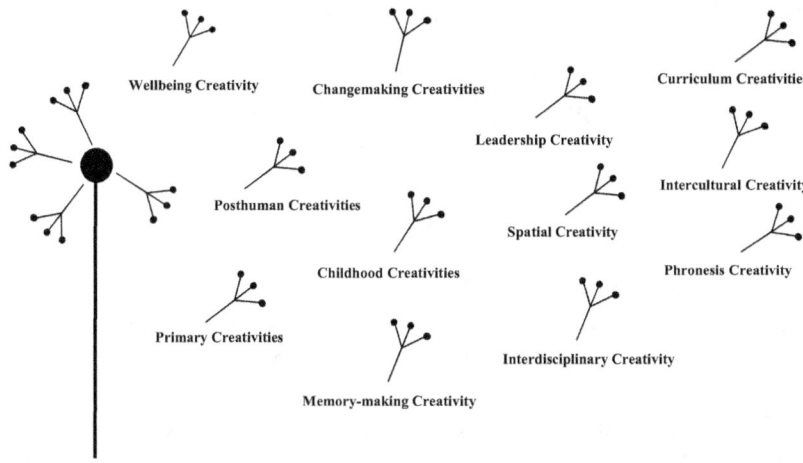

Figure 1.1 Multiple and diverse creativities as seeds of change

educational modalities has intensified. These challenges include shifting and blurring divisions between subject areas; the need to actively engage all pupils in blended face-to-face and online learning; the widening gaps of inequality; and the necessity of rethinking the very structures and routines of day-to-day school life.

- How can primary school communities decide together what and whom they are capable of becoming and re-invent themselves through diverse creativities to empower social, cultural, and environmental changes and sustainability?
- How can primary school communities transcend the negativity of fake news, the force that is social media, and the onslaught on democracy that is silencing people?
- How can primary school communities forge new pathways for their children, for themselves and the communities they serve?

These are imperatives that pervade all contemporary primary educational discourse. These are the imperatives of hope which fuel the unique opportunities arising from sculpting new creativities in primary education advanced in each of the chapters of this book.

So, we ask, *what* changes might help in diversifying and sculpting new creativities as seeds for change? How might new creativities open up the space and time for unlocking research and inspiring change in primary education? How does 'sculpting' speak to the performative agenda of new creativities in shaping and moulding new and re-imagined practices in primary education? And, importantly, given this amazing opportunity to decide together, what do learning communities need to initiate *new* pathways for ecological change in and reforming of primary education?

Creativities we teach by: co-authoring hope

Primary educators' work involves teaching creatively and teaching for creativity. Some of the most influential research informing and transforming practice in primary education includes the work of Anna Craft (2015). Her work invites teachers to seek innovative ways to shape the curriculum in response to children's needs. She introduces new understandings of how teaching for creativity and teaching creatively manifest differently. Importantly, she argues that we need 'possibility thinking' when we consider how creativities enable more *hopeful futures* for children.

Newspaper headlines, Twitter feeds and the educational press indicate a growing appetite for fundamental change in education in the UK and elsewhere; a desire to create a new normal (see Figure 1.2).

We can also reflect on the extensive research conducted on creative teaching and creative learning (see for example, Fenyvesi et al., 2020), which examines features of a creative pedagogical stance and creative curricula in primary education and the need to engage learners differently, in both individualised and collaborative creativities, where arts, sciences and mathematics creativities meet and matter (Burnard & Colucci-Gray, 2020).

Then there is the idea of creativity emerging from an interactive network of creative agents, where creativity is no longer vested in an individual and exercised through a chain of command that runs the traditional model of authoring something new. Rather, it is the product of a dynamic and interactive process of collaboration, the property of a creative ecology (Harris, 2016). We can also think about the systems of *distributed creativity* (DeZutter, 2011), *intercultural creativity* (Tang, 2019) and forms of *group creativity* (Sawyer, 2003), which bring the operation of face-to-face collaboration into sharper focus. There is also *participatory creativity* (Clapp, 2016), *everyday creativity* (Szabo, Fenyvesi, Soundararaj, & Kangasvieri, 2019) and *individual creativity* (Hermida, Clem, & Guss, 2019). These diverse creativities offer a widening of the possibilities for re-seeing and re-thinking; for sculpting new creativities in primary education.

Increasingly, primary educators are keen to apply educational research to the task of, and necessity of, reauthoring change – thinking of new strategies and transforming some of the existing structures and products of primary education which have been complicit in the production of stale and outmoded practices.

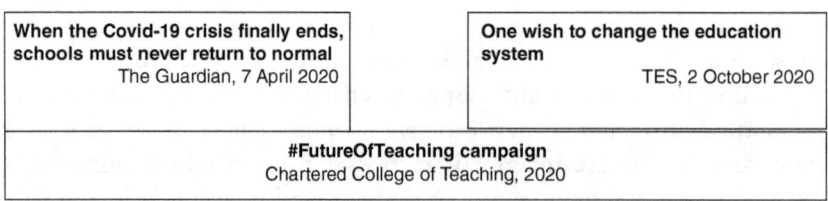

Figure 1.2 Examples of education headlines in 2020

There is change afoot for discarding, disassembling, and deconstructing the contested spaces and practices that lack a way to effect change in educational systems which are often bound to political systems and pressures.

Now, if *sculpting new creativities*, as we argue throughout this chapter (and book), is the means by which *research is unlocked to initiate change*, and *if the work of primary educators is to creatively apply the latest and shifting educational research and thinking*, transcending paralysing policy that creates doubt and uncertainty, then how can we reformulate change agendas in primary education? How can we inspire primary headteachers to undertake the formidable task of reconfiguring aims and expectations, and mobilise new ways of co-authoring change-making practices in and through research together for future-making education? And how do we learn to support and scaffold new ways of knowing, being and doing, to enhance children's distinctive and diverse styles of creativities, to create quick and nimble change solutions and alternative ways into new subject disciplines, and new ways of working collaboratively and at the individual level? These are exceptionally important questions in the name of innovating primary education.[1]

It is more important than ever that we (as humans as well as educators) are able to adapt to the unexpected and unknown; more than that, that we are able to shape how we and others respond to the unexpected and unknown. In other words, we do not know what we are preparing pupils for; what we do know is that whatever the immediate, medium, and long-term future holds, we have a role and a duty to enable and empower our pupils to be confident, independent, thinking, discerning, and resilient problem solvers and creatives.

Creativities we lead by: re-imagining hope

But how? With so many perceived barriers to achieving the school, classroom, curriculum, and opportunities for our pupils to which we aspire, can we effect such transformational change? If we carry a vision of a hopeful future for our children, we must ask questions and hypothesise that there can be a different way. *Creativities of hope* are born out of this desire to think about things differently or to find new ways. They offer us research-informed ways to re-imagine our education system at both a national and local level, in individual schools and across clusters and in anyone's classroom. By unlocking research we can develop our understanding of the ways in which diverse creativities can re-empower, re-ignite and re-invigorate those creativities of hope so that we can consider the realms of the possible which can positively affect children, educators, schools, and wider communities.

Here there is an important point for leaders, primary educators and children which speaks to the fear of public failure. Primary educators tend to be risk averse when it comes to setting up learning cultures. Risk taking is feared because it involves failures and mistakes. The fear of failure and mistakes makes people stick with familiar ideas and solutions rather than try different and possibly better options. We know that mistakes help us improve. If children hold such a view, they are likely to realise that failures and mistakes are normal and that there are opportunities to progress. This will encourage them to participate in more challenging learning activities. So, what does this mean for leaders and educators in primary schools? It is critical that creativity is demonstrably valued and celebrated and that intellectual risk taking is supported and encouraged. This might require reconfigured leadership so that structures not only regulate, but define and enable educators and communities to enact diverse creativities. Leaders, of both schools and classrooms, need to reflect on whether the ethos and systems which have been established support pupils and educators to be comfortable with uncertainty and facilitate time and space for such enactments. Unlocking research shows us not only that hope and affect are enhancers of creative performance but that, through the enhancement of diverse creativities in our settings, meaningful change to our systems, our environment, our curriculum and our professional training and learning can be achieved.

So, how can leaders inspire and counteract fear of risk taking when embracing diverse creativities in primary education? This needs to be considered at three levels. First, at the strategic level, it is about how diverse creativities are defined, framed and embodied in/as discursive parameters that construct the concept of 'creativity' and diverse creativities in strategic decisions (for example, at curriculum level). Second, at the system level, it is about how whole-school practices (specific policies, timetabling, assessment) work to operationalise and differentiate diverse creativities. Thirdly, finally, at the individual and social level, it is about how individuals can collectively choreograph and highlight multiple creativities to co-create new conditions and practices of possibility. So, how does this help reformulate the ways in which diverse creativities can be engaged to support change in primary education? Here is one such example.

Box 1: Storying a school's leadership in facilitating a creative ecology

When Michelle was a headteacher, she worked with the children, the staff, and the wider school community to co-construct a culture where creativity was actively encouraged for its pedagogical significance, to (co-) create new and impactful structures, processes and provisions, and as means with which to retain autonomy and control of government edicts. Thinking differently about the systems level of school practice was essential since these elements needed to support the cultivation of this culture. For instance, reimagining accountability structures was an important part of developing teachers' individual professional autonomy to be innovative and take risks. This impacted meaningful change through more creativities being generated across the curriculum, all of which materialised the possibilities for reconstructing the learning culture for future-making education.

> Although achieving meaningful change was not always straightforward, fostering a creative ecology at the strategic, system, and individual level resulted in a greater, shared capacity to respond to, to be resilient to, and to adapt to its challenges.

Creativities we identify with

The need to work creatively pervades all areas of work in primary schools, and it could be argued that the need to work more creatively has never been more pronounced. Grasping the opportunity to create a new normal, for us to reimagine our schools, our curricula, our pedagogies, engagement with our pupils, our communities, and with each other as educators will give rise to a complex school ecosystem which can bring about transformational change.

We have an ethical *response*-ability to heed the call for a different stance towards primary education, which is open to creating new practices evidenced in the latest studies, which more and more frequently emphasise the role of creative self-beliefs. According to these studies, creative self-beliefs qualify creative achievements, at least to some extent, but are also significant for lower-level creativity, including creative thinking or solving everyday problems. Creative self-beliefs describe people's convictions about their own abilities and the nature of those traits that are of key importance for activities that require creativity (Beghetto & Karwowski, 2017).

We aim to challenge the myths and (mis)understandings that some teachers are creative and some are not creative – if we want educators to identify with diverse creativities in their classrooms and their schools we need them to identify with creativity (a mindset) and also see that they already possess the required 'skills' and mindsets. Creative self-awareness refers to an individual's perception of their strengths or weaknesses within the frame of creativity and the possibilities of changing those. It also encompasses creative metacognition – a combination of self- and contextual knowledge used in decision making about one's own creative functioning as well as one's conviction about the nature of creativity, known as creative mindset (Beghetto & Karwowski, 2017).

Creative mindset refers to a subset of implicit theories of creativity; more specifically, mindsets deal with the perceived roots of creativity and its perceived stability (fixed mindset) versus changeability (growth mindset). Some individuals (so-called entity theorists) tend to view creativity as a fixed, trait-like characteristic and do not believe that it can be changed, when others (the so-called incremental theorists) view creativity as a malleable competence that can be successfully trained. This speaks to the agenda of 'teaching for creativity' and encourages educators to challenge their views of each other and their pupils about perceived creativeness (Beghetto & Karwowski, 2017).

These are all important research findings about the need to inspire primary educators to view themselves differently. Educators are innately creative beings;

it is not something we need to learn to be or strive to become. We enact diverse creativities every day because we are typically looking for new ways of looking at things to improve our provision, develop our practice and respond to the needs of our pupils and our communities. We do this as part of our classrooms', our schools' and our own professional evolution and we do this because we are and need to be reflexive and responsive to external influence, invariably beyond our control. Primary school educators are creators and change makers because what they do does have an impact; they make a difference. What if every primary school educator left school every day feeling like a creative? Think of the possibilities. Recognising (creative) educators as creative learners too empowers educators to think creatively and so to teach creatively, and to teach for creativity, taking risks and thus realising creativities of hope.

So, creativity is not an innate, invariable talent: on the contrary, it is a plural, multidimensional, participatory enactment. Research has shown that children can leverage considerable influence and genuinely engage as co-authors in and of their learning (as evidenced in Chapter 8 and Chapter 11 of this book). It is important for educators to reflect on how they can and should give children autonomy so that their understanding of the world, and their place in it, helps them to feel safe, reassured and empowered about their future. We are seeing, around the world, that children are increasingly making their voices heard, and they are becoming active at local and even global levels. Many primary-age children are highly motivated and are able to use their enthusiasm and motivation to effect change by motivating the adults in their lives to make positive changes. To develop diverse creativities and whole-school creative ecologies, the learning environment should encourage the community to explore, be open to new ideas, take risks, and be imaginative and curious. While some of these features can be perceived as potential threats in terms of classroom management and teachers' self-efficacy in the learning environment, an inclusive learning environment should encourage children to explore, to be open to new ideas, to take risks and to form positive relationships (Cremin & Chappell, 2019).

In the next section, we feature an international project in which educators from across Europe formed a professional learning community to reimagine what happens when we posit a certain complementarity between collaboratively constructed 'everyday creativity' and 'transdisciplinary creativity'. What if diverse creativities can be integrated as central to classroom practice? What if education is the means by which a society ensures its own future? Then how might diverse creativities offer different answers to the kinds of future-making education that primary education should entail?

The 'everyday creativity' of teachers' professional learning

'Everyday creativity' is about real-world learning. It is fostered by seeking a better understanding of the inter- and transdisciplinary collaboration that is inherent in the transformation of STEM into STEAM to address the shortcomings of curricula that are still largely subject-based. It relates to one's grasping of one's life as being of the world, not 'a part' or 'apart' from it, and of opening up a path which invites participation. Everyday creativity is about how we come to live and think together, to create together, to teach and learn together, transcending a view of 'subject' silos and developing enactments of new learning co-created by the teachers and children in the process of performing 'everyday creativity', 'group creativity', 'collective creativity', 'mathematical creativity', 'musical creativity' and so on in the classroom. Here each creativity interpenetrates another, looping around and through one another, and establishing a 'creative ecology' or ecological assemblage.

In a European Union Erasmus[2] + study of teachers' professional learning, 20 teachers from Hungary, Italy, the Netherlands, and Romania were invited to work together to rethink what constitutes 'everyday creativity' in the classroom.[3] The teachers' handbook, an online publication called *Everyday creativity: Boosting creative resources with Finnish models of education* (Szabo et al., 2019),[4] offers a set of brilliant published materials sharing details of a teacher education enquiry, illustrating and outlining a vision of creative ecologies that emerged in the learning community of the project.[5] The researchers asked:

- How do teachers discursively reconstruct their pathway of learning?
- How did the teachers in the study reflect on diverse creativities and the environment (human and material alike) in which they developed their follow-up projects?

The handbook shares teachers' self-reflective course assignments as well as their reports on their experimental and exploratory follow-up projects. This illustrates how teachers' reflections can become shared narratives through which teachers discursively reconstruct not only their professional identities, but also their visions of diverse creativities and their perceptions of the local ecologies they practise as part of their professional learning communities. The course included a module on 'Developing learner-centred indoor and outdoor environments', which offers several tools for creative co-creation in local ecologies of learning.

The first stage of exploration of already existing learning environments set the ground for the reflection on local educational policies (for example, who has the right to display something on the wall, to introduce new arrangements of furniture, to propose tasks, and so on; Szabo et al., 2019), which then led to new types of processes and products, such as re-designing activities in which pupils are tightly involved. This involved pupils, their parents/carers or teacher colleagues in classroom design as a game-changing innovation which built on preferences and viewpoints that might be missing from the teacher's personal/professional practice.

The teachers transformed learning environments, for example, a new setting with pupil-influenced design, calling external explorers and local community members alike to rethink the material environment and renew local educational practices in terms of modalities, practice principles and forms of authorship. They co-created innovation which led to a new set-up becoming the point of departure of further renewal – thus launching a cycle of iteration (akin to design thinking or participatory action research) in creative renewal.

Teachers were invited to submit videos in which they tell the story of the transformation of a learning environment of their choice. By defining the modality of the assignment, the goal was to make teachers observe their work environment (that is to say, the school) in a mediated way, that is, through the lens of a camera, to enhance teachers becoming an observer. Asking teachers to tell a story of transformation, the aim was to assemble narratives in which teachers position themselves in the coordination system of pedagogical practices and local community relations.

In the figures that follow, we highlight some aspects of teachers' assignments and videos (the narratives present the transformation in retrospect; sometimes the transformation of the learning environment happened a long time ago).

Figure 1.3 The spirit of a school by Alpár Ferencz-Salamon, Romania (https://bit.ly/2Y8aX5s)

'Students have played a major part in designing the school environment'.
'Our theatre room has a major role in enhancing communal feeling'.

Figure 1.4 Student community space by Enikő Tankó, Romania (https://bit.ly/2RzBPsG)

'A former classroom turned into a community space for students'.
'It is an open space with colourful pillows, bean bag chairs and seats which can be rearranged'.

Figure 1.5 Sense of Joy by Boglárka György (https://www.youtube.com/watch?v=CfyWiyrj2ZE)

'To create a space where kids feel encouraged to express themselves, even if they have unconventional ideas'.
'Using many colourful, different-sized spheres in the classroom keeping the openness, lightness of space in creating an engaging space for students'.

Figure 1.6 Teachers as designers by Mária Szidónia Ráduly (https://www.youtube.com/watch?v=ZHp8TFMpJP8)

'The classroom is divided into centres, one for each subject. In these centres, children have the opportunity to collaborate and help each other'.

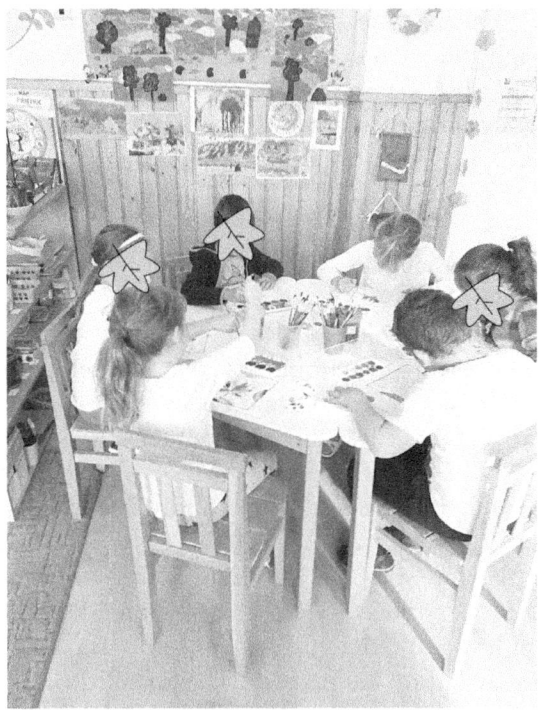

Figure 1.6 (Continued)

Figure 1.7 Flexible classroom by Edit Páll (https://www.youtube.com/watch?v=ZF14YdrGdZU)

'The layout of the classroom can be changed according to the activity and needs of the teaching'.

While the participants explored their own classrooms from an external perspective through the videos, the module portfolios combined their observations in their own Finnish schools and then led to comparisons between their own education system and other systems. The module portfolio 'The spirit of Finnish schools: Developing learner-centred indoor and outdoor environments', was completed with a focus on:

- 'maker spaces' inside and outside the schools;
- mentoring;
- inspiring spaces and solutions;
- mobility in learning environments (e.g. dynamics of changing classrooms, moving inside the classroom); and finally
- hidden curriculum in learning environments.

Participating teachers were assigned an individual follow-up project that would enhance 'everyday creativity' in their local school environment and community. The participants were first asked to identify a pedagogical challenge relevant in their local context. Then they planned a local action to address the challenge, implemented the plan in collaboration with colleagues, evaluated the implemented action, and assessed sustainability and future actions. Teachers submitted written reports on their follow-up projects and those reports were condensed for the published handbook. Follow-up projects were organised by the types of changes that the teachers initiated in their local school communities and by the main goals identified from the teachers' reports (see Szabo et al., 2019, pp. 86–89). Five of the follow-up projects included the creative transformation of a learning environment. In this study, we learn how 'everyday creativity' meets 'transdisciplinary creativity' with regards to doing differently, seeing and responding differently, and allowing us to be open to what is beyond, outside and across disciplines.

Rethinking the ecology and contribution of new creativities to primary education

In primary education we often think about school practices as separate entities that are made, unmade and lived through the existence and negotiation of hopes and practices. These 'new beginnings' are often conceived in response to external influences, which may result in schools bringing about change that feels enforced rather than change that is chosen. This can sometimes result in change feeling finite and superficial rather than meaningful and transformative. So how do we make the system more creative? Where change is meaningful and sustainable? And how can we use creativities to make the system evolve? By unlocking research, we can challenge the dominant stories we have come to know about change in schools and open up new possibilities for whole-school change.

Thinking of whole-school changes not as separate entities but as enactments of multiple beginnings empowers educators to take charge of the change agenda in schools and think about it in a different way. We can achieve this by moving away from the notion of change as a linear narrative, towards seeing it as new beginnings which get produced and conceived in multiple ways, and which are continuously reconfigured by multiple and diverse creativities.

Arguing for a new way to enact whole-school systemic change creatively and sustainably, Anne Harris (2016) has advanced the concept of 'creative ecologies' which vibrantly and productively entangle in professional learning communities, such as primary education. Refraining from advancing one-off creative events in a school, or seeing creativity as the reserve of the arts, or generic conceptions of creativity, Harris's research foregrounds creativity's inherent nature as multiple, relational and active. It focuses on pluralism, where nothing is singular, static or unified, but always many, evolving and interwoven.

Creative ecologies (Harris, 2016) takes into account the entire context and community of various stakeholders that are engaged in primary education. The model summarised in Figure 1.8 includes five loci which are all interrelating – as products, processes, partnerships, policies, and the physical environment – and that are all, always and already, interwoven and interconnecting to (em-)power school policies, systems, and practices.

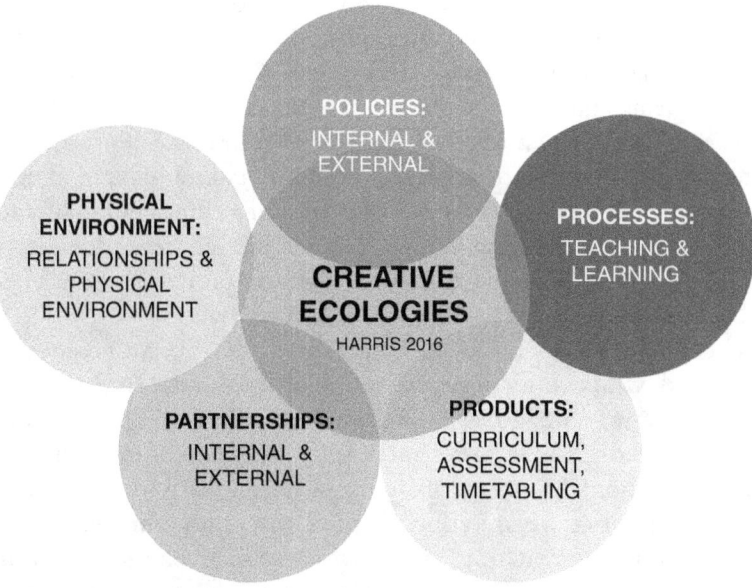

Figure 1.8 Creative ecologies (adapted from Harris, 2016)

Viewing primary schools as creative ecologies is critical to each professional learning community, seen as dynamic configurations bringing into confluence a multiplicity of discourses and understandings about what is perceived to be significant and worthy of change and at the core of our 'everyday experiences' and 'everyday creativity' as teachers and learners, as well as citizens and consumers of knowledge in contemporary societies. We do so by seeking to develop the educational space as a site for pluralist dialogue across policy, systems and practice with the aim of gaining deeper understanding of how we can catalyse and (re-)configure change; that is, enactments of diverse creativities that provide provocative, fresh and diverse educational experiences.

For primary school educators, ways of developing whole-school approaches to learning and teaching creatively, and learning and teaching for diverse creativities, involves recognising that primary schools can be sites for re-imagining and re-operationalising radical change in professional learning communities. We can unlock research and use it to better understand and inform our practice, rather than defend it. Thus we can move beyond neoliberal notions that separate research, practice and 'workplace readiness' and move toward an environmental, ecological, more holistic approach to catalysing change from the ground up in professional development for practising teachers (and in teacher training programmes).

With Harris' (2016) creative ecologies model at the centre, our theoretical framework (see Figure 1.9) proposes a scaffold from which to rethink an ecology of primary education infused by multiple and diverse creativities. Through this model we seek to demonstrate how policies, processes, products, partnerships, and a physical environment could be developed with the potential to affect meaningful change in classrooms, schools, and beyond. The framework seeks to invite a way of configuring and co-authoring, with multi- and inter-stakeholders, collaborative *activities* to sculpt new normals in our schools, our classrooms, and in our education systems such as exploration, play, hypothesising, and making connections. These activities promote *participatory creativity*, or doing things differently together, highlight the importance of interconnection and interconnectedness in (co-)authoring change to bring about practices which are co-produced, interrelated, relational, and communicated in ways that are co-constitutive.

The final layer in Figure 1.9 highlights the diverse creativities featured in this book, which offer different ways of (co-)authoring to prompt thinking which reviews, reimagines and redefines the foci of schools. These creativities are signposted chapter by chapter so you can explore them in more depth later in this book. Through enacting diverse creativities, the focus shifts from which creativities we are educating for, or simply with, as we engage in creative learning and teaching, and moves towards seeking ways of understanding the nature and the logics of knowing-being-doing differently as professional communities.

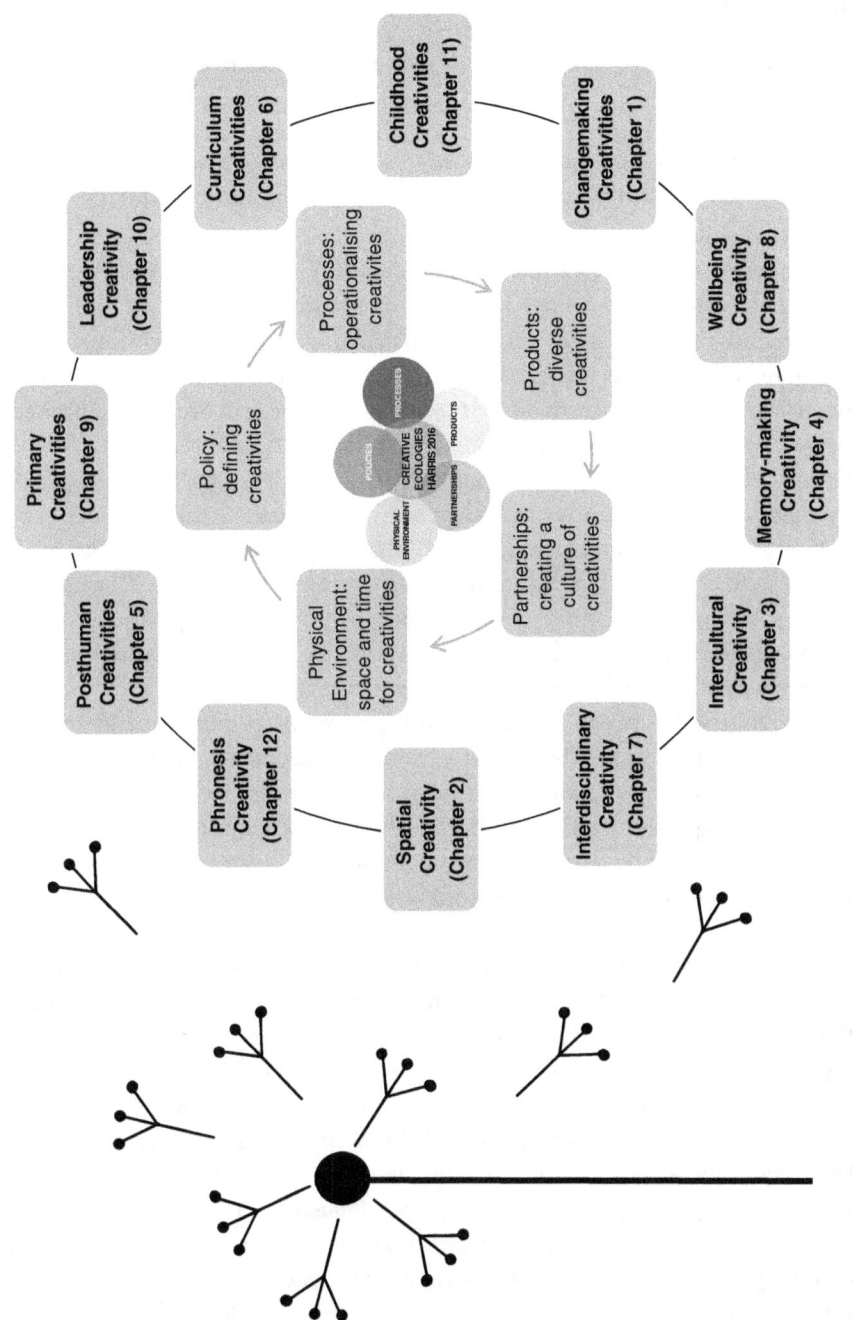

Figure 1.9 Co-authoring new creativities from innovative research-informed practice

A summary of key points about the contribution of diverse creativities to primary education

- Unlocking research can enable us to challenge what constitutes 'creativity' and the expansion of 'creativities' as inherently pluralistic where nothing is singular, static or unified, but always many, evolving and interwoven (see particularly Chapter 4 by Lee and Stepney, Chapter 5 by Anne Harris, Chapter 7 by Hickey-Moody, Cook and Portelli, and Chapter 8 by Fenyvesi, Brownell, Sinnemäki and Lavicza).
- Unlocking research can enable us to (co-)author change and to move away from the right-wrong dichotomy, as well as to re-think the roles of educators and learners, since working towards more sustainable societies requires practices that are co-produced, interrelated, interconnected, relational and communicated in ways that are co-constitutive (see Chapter 4 by Lee and Stepney, Chapter 6 by Loughrey and Gerver and Chapter 7 by Hickey-Moody, Cook and Portelli).
- Unlocking research in primary schools means unleashing possibility thinking by envisioning possibilities that may seem unrealistic at first glance, but hold the potential for innovative solutions that are all, always and already, interwoven and interconnecting, and (em-)powering change to school policies, systems and practices through co-creation of possibilities spaces and collective phronesis (see Chapter 2 by Bellfield, Dyer, Synalska and Erskine, Chapter 5 by Anne Harris and Chapter 12 by Julia Flutter).
- Unlocking research can identify diverse ways of balancing the sometimes-opposing requirements that dictate the implementation of strict benchmarks alongside creative leadership and innovative practices (see all chapters and particularly Chapter 3 by Biddulph and Burnard, Chapter 6 by Loughrey and Gerver, Chapter 8 by Fenyvesi, Brownell, Sinnemäki and Lavicza, Chapter 9 by Gray, Colucci-Gray with Robertson, and Chapter 10 by Crawford, Outhwaite and Crawford).
- Primary schools can be sites for re-imagining and re-operationalising radical change as in intercultural and interdisciplinary creative learning communities (see Chapter 3 by Biddulph and Burnard, Chapter 7 by Hickey-Moody, Cook, and Portelli, and Chapter 11 by Murris, Peers and Woodward) and activating holistic pedagogic creativities which emphasise health and wellbeing (see Chapter 8 by Fenyvesi, Brownell, Sinnemäki and Lavicza).
- Primary schools are intercultural sites filled with communities whose creative *self-belief*, *creative self-awareness* and *creative mindsets* all bring agency to an ecological approach to primary education in order to re-think how creativities of change in primary education can be understood in terms of processes of whole-school co-inventions (i.e. creative ecologies) (see all chapters in Part 1, particularly Chapter 3 by Biddulph and Burnard, and Chapter 5 by Anne Harris) and sculpting 'change' differently (as voiced in Part 3 Chapter 10, Chapter 11 and Chapter 12).

If we want to prepare children to grapple with the future and to know and hope in new ways about a world that is complex and generative, yet one we will help to generate, then we need to be clear and confident about what this means, including practising diverse creativities of hope. Together we can rethink and create ways of articulating and creating hope as new ways to access and mobilise whole-school change, resources, and creativity-related processes, values, and experiences. This will empower and educate the whole community to develop the capacities to act and inspire, and to release and sustain their own diverse creativities to decide together what they are capable of becoming and their relationship with the future.

Earlier in the chapter, we introduced the imperative of supporting conversations about ways in which diverse creativities can be embedded in the learning cultures of a school ecology to bring about the changes that we hope for and aspire to. By unlocking research, we can empower educators with a new vocabulary not just to articulate their hopes with, but to realise them too. Here, we invite you to engage in community unlockings of research in practice as starting points to explore some ways in which your school might begin the conversation. This will enrich the understanding of the processes through which primary education might embrace new creativities as important paths to establishing change.

Unlocking research in practice: provocations for group discussion

1. How can primary educators play a key role (for example, alternating between showing children what diverse creativities look like and encouraging children to think about their own diverse creativities) in encouraging and celebrating diverse creativities across the school and within the classroom?
2. What would primary school/children's learning look like with 'everyday creativity' and 'transdisciplinary creativity' embedded to support a more holistic, embodied, and relational growing of wellbeing and for living sustainable lives?
3. Given that it is primary educators, not politicians, who determine the nature and quality of children's learning, how can primary educators encourage and translate diverse creativities to every child's education and into every classroom experience?
4. What kinds of creativities matter to children in your school? Which creativities lie at the heart of the curiosity of the young and their openness to the world? What forms of co-authoring/co-designing appear to live in the space of children's worlds that are of interest to and distinctive to the digital age?
5. What is the potential of sculpting new creativities as seeds – for taking a participatory approach, engaging as co-authors and co-designers with/in our community – of change-making education and future-making education?

Notes

1 For further reading about particular conceptions of creativity or particular theories about how creativity is performative and productive of generative possibilities in primary education including: (a) how we navigate multiple creativities in primary education classrooms inspired by transdisciplinarity or reconfiguring STEAM boundaries and subject disciplines; (b) disrupting the outcomes-based models of schooling by mobilising the kinds of arts-based educational innovations that STEAM offers; and (c) taking ownership of recommendations from commissions, reviews and testing and Ofsted frameworks, see Burnard et al. (2017).
2 See Erasmus+ | EU programme for education, training, youth, and sport (europa.eu)
3 See Everyday Creativity (creativeschools.eu)
4 See Everyday Creativity - TEACHERS' HANDBOOK (creativeschools.eu)
5 To find more about this project, use this link to hear a keynote speech by Tamás Szabó in which he talks about the Everyday Creativity project in the wider context of teacher education: Toward the renewal of spatial practices for multilingualism: Applying a schoolscape approach - YouTube

References

Beghetto, R. A., & Karwowski, M. (2017). Toward untangling creative self-beliefs. In M. Karwowski & J. C. Kaufman (Eds.), *Explorations in creativity research. The creative self: Effect of beliefs, self-efficacy, mindset, and identity* (pp. 3–22). Cambridge, MA: Elsevier Academic Press. http://doi.org/10.1016/B978-0-12-809790-8.00001-7

Burnard, P., & Colucci-Gray, L. (Eds.). (2020). *Why science and arts creativities matter: (Re-)configuring STEAM for future-making education.* Amsterdam: Brill-I-Sense.

Burnard, P., Dragovic, T., Jasilek, S., Fenyvesi, K., Rolls, L., Durning, A., & Biddulph, J. (2017). The art of co-creating possibility spaces for fostering STEAM practices in primary education. In X. Du & T. Chemi (Eds.), *Innovation and change in education cross-cultural perspectives* (pp. 247–281). Gistrup, Denmark: River Publishers.

Clapp, E. P. (2016). *Participatory creativity: Introducing access and equity to the creative classroom.* Abingdon: Routledge.

Craft, A. (2015). *Creativity, education and society: Writings of Anna Craft.* Stoke-on-Trent, Staffordshire: Trentham Books.

Cremin, T., & Chappell, K. (2019). Creative pedagogies: A systematic review. *Research Papers in Education.* Advance online publication. https://doi.org/10.1080/02671522.2019.1677757

DeZutter, S. (2011). Distributed creativity in performing groups: A case study. In C. Lobman & B. O'Neill (Eds.), *Play and culture series volume 11: Play and performance* (pp. 237–260). Lanham, MD: University Press of America.

Fenyvesi, K., Lehto, S., Brownell, C., Nasiakou, L., Lavicsa, Z., & Kosola, R. (2020). Learning mathematical concepts as a whole-body experience: Connecting multiple intelligences, creativities and embodiments with the STEAM framework. In P. Burnard & L. Colucci-Gray (Eds.), *Why science and art creativities matter: (Re-)configuring STEAM for future-making education* (pp. 300–336). Amsterdam: Brill-I-Sense.

Freire, P. (1995). *Pedagogies of hope.* London: Bloomsbury.

Gardner, H. (1983). *Frames of mind: The theory of multiple intelligences*. Basic Books.

Harris, A. (2016). *Creative ecologies: Fostering creativity in schools*. creativeresearchhub.com.

Hermida, Y., Clem, W., & Guss, C. D. (2019, September 18). The inseparable three: How organisation and culture can foster individual creativity. *Frontiers in Psychology*. https://doi.org/10.3389/fpsyg.2019.02133

Sawyer, K. (2003). *Group creativity: Music, theatre collaboration*. Erlbaum Associates.

Szabo, T., Fenyvesi, K., Soundararaj, G., & Kangasvieri, T. (2019). *Everyday creativity: Boosting creative resources with Finnish models of education. Teachers' handbook*. University of Jyvaskyla. Retrieved from https:/tinyurl.com/everyday-creativity-book

Tang, M. (2019, September 4). Fostering creativity in intercultural and interdisciplinary teams: The victory model. *Frontiers in Psychology*. https://doi.org/10.3389/fpsyg.2019.02020

CHAPTER 2

Using school corridors to support learning: spatial creativity driving primary education

Thomas Bellfield, Emma Dyer, Karolina Szynalska McAleavey and Ben Erskine

Introduction

School environments can be designed and developed over time to enrich teaching and learning across the whole curriculum, whether in formal, informal or hidden spaces. In some schools, however, the educational focus often falls exclusively on teaching and learning activities. The design of the buildings and classrooms in which they take place and their relevance to educational experience and outcomes are rarely considered or explicitly acknowledged by teachers and school leaders.

Questioning and shaping the relationship between education and the environments in which it takes place *can* strengthen relationships between staff, students, education (as experience), school (as institution) and their wider communities. However, its success most often depends on a combination of *who, how, when* and *why* things are done rather than any specific outcome. This work can take many forms. It might require designing and building new physical spaces, from small extensions to whole new buildings, or adapting existing spaces. It might also involve using timetables to develop innovative ways of using spaces or animating a school's use of space through specific pedagogies. Such work might be undertaken at different points in a school's life with the involvement or exclusion (intentional or not) of different members of the school community. It might be of varying duration, reactive or proactive, and occur once or repeatedly. The effects can be diverse, immediate and delayed, intentional and unintentional, known/able and unknown/able. Ideally, however, this work matters most when it unfolds through collaborative approaches with different specialists working together.

Accordingly, our aim in this chapter is to encourage and support those who work in and with schools to *engage proactively and creatively with the relationship between education and the environments in which education takes place*. It is this *work*, in all its diversity, that we refer to as (practices of) 'spatial creativity'. As a group of four – two architects, an education advisor and a headteacher – we have been building on the example of the headteacher's own school, Fulbridge Academy, in particular, the decorated network of school corridors, to ask what else the concept of creativity, with respect to spaces beyond the traditional classroom, might suggest in a primary school environment. This chapter began in conversation with Ben Erskine, Fulbridge Academy's headteacher, who guided us through the evolution of the Fulbridge corridors and his team's motivation in incorporating them into the creative curriculum. Ben's thoughts form the basis of the first part of this chapter and are tightly woven within the main text, to which we have added excerpts from our original conversation. To this, we bring our background of academic research in architecture and education and our individual specialities of reading and literacies, of collaborative space-making with students, and of international examples of educational architecture and design. We aim to offer an alternative to the current, prevalent approach in English schools that favours construction according to centrally coordinated standardised drawings and specifications and the prioritisation of 'value for money'. We also suggest some useful texts that we hope you might be persuaded to delve into. These include a text about reading and the body (McLaughlin, 2015); a guide to co-design with students (Hofmann, 2014); and a proposal that cities in themselves should be viewed and used as schools, with urban design centres created to support students in their individual interests (Ward & Fyson, 1973).

The evolution of Fulbridge Academy's corridors: planning a creative approach

> *… that was 'the thing' to have, a thematic or creative curriculum [. . .]. So we took that a step further and thought, the amount of children we've got in the school who have a very deprived background, therefore haven't even been to the nature reserves or the big park in Peterborough, how are they ever going to understand what it could look like in the war time or the truce time? Even we find that hard to understand as an adult with a lot of experiences.*
> (Ben Erskine, Headteacher, Fulbridge Academy, November 2020)

As with many English primary schools, the corridors of Fulbridge Academy are a dominant feature. Built in the 1930s with a single 100-metre corridor, the original building has been extended several times to accommodate a growing community and now has around 250 metres of corridors. For well over a decade, Fulbridge Academy has been developing a thematic approach to the decoration of every corridor in the school. This process began when the Senior Leadership Team (SLT) introduced a creative curriculum through which all subjects, including science and maths, were delivered through the lens of individual topics. Initially, semi-permanent role-play areas linked to ongoing topics, such as a Greek agora, were created inside classrooms to give students the opportunity to familiarise themselves with some of the relevant landscapes, architectural structures and objects. Gradually, the decorations moved out of the classrooms and into the uniformly 'horrible yellow' corridors and a carefully planned programme of curriculum-led internal decoration of these circulation spaces began to ensure that every aspect of the curriculum was represented in them.

The transformation of the corridors by professional artists, as well as school staff, with paint, furniture and other props was intended to provoke curiosity and invite a deeper level of engagement with each topic. Corridors began to function as sites of immersive experience, although they also retained their original purpose as circulation space. During lessons, whole classes were taken to the appropriate area of a themed corridor that connected with the topic being studied, for instance, a domestic setting in 1940s Britain during an air raid (see Figure 2.1). As corridors developed into a very different type of learning arena from the school's classrooms, the decor of each classroom was deliberately stripped back to encourage processing skills and working memory to function effectively without the distraction of displays and decoration. Integral to the way in which the curriculum was planned and delivered, the corridors now connected subjects such as history, geography, science and maths with art and design (see Figure 2.2, Figure 2.3 and Figure 2.4).

Figure 2.1 A corridor decorated with items from World War 2 in England. A drawing room inspired by the Sherlock Holmes series of stories is visible in the background

Using school corridors to support learning

Figure 2.2 The 'green' corridor. Adjacent to the school's entrance, it combines dinosaurs and fairy tale characters. It is a tactile environment with a magical atmosphere

Figure 2.3 Where two corridors meet, the contrast between the divergent themes results in a charming and incongruous visual mosaic. Here a Victorian-era house meets a polar scene

Figure 2.4 Disney meets outer space

When, 5 years ago, Ben Erskine took over as headteacher, the delivery of the whole school curriculum, through a topical lens, was modified to exclude maths and science from having to be taught thematically.

> What constrained teachers was the fact that they were trying to teach reading, writing, science and everything and linking these to 'the Tudors' which isn't always easy.
> (Ben Erskine, Headteacher, Fulbridge Academy, November 2020)

Alongside this development, a new vision for the corridors was planned to enrich the teaching of literature and literacies across the school, enhancing classroom-based teaching by constructing and illustrating the settings of a selection of key texts into the corridor spaces (see Figure 2.5 and Figure 2.6). This new emphasis on illustrating settings from books in the decorated corridors had two foci: to communicate the value and pleasure of reading to every member of the school community and to 'close the gap', that is, to reduce the speech, language and communication attainment gap between children who are socio-economically disadvantaged and their peers (Early Intervention Foundation, 2018).

> … because we already had the corridors set up, they started to evolve into environments that children could go to to start to understand what it would be like if they were in the book with the characters. It makes it really hard if you've not experienced [different environments and atmospheres].
> (Ben Erskine, Headteacher, Fulbridge Academy, November 2020)

Using school corridors to support learning

Figure 2.5 The Hogwarts Express from the *Harry Potter* series. This part of the corridor leads into the inside of an Anderson shelter

Figure 2.6 A room at 221B Baker Street, the fictional address of Sherlock Holmes. The reflection in the mirror captures the Roald Dahl themed section behind it

In recognising that a considerable proportion of students at the school had a limited range of life experiences, the SLT saw the corridors as an opportunity to introduce them to new types of landscapes, such as an arctic scene or farmyard. Additionally, a significant percentage of the cohort were not yet fluent in English, which might also lead them to struggle with unfamiliar vocabulary found in key texts. The SLT was confident that the highly structured teaching of phonics and literacy in the classroom would enable children to decode new words but also recognised that, without understanding their meaning, access to the wider curriculum would be limited. They envisaged that creating story settings in the corridors could help children to assimilate unfamiliar words in a graspable, relatable way and they set about curating a portfolio of high-quality texts for each year group. Each class was then allocated a series of books for the year, which they would read and write about together in the classroom, visiting the fully realised corridor settings to enrich their understanding of these texts.

The decorated corridors of Fulbridge Academy offer an example of an innovative, creative practice that a school has persevered with and developed thoughtfully over a number of years. The decorations express the school community's consensus about the role of the physical space of the school, which is also consistently communicated through social, teaching and learning practices. They are a learning resource created congruently with the curriculum that creates opportunities for exciting encounters. The level of maintenance of the decorations is indicative of the community's level of care and applies to all parts of the school's circulation spaces, regardless of their age and condition.

Reading and the body: reading as a spatial/bodily practice

Reading is a spatial practice. The physical context of reading influences one's experience of a text and its interpretation. Emeritus Professor of English at Appalachian State University, USA, Thomas McLaughlin, in his book *Reading and the body* (2015), develops a new theoretical perspective of reading as a spatial, as well as bodily, practice. He details the ways in which this understanding of what it means to be a reader has been widely neglected in favour of a cognitive-psychological perception, as if reading only pertains to the brain and the eyes, with little acknowledgement of the rest of the body or the spaces in which reading occurs. McLaughlin explains that the practice of reading makes many procedural demands upon individual parts of the reader's body which then need to be habituated, that is, to become second nature, to achieve fluency. He then expands this concept to the spaces around the reader.

McLaughlin suggests that fluent readers often deliberately create spaces around themselves, enhancing 'a cocoon of personal space that other people hesitate to invade' (2015, p. 31). Beginner readers, however, have a far more difficult task in protecting themselves from distraction and interruption due to the additional procedural demands that are required to learn to read; not least because they must, in almost all instances, learn to read aloud. Beginner readers must coordinate the tongue, the lips and the voice with their eyes and ears as they assemble the words on the page while stilling their limbs sufficiently to focus on pages that they must turn with their fingers in the appropriate direction. It is only once these operations are easily orchestrated by the body that an awareness of the physical process of reading starts to reverse itself to the extent that a reader can ultimately surrender an awareness of their bodies and their surroundings, and lose themselves in a text.

A lack of familiarity with the concept of the bodily and spatial nature of reading and of learning to read, even amongst teachers who teach reading, may be due to the fact, as McLaughlin establishes, that our awareness of this complex physical process diminishes as we become more accomplished readers. Merleau-Ponty, the French philosopher of phenomenology, who explored in depth the relationship between the body, the world and our perception of it, describes the erasure of the reading body in its space as 'an oblivion':

> The wonderful thing about language is that it promotes its own oblivion: my eyes follow the lines on the paper, and from the moment I am caught up in their meaning, I lose sight of them. The paper, the letters on it, my eyes and body are there only as the minimum setting of some invisible operation.
>
> (Merleau-Ponty, 2002, p. 466)

McLaughlin offers an explanation for why reading promotes this erasure of the body and the spaces around it in fluent readers, suggesting that 'the concentration necessary for reading is so intense that it is vulnerable to a distracting place and responsive to a supportive space'.

(2015, p. 34)

The impetus by the staff of Fulbridge Academy to represent treasured books across the walls of their corridors acknowledges, even if implicitly, the obstacles to reading for pleasure faced by beginner readers, in particular, the struggle to comprehend and consequently to enjoy a text if much of the vocabulary is unfamiliar. Graham and Kelly, in their classic text for teachers and teaching students *Reading under control* (2008), relate the exasperation and anger that many children express when they realise that 'although they find reading difficult and disagreeable, that reading can bring so much pleasure, knowledge and satisfaction to those around [them]' (2008, p. 150). Children do not often have the opportunity to read in the corridors of Fulbridge, due to issues of supervision and space. However, the aim is to restore the pleasure and joy that can be found in books through illustrations and objects, while also addressing the gaps in vocabulary relating to experiences of places that some children may have missed, due to 'a lack of vital early literacy experiences' (p. 150). This is important because children's enjoyment of reading is widely recognised as a predictor of educational achievement. The National Literacy Trust's research into reading trends in the UK in 2019 found:

> [T]wice as many young people who don't enjoy reading read below the average expected for their age compared with their peers who enjoy reading. Conversely, nearly four times as many young people who enjoy reading read above the expected level compared with their peers who don't enjoy reading.
>
> (NLT, 2019, p. 13)

Using spatial decoration to address disadvantage through oracy at Fulbridge

By representing story settings spatially in the corridors from texts that children will read in their classrooms with their teachers and adding unique physical objects that relate to them, the Fulbridge team proposes to stimulate the curiosity of children to develop a range of vocabulary that can help them unlock texts. In doing so, the SLT also acknowledges a strong link between poor oracy skills in English and disadvantage within the English education system.[1] Similarly, neighbourhood poverty and low family income, along with low levels of literacy within families, are also associated with the quality of children's academic achievement and can strongly influence parents' ability to create a stimulating home environment for learning (EIF, 2018). Fulbridge Academy serves a community with a significant level of low income and poor language skills in English.

It has been well established in the research literature that the acquisition of strong language skills in the early years of a child's life is one of the most significant predictors of educational success. In a report into the role of language in children's early educational outcomes, Roulstone, Law, Rush, Clegg, and Peters (2010) contend that children's success at school is not only governed by their social background, but their communication environment before their second birthday and language at the age of 2 years also have a strong influence.

Without a structured input, children will only use the vocabulary that they already have. Role play in the corridors, modelled and supported by adults, can boost their vocabularies. Through their encounters with the illustrated corridor spaces at Fulbridge, the hope is that children can start to build the wider vocabulary that many have missed in early childhood.

Sculpting spatial creativity: working with/within limitations

Fulbridge Academy offers an example of sculpting spaces creatively: a practice that enhances teaching and learning potentials (specific to reading) through the proactive and creative use of the school's built environment, specifically its circulation spaces. As with all practices, however, it has particular limitations that must be considered.

Decorations are applied to an existing surface and their potential is limited by the constraints of the building's structure and geometry. At Fulbridge, this limitation is caused by relatively narrow corridors. As decoration in itself cannot create

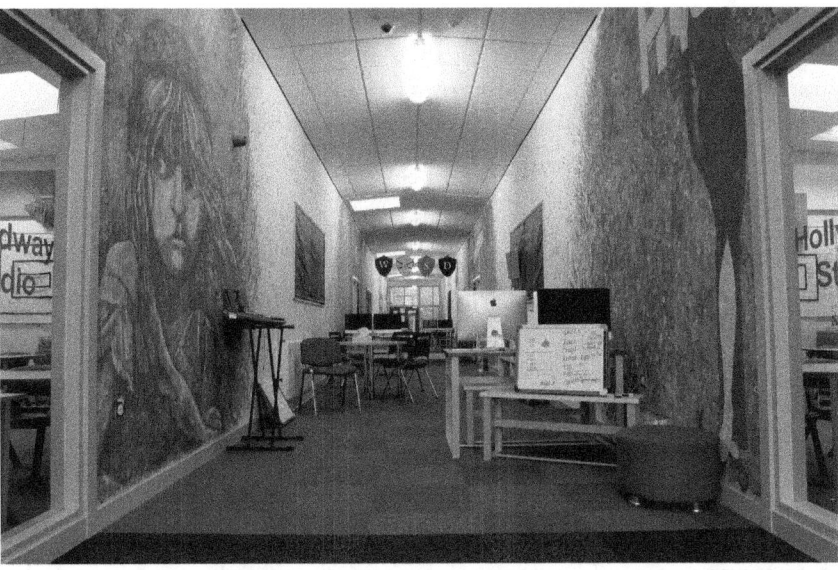

Figure 2.7 'Learning street' in Fulbridge Academy's new building, where the corridors are wider than in the original building

additional space, it must strike a balance between evoking a particular fictional or historical setting and providing an appropriate and safe space for circulation. The requirements of these two functions may conflict; for example, evoking the Hogwarts train that takes Harry Potter to school (see Figure 2.5) is achieved by representing elevated train tracks using a richly textured uneven floor surface, which can raise concerns about safety and equality of access. The balance struck between artistry and safety must also be dynamic as it means different things to different people: needs and perspectives will differ between individual children, as they do between adults. They will also differ between children and adults.

Decorations are material things and, as such, are ascribed levels of quality. The specification of materials, including the quality of workmanship, must meet a number of legal requirements to ensure their safety, including protection from accidental impact and fire safety. The decorative sets must be regularly maintained, potentially costing additional resources and feeding back into the balance of what can be achieved. However well-intentioned, inappropriate and poorly built and maintained spaces can have a negative effect on pupils' learning.

Sculpting spatial creativity: the potential of corridors, atria and learning streets

In older school buildings like Fulbridge, the addition of extensive corridors was a by-product of the increased complexity of a layout that reflected the changing social structures and demands of the curriculum. Importantly, the historic and current definition of corridors within mainstream school design guidelines reflects and reinforces this: corridors are 'non-net areas', that is, supportive but not 'usable' spaces for anything other than their intended function of circulation. Depending on the prevailing convictions of policy makers about the efficacy of spaces designed for education and available funding, corridors have accounted for different percentages of the total net area of the school: 7 per cent in primary school buildings in the late 1940s, 20 per cent in schools in the early 1950s and in the last decade, and 30 per cent in more generously funded buildings (e.g. those built during the English government's Building Schools for the Future Programme, 2003-2010).

Today, alongside their circulatory function, corridors are most commonly used in schools as ad-hoc teaching spaces or pastoral support spaces where small groups or individuals are given support by classroom assistants, special educational needs coordinators or counsellors. In this context of diverse use, corridors designed specifically and only for circulation are unsuitable and inefficient: unsuitable because their limited design brief makes them too cramped, too exposed to noise and interruption, too cold or too dark for wider use; inefficient because, although their limited functionality for circulation leaves them empty for large parts of the school day, they are spaces that must still be maintained. The use of corridor spaces for the education and pastoral support of children ignores these faults, making them potentially harmful or, at least, undermining the interactions between children and adults that take place there. Of course, many schools feel that they have no choice but to support children's education and wellbeing in these spaces because there are limited numbers of specially designed small-group rooms to meet the needs of the children in their current cohort.

For these reasons, many celebrated contemporary school buildings pay particular attention to the enhanced design and function of circulatory spaces by limiting the need for corridors or avoiding them altogether (e.g. Hellerup School, Copenhagen, Denmark). Atria and learning streets are architectural forms that create generous open circulation spaces. With thoughtful design, these can aid navigation and creative interactions; are suitable for a range of uses such as teaching, performance, assemblies, dining and play; and can also be an identity-building metaphor for the whole school community. They are approaches to sculpting space creatively that echo the concept of 'built-in variety' developed by the architects/educationalists Mary and David Medd (e.g. Burke, 2013/2016) and are exemplified in many of the schools they designed (e.g. Eveline Lowe Primary in Southwark, London, 1963-66). The idea that spaces should be designed for multiple and flexible uses, including for bodies of different proportions and abilities, is by no means a new one.

Atria frequently feature exciting spatial arrangements such as dual-functional staircases/seating areas or tiered auditoriums; they are often compared to 'heart spaces'. Learning streets, however, distribute this space and functions throughout a school. Learning streets retain a core circulatory purpose yet are also designed to be *properly* suitable for a range of other uses, such as teaching, library or reading space, computer stations and storage. It is critical that such spaces are designed so that the environmental and technical attributes (e.g. temperature, lighting, acoustics, colour, materials, dimensions) are suitable for and can be tailored to multiple specific uses/users. Atria and learning streets are not mutually exclusive: the University of Cambridge Primary School's (UCPS) 'ring' design includes an internal learning street that encircles an external courtyard (atrium). The Fuji Kindergarten (2007) by Tezuka Architects is similar in design; however, unlike UCPS, no formal distinction is made between circulation and teaching spaces.

Although these two examples might appear innovative in the context of mainstream school design, particularly in the UK, the ideas that underpin them are far from new. For instance, the architect Hans Scharoun compared the organisation of his 1960s primary school building in Marl, Germany to a mini-city with its 'learning houses' (classrooms) which collectively formed 'neighbourhoods' (larger areas) with public spaces (circulation) (Blundell-Jones, 1975/2012). Learning streets are also a prominent feature of the schools designed by eminent Dutch architect Herman Hertzberger:

I think a school should be like a small city. In a city you have small places, large places, all sorts of secluded and semi-secluded places; you have vistas and you have all sorts of activities. In effect, these pupils are not yet of an age to go into the city and explore the life of the city, but they should explore life through the school, so you must create as many conditions as possible in the school so that they experience the world through the school building (Dyer, 2016, para. 32).

A notable example, contemporary with Hertzberger's vision, is the Gelsenkirchen Bismarck EGG school near Bismarck, Germany, by the architect Peter Hübner (Hübner, 2005).

> Taking the principle of designing a school as a city further is SCABAL architects' unrealised proposal for a High Street School. Here, school spaces are located throughout a city with use shared by and negotiated between multiple schools, residents and office workers. The streets of the city form the only 'corridors' between them. Even these two examples are not new ideas, having been advocated three decades earlier by the Italian architect and academic Giancarlo De Carlo (1969) in his influential essay 'Why/how to build school buildings'.
>
> (see also Wood, 2018)

A final example worth mentioning is that proposed by the educators Colin Ward and Anthony Fyson in the 1970s, most notably through the publications *Bulletin for Environmental Education (BEE)* (edited by Ward, 1971-1980; see Perez-Martinez, 2020) and *Streetwork: The exploding school* (Ward & Fyson, 1973). Rather than calling for schools to be designed as cities, they aimed to demonstrate that the city itself can be a school. They did this by supporting students and educators in realising the city's educational potential: publishing materials (BEE pamphlets) and establishing physical centres, staffed and stocked with physical resources, while some even had dormitory provision.

The earlier examples of spatial creativity describe how schools might be reconceived to minimise inefficient spaces such as corridors, and instead to promote spaces that support creative collaborations. The design and construction of new buildings is, of course, a luxury and the majority of schools and teachers will necessarily only have resources to undertake relatively minor adaptations. This need not limit the potential to imagine creative changes to the building, however, as Fulbridge's use of decorated corridors demonstrates. In the following section we offer some further examples of spatial creativity, appropriate to the context of existing school buildings; these are intended to inspire and to provoke reflection on what might be possible in one's own school.

Spatial creativity: working with/within existing buildings

Typically, school buildings last far longer than planned for or anticipated. Shifts in policy, fluctuations in student numbers and changing educational and pastoral needs can happen relatively quickly. This can result in a pressing need for more space, often straining resources.

Building projects in existing schools frequently happen at speed and are often squeezed into holiday periods to minimise disruption. Limited resources (e.g. allocated funding) means that time allowed for design teams and members of the school community to collaborate is also minimised. Indeed, the introduction of new software packages such as StatLog aims to actively cut school staff out of such processes. Failing to include stakeholders in school building projects can result in poorly and narrowly conceived projects. Often, construction is simply the wrong answer, and adaptations to timetabling or spatial planning would be more appropriate.

There is a wealth of precedents, both historic and contemporary, that clearly illustrate the benefit of taking a slower, more considered approach involving careful consultation with staff and pupils. Die Baupiloten is an example of such an endeavour. Conceived as a collaborative 'study reform project' between Susanne Hofmann Architekten (now die Baupiloten Architektur) and the Technical University Berlin's architecture faculty, it was led by the architect Susanne Hofmann.

The project by Die Baupiloten at the Erika Mann Elementary School 1, Berlin (2003-05) involved the transformation of nineteenth-century corridors to provide dedicated spaces for 'learning and living'. It began with children creating three-dimensional scenes in shoeboxes using craft and recycled materials. This provided a platform for students and architects to discover, explore and communicate different spatial, atmospheric and programmatic ideas. Using narrative helped to support the iterative process, with architects independently developing ideas between workshops with students. Once the architects had developed the agreed design brief into initial spatial concepts, articulated as scale models, students used role-play to test and develop specific design elements. These games led to further scale models. The whole process unfolded over several months, allowing initial ideas to settle, grow and shift. The final design was based on a story developed by students about a Silver Dragon World and led to a transformation of the school corridors with themes such as Stardust Diving, Breath of Gentle Air, The Throne on the Beat of the Wings, and Flying on the Dragon's Tail. Additions included soft, illuminated sculptures; hanging fabric retreats; plants; and wall-hung seats and desks, extendable through folding and sliding elements.

Die Baupiloten's methods use simple and cheap materials, are suitable across a range of ages and can be readily adapted. These are described in a clear and instructional manner in Hofmann's 2014 text *Architecture is participation*, as well as on their website.[2] Many more examples of 'spatial creativity' in practice, including some from the UK, can be found at the excellent online resource *Designing with Children*[3] and at The Sorrell Foundation programme archive[4] (particularly the Joinedupdesignforschools and Young Design programmes). *Build Up*[5] and *Matt + Fiona*,[6] for example, offer starting points for involving children in design and construction. It is also worth noting, however, that achieving *meaningful* participation that is educationally transformative depends on more than following a method, even if successfully used elsewhere. Use must continually be considered, and it is to this we turn next.

Paying attention to 'use'

Beginning with the example of Fulbridge Academy's use of decorated corridors, we have described different ways in which a school, whether new or old, well-thought out or poorly constructed, might sculpt spaces creatively, including some of the educational potentials and practical problems of doing so. Common to these examples is that *how* and *why* we design and use school buildings communicates and reflects our educational and social values. These values will always change and overlap, sometimes conflicting; school buildings – as relatively permanent structures – must, therefore, have the capacity to accommodate change. With respect to the design and use of school corridors, for instance, hidden spaces can hinder sightlines, making the (required) supervision of pupils difficult, while narrow corridors can impede pupil movement, cause jostling between pupils and may exacerbate bullying. Yet there are also many reasons why the inclusion of hidden (or private, therapeutic) spaces is critical, especially those related to the mental and emotional health of pupils who need a safe space to self-regulate, attend counselling sessions or have a medical need attended to. Being proactive in continually attending to one another's needs, therefore, enables a school's many constituents to benefit their collective community.

Thus far, we have discussed *use* in terms of what can and cannot be done in a particular space. However, *use* also suggests a lens through which educational environments can be continually questioned and adapted. As the British/Australian feminist scholar Sara Ahmed puts it:

> Use provides a way of philosophizing from the everyday, a way of thinking about what we are doing as we are doing it. When we say something is being shaped by use, we are also talking about who can use what, when, and where. A consideration of use allows us to show [and discover] how a world can be [and is] shaped by what seems to be the smallest thing: how worlds are shaped from the bottom up.
>
> (2019, p. 65, original emphasis)

In interrogating *use* Ahmed makes her arguments by using a number of objects. We re-use some of these here to highlight some ways in which considering *use* matters when designing and/or inhabiting schools.

Signs, which can be small or large, as can their scope and effects, are often in the form of *use instructions*. In saying what a room (for example a classroom) should and should not be used for, a sign also says *who* should and should not use a room and when (Ahmed, 2019, pp. 28–31).

A sign need not be written or in the form of a symbol. A door controlled by a code or a window placed at a particular height can be signs; so can a set of steps, or a timetable. With no alternative provision made, a set of steps tells users who find steps difficult that they are not welcome, even when other signs might claim they are. A high-level window or carefully placed door can prevent a child from looking in or out, whilst maintaining adult sightlines. A timetable might dictate where is used for what, when and by who; combined with scarce resources, this can be devastating.

Established norms can also be signs. Ahmed likens social norms to 'comfortable chairs' (2019, p. 43): the way an institution – *a school* – or piece of furniture – *a chair, a door-opening device, a classroom layout* – functions for certain people but not for others. As each is used (in design and inhabitation), they become ever calibrated towards those that (can) use them, making use, and change of use, ever harder for those who do not happen to fit (pp. 43–44).

Signs of authority and ownership instruct that not anyone can permit use and that not all uses are permitted (2019, pp. 33–35). The need to ask and receive authorisation, as well as the knowledge and ability needed to do so, might be enough to prevent a request being made. How, why and by whom authorisation can be given and received are important questions, easily overlooked by those in power, sometimes deliberately so. Can a child who is struggling to read within a noisy classroom environment or who finds a hard floor particularly uncomfortable take themselves off to find a more suitable space? Not fitting can be a reason to pretend to fit, even when harmful (2019, pp. 159–163).

An absence of authorisation does not necessarily prevent *use*. An important kind of use described by Ahmed is that which occurs when authorisation is denied or when seeking authorisation is not possible. In such situations *use* might be noticed and prevented, but it might also go unnoticed or be tolerated by those in power. Where it continues, Ahmed describes how *use* can, over time, affect how things are used and by whom, and how this can affect balances of power and shift norms. She suggests the term 'queer use' here: referring to 'how things can be used in ways other than how they were intended to be used or by those other than for whom they were intended' (2019, p. 44).

This is why *paying attention* to use, continually, is critical; why doing so must be a proactive attitude, rather than a scheduled chore, that is encouraged and supported with processes that enable open, critical questioning and flexible change.

Conclusions

In this chapter we have built on the example of the decorated corridors of Fulbridge Academy to highlight ways in which schools might explore practices of spatial creativity for and with their communities. We have suggested that this might be possible through a radical redesign of the school space (atria and learning streets) or a more modest but equally imaginative rethinking of how current spaces are used through participatory design with students and staff.

We recognise that the simple redecoration of corridor spaces will have some limitations, since the function for which they were originally designed (i.e. circulation) will constrain the way in which they are used, unlike some of the other purposefully designed learning spaces that are integral to imaginative, new school buildings.

The government agencies who procure school buildings in the UK have in recent decades been slow to consider any radical deviation from the most modest, modular form of school buildings that are designed to be delivered as cheaply and quickly as possible. Architects working in school design in England were side-lined by the then-Secretary of State of Education, Michael Gove, in 2010 as unnecessary to the school building enterprise. There are many examples outside the UK, however, of architects and educators working together to create thoughtful, imaginative spaces for children and young people's education, and we have given a few examples of this in our earlier reflections about learning streets. The writings of Giancarlo De Carlo, Herman Hertzberger and Colin Ward, all cited earlier, also offer a very different way of thinking about education and creative spatialities, and these texts are accessible and available without having to leave one's country to see other schools. The example of Die Baupiloten demonstrates how architects can work *with* schools, *with* teachers and students, to effect imaginative yet practical adaptations to school buildings rooted in the combining of different knowledges and imaginations.

Returning to the example of Fulbridge, there are further steps that its school community might want to take to develop their creative/spatial offer further. They already recognise how important it is for their students to learn to read proficiently and fluently with understanding of what they are reading. They have chosen to expand their reading programme to their corridors, where they use illustration and decoration to familiarise children with story settings, to broaden their vocabularies and improve their oracy. A next step might be to explore some of the research literature about reading as a whole staff to consider the many different paradigms of reading beyond the cognitive-psychological approach that is promoted by the Department for Education. As a school, they are intuitively exploring a bodily-spatial approach to reading through their corridor decorations. Working with a wider range of reading paradigms may inspire them to make further changes. An accessible book that introduces these paradigms and provides carefully explained, practical examples of them is Kathy Hall's *Listening to Stephen read* (2002). This text might usefully form the basis of professional development sessions for all staff involved in reading and writing with students. The first chapters of Gabrielle Cliff Hodges's book *Researching and teaching reading: Developing pedagogy through critical enquiry* (2015) also offers an excellent introduction for teachers and teaching students to different ways of approaching reading, beginning from a perspective that reading is 'a human, ideological construct with no correct answers about what it comprises' (Cliff Hodges, 2015, p. 17).

Fulbridge's decorated corridors are the result of an intuitive approach that evolved over a relatively long period of time. Perhaps because the project was practice-based rather than research-led, Fulbridge is yet to engage in an evaluation of their effectiveness. There are a number of useful and child-friendly methods that they could use to capture students' experiences of their environments and elicit their views. Participatory research with staff and children should result in a more active engagement in future decisions about the corridor spaces. This absence of evaluation also shapes the corridors' form and use. Where practices are initiated, designed, built and managed by a particular group of users (e.g. senior adult members of school staff), well-considered, formal methods of evaluation are the only way to establish an understanding of how spaces affect those who use them. In the school designed by Peter Hübner alongside the school's students, this participatory approach is expected to have a stronger impact on learning and wellbeing because students are included from the beginning. Although the students of Fulbridge might be not expected to decide which key texts are chosen for teaching, this should not preclude them from involvement in related choices about their spatial-educational environment; for example, the decoration of the corridors.

Unlocking research in practice: provocations for group discussion

1 Instigate a practice of spatial creativity: for example, a whole-school design project about circulation spaces. What would your school be like without corridors? Could staff/students explore models of other types of schools (like Hellerup in Denmark) or Hertzberger's schools in the Netherlands, or even, post-pandemic, visit schools that use atria and learning streets?

2 Locate the purpose of spatial creativity by considering how the school's environment can contribute to teaching and learning. For example, who is responsible for displays in your school corridors? How coherently are displays managed across the school? Do they link with curriculum areas and represent the ethos and values of the school? What do students think about these displays?
3 Evaluate a practice of spatial creativity: for example, staff could be led on guided tours of the corridors by some of the youngest members of the school. Students could also take photographs to share what they pay attention to and what designs and decorations look like from their perspective. What can adults learn from seeing these spaces from a child's height/point of view?
4 Investigate different ways of understanding what it means to read and to be a reader in a staff professional development session.
5 Invite a group of architecture students into the school to work with children and staff on ideas for improving parts of the building. There need not be a plan or budget for actual construction in place, as long as this is made very clear from the start.[7]

Notes

1 Although children for whom English is not a first language often thrive in school (since being fluent in two or more languages can give them many advantages), if they enter school with little or no English language, they may take up to 7 years to achieve fluency in English. This is important to acknowledge because the national curriculum is exclusively taught in English and, if their families do not speak English, they may be additionally disadvantaged by arriving at school with poorly developed oracy skills in English.
2 See http://www.baupiloten.com/en
3 See https://www.designingwithchildren.net
4 See https://www.thesorrellfoundation.com/programmes/
5 See http://www.buildup.org.uk
6 See http://mattandfiona.org
7 This final recommendation echoes those made in Chapter 18 of the Cambridge Primary Review Final Report (Alexander, 2010). The work advocated would build on that undertaken through The Sorrell Foundation's Joinedupdesignforschools and Young Design programmes, as well as more recent work, such as that by Die Baupiloten.

References

Ahmed, S. (2019). *What's the use? On the uses of use*. Durham, NC: Duke University Press.
Alexander, R. (Ed.). (2010). *Children, their world, their education: Final report and recommendations of the Cambridge Primary Review*. Abingdon: Routledge.
Blundell-Jones, P. (2012, October 22). 'Marl School in Germany by Hans Scharoun'. *The architectural review*. (Original work published March 1975). Retrieved from https://www.architectural-review.com/buildings/school/marl-school-in-germany-by-hans-scharoun

Burke, C. (2016). *A life in education and architecture: Mary Beaumont Medd*. (Original work published 2013). Abingdon: Routledge.

Cliff Hodges, G. (2015). *Researching and teaching reading: Developing pedagogy through critical enquiry*. Abingdon: Routledge.

De Carlo, G. (1969). Why/how to build school buildings. *Harvard Educational Review, 39*(4), 12–35. Retrieved from http://www.hepgjournals.org/doi/abs/10.17763/haer.39.4.r1163153200753u4

Dyer, E. (2016). Interview with Herman Hertzberger (2016). *Architecture and education*. Retrieved from https://architectureandeducation.org/2016/02/03/interview-with-herman-hertzberger/

Early Intervention Foundation (EIF). (2018). *Realising the potential of early intervention*. Retrieved from https://www.eif.org.uk/report/realising-the-potential-of-early-intervention

Graham, J., & Kelly, A. (2008). *Reading under control: Teaching reading in the primary school* (3rd ed.). Abingdon: Routledge.

Hall, K. (2002). *Listening to Stephen read*. Berkshire, UK: Open University Press.

Hofmann, S. (2014). *Architecture is participation: Die Baupiloten – methods and projects*. Berlin: Jovis.

Hübner, P. (2005). *Evangelische Gesamtschule Gelsenkirchen-Bismarck: Kinder bauen iher schule / children make their school* (bilingual ed.). Stuttgart: Edition Axel Menges.

McLaughlin, T. (2015). *Reading and the body: The physical practice of reading*. London: Palgrave Macmillan.

Merleau-Ponty, M. (2002). *Phenomenology of perception* (C. Smith, Trans.). Abingdon: Routledge.

National Literacy Trust (2019). *Children and young people's reading in 2019*. Retrieved from https://literacytrust.org.uk/research-services/research-reports/children-and-young-peoples-reading-in-2019/

Perez-Martinez, S. (2020). Deschooling architecture. *Contemporary Journal, 2*. Retrieved from https://thecontemporaryjournal.org/issues/critical-pedagogies/deschooling-architecture

Roulstone, S., Law, J., Rush, R., Clegg, J., & Peters, T. (2010). *Investigating the role of language in children's early educational outcomes* (Research Report DFE-RR134). Department for Education. Retrieved from https://assets.publishing.service.gov.uk/government/uploads/system/uploads/attachment_data/file/181549/DFE-RR134.pdf

Tezuka Architects. (2007). *Fuji Kindergarten Project by Tezuka architects, Toyko, Japan*. Retrieved from https://www.architonic.com/en/project/tezuka-architects-fuji-kindergarten/5100019.pdf

Ward, C., & Fyson, A. (1973). *Streetwork: The exploding school*. London: Routledge and Kegan Paul.

Wood, A. (2018, June 28). Giancarlo De Carlo: How to keep educational architecture human or creative anti-institutionalism. *Architecture and Education*. Retrieved from https://architectureandeducation.org/2018/06/28/giancarlo-de-carlo-how-to-keep-educational-architecture-human-or-creative-anti-institutionalism/

CHAPTER 3

Storying the journey to new spaces of intercultural creative learning

James Biddulph and Pamela Burnard

Introduction: why storying matters

The world is full of stories – they are powerful and essential characteristics of human societies. We tell stories about ourselves and our communities. We tell stories that present our trials and tribulations through yarns that weave together the past, the present and our interpretative hopes for the future; to create memories and to confirm our place on the earth: stories circulate endlessly, sometimes within small networks of friends and family, sometimes they travel over long distances and assume socially significant proportions. What happens when these personal stories are spoken and analysed? What happens in the story crafting that brings new insights, disruptions or revelations? And beyond the self, what happens when we listen to children's family stories and better understand their lived experiences out of school? What transformations can take place?

Storying, as with storytelling, is an insightful methodological approach and tool used in education research that disassembles conventions of research, such as interviewing where there is an interviewer and a subject being interviewed. Storying gives voice to the marginalised and enables a profound understanding of the significance of stories and storying in the production of knowledge. Both teachers and researchers are interested in children having the space to speak their own personal stories, in their own way and time. However, the dense UK primary curricula and scarcity of time in schools reduces the opportunities for teachers to understand the themes that children say are meaningful.

This chapter provides an example of the power of hearing stories. It documents James's story as an educator who problematised his experiences working in a multi-ethnic, multicultural, socioeconomically diverse community in East London.

With an interest in creative learning and the diversities within the school community, his story involves reconceptualising, moving beyond the comfort of the classroom and school domain, towards children's family homes. There are five main sections to the chapter: firstly, we define creative learning and secondly define interculturalism, and we discuss why they are important; thirdly, we describe how creative journaling can deepen self-awareness in trying to make sense of 'other people'. This then introduces the doctoral study, describing a study of creative learning that moved beyond school research to be situated, instead, in ethnic minority immigrant children's family homes. Finally, we look beyond what we found out to future-making and future-possibilities thinking.

Before we begin, we thought we should explain who we are and how our stories crossed paths in 2001. Pam is a professor with expertise in the arts and creativities. James is a primary headteacher. We met in 2001 when James was studying for his Postgraduate Certificate in Education, and Pam was his lecturer and tutor. Both play the piano. We are both passionate musicians who have enabled music making in education in different ways. Pam supported James throughout his career, guiding and cajoling him to continue his studies and eventually work towards a doctorate, which he completed in 2017. Journeying together is a metaphor for the purpose of the *Unlocking Research* series: bringing together the interaction of research and practice; inspiring research-informed practice and practice-influenced research; and showing that research that is unpacked and articulated for practice can produce profound shifts, re-awakenings and new imaginative possibilities.

Why creative learning matters

Throughout this edited book, there are various definitions of creativities. Drawing from the literature about creativity, the question of making sense of *creative learning* became the focus for James's study. Historically, the term 'creative learning' emerged from policies to do with creativity in education rather than from research. It also emerged as distinct from, but related to, creativity; it was non-systemically ascribed, under-theorised and contested (Burnard, 2007). We also note that most of the research was centred on school contexts. It was quickly evident that there was a research imperative to consider creative learning in spaces outside of school. So, what could creative learning be? Creative learning involves co-creating (thinking/doing/being/acting/experiencing together) a learning culture for each learner within a professional learning community which aims to provide the opportunity to make decisions and co-make spaces in which everyone feels comfortable about taking risks, and to allow individual and community choices and actions to affect outcomes. Creative learning is a particular kind of learning path where learners are actively involved in creating learning opportunities. Our review of the literature suggested that there were four repeating themes mixed together in definitions of creative learning: *possibility thinking, playfulness, notions of identity and agency*, and *the creation of something new*.

However, the universalised assumption that creativity (and by implication creative learning) are 'good things', needed exploration. Creativity, and by implication creative learning, is defined through the assumptions of the dominant groups in society. What is seen as 'normal' is defined through the eyes of White culture, typically well-educated (and in the UK upper middle class), and thus attempts at universalisation perpetuate the deafening silence of those whose voices are not presented, or even *represented*. Misrepresentation and homogenisation seem more common. And, often, creativity is seen as an educational panacea for the problems in a socially unjust education system. The capitalist belief in the 'intrinsic goodness' of creativity, as product driven, to develop a future workforce, is undermined by the fact that it is the dominant monocultural voice that articulates its value. So, with its universalisation there is an inherent hierarchy and structured inequalities. Seeing creative learning as a dynamic and fluid concept brings to light the importance of diversity and holding a critical awareness in mind: that there are missing voices in definitions of what it is and what it could mean for those engaged in it.

Why interculturalism matters

We live in rapidly changing communities (Cantle, 2012). Schools are microcosms of this social complexity. Between 1993 and 2013 the foreign-born population in the UK more than doubled from 3.8 million to around 7.8 million. Such data indicate common assumptions when we refer to diversity: it is about the Other, about ethnic minorities, and about groups that are foreign to the main community. The increased cross-cultural exposure can reveal ways in which diversity 'rubs against and challenges our prejudices' (Hofvander Trulsson & Burnard, 2016, p. 123) – but also that the term diversity needs to be problematised.

Before exploring the concept of interculturalism in relation to creative learning, we first delineate the terms *multi*-culture and *inter*-culture. For decades, the terms 'multicultural' and 'multiculturalism' were associated with the politics of identity (Modood, 2007) and the representation, rights and status of different groups of people. This evolved as the migration of communities and empowerment of groups (for example, women's rights, LGBTQ+ rights, human rights, First Peoples' rights) required changes to thinking about culture and diversity (Kelly, 2002). Within education, the multicultural movement was a central policy agenda, designed to develop community cohesion in the context of a 'melting pot' of multiple cultures. The inclusion of minority ethnic groups, in other words, presented *problems* for educators and wider society.

Importantly, the difference between multiculturalism and interculturalism indicates a position and mindset about diversity. Multiculturalism attempts to recognise the identities of different cultures, essentially about ethnicity, faith, nationality, language or any other dimension that has a social or political salience. Multicultural policies aim to negotiate 'accommodations' between the 'host' majority community and the other groups, with the resulting perpetuation of difference and a sense of 'other-ness'. Conversely, interculturalism does not lock in the notion of a binary radicalised divide – a them and us discourse – but instead is more about 'the creation of a culture of openness which effectively challenges the identity politics and entrenchment of separate communities, based upon any notion of "otherness"' (Cantle, 2012, pp. 142–143). As a dynamic process, therefore, it promotes difference as something to be embraced rather than feared, recognising that, through connection and dialogue, tensions and conflicts can arise as a necessary part of societal change. Moreover, the term 'intercultural' acknowledges the complexity of locations, identities and modes of expression in a global world, and the desire to raise awareness, foster intercultural dialogue, and facilitate understanding across and between cultures.

One of many global educational imperatives is to further understandings of and engage critically in what constitutes intercultural. Teachers play a significant role in this undertaking. Intercultural practices shed new insights into shared cultural and intercultural futures that need to be re-imagined and co-created with principles that include ethical obligations, exploration, openness and reflexivity. This leads to embracing a multi-perspective world view that addresses and celebrates the embodied nature of intercultural teaching practices: a world view that is continually constructed, dynamic and fluid, existing both within and between locations, and that connotes a particular type of ethical educational *space*.

We could also consider the place where two cultures meet as a cultural interface; a place where all interested people can meet to create knowledge based on a melding of multiple standpoints. Theory challenges practice. It pushes and nudges and makes the comfortable feel uncomfortable. For critical theorist Hélène Cixous, being intercultural is being two – the nature of the being is intersubjective, inter-corporeal and in-between. What does this mean and could it apply in primary education practices?

As we will see, for James's study, the educational researcher's typical way of describing the research seemed insufficient: what was his response-ability? How did he question his power as a white, male, educated, professional educator and researcher? For example, social and educational researchers talk about 'entering the field' and 'gathering' data as if venturing into the world to harvest material for processing (analysis) before its eventual distribution and consumption by a society hungrily seeking new information to build up its body of knowledge and increase its capacity for growth and improvement (Flutter, 2016). However, for education practitioners researching their own professional practice, and their journey into and focus on 'interculturality', as James was, it feels much more fluid and uncertain than being on dry land. These researchers need to locate and address the overlap of their practice and ethical agendas in educational research. In James's research the children were not participants – they were children with meaningful lived experiences. The experiences and insights of creative learning in their homes was not data – it was how they lived their lives. The field was not an abstract place of study – it was intimate and valued family homes. With growing intercultural awareness, James's study took a turn to consider the internal reflections and disturbances and to bring these out into the open as valuable aspects of documenting the research journey. In the next section, we describe practical methods used by James for developing reflexive approaches using journaling and a method created by Pam called *rivers of experience*.

Creating reflexive practices

Journaling

Writing a journal is a commonly accepted method for ethnographic research. It is also a way of documenting the 'me search' in how a teacher or researcher or researching teacher position themselves, bringing to the fore their hopes and fears for a project or moment and as a way of problematising issues that arise (Gray & Malins, 2004). Through the process, there is value in asking questions of oneself: about how we locate ourselves, and how much we reveal about ourselves in our professional and research lives, and to reconcile the different roles and positions we occupy as educators – whether academic or practitioner (Burnard, Kelly, & Biddulph, 2010). Moreover, Winstanley and Moule (2021) talk of the vital importance of educators learning and experiencing the process of writing and creating confident, well-articulated expressions of experience. In this chapter, James presents examples of his 'me search' as he grappled with rethinking the separation of self from research (see also Phillips & Bunda, 2018). Extracts from his journal reveal the challenges he faced as a professional and a researcher. James's use of journal writing allowed him to engage with the experience of researching in children's homes, with an ongoing process of critique and raising questions about his own assumptions. Journaling is a valuable process for both adults and children.

How do I start writing a journal?

The first task is to purchase a blank book. We would recommend an A4, hardback, art book without lines, because there is a sense of value and importance given to the emerging contents unrestrained by lines. The lack of lines gives opportunity for all possibilities. There are many different techniques to start. Julia Cameron (1993) suggests writing for 3 to 5 minutes every morning. These morning pages encourage the releasing of imaginations (see Box 1).

> **Box 1: Starting a journal practice: morning pages**
>
> Morning pages are a technique to help people start to write. Simply put, it involves writing three pages of longhand writing. This is done first thing in the morning and is strictly a stream of consciousness (i.e. not over-thinking,

> but just writing whatever comes into your head). Julia Cameron explains these important 'rules':
>
> - Write every day.
> - Write three pages.
> - Write in long hand with paper and pen and do not type.
> - These daily meanderings are not intended to be inspiring or groundbreaking prose.
> - The daily writing can be positive or negative in its content. It does not matter.
> - The purpose is to get the hand moving over the paper and to write down words and sentences in your head.
> - Do not read over what you have written.
> - Just write. And do it daily. Three pages!
>
> See Cameron (1993, pp. 9-18).

When a new habit of writing is formed, we suggest you become conscious of the significant moments in your professional life. When these occur, for example, a moment when a child surprised you, spend 10 minutes writing what happened. These questions could guide your writing:

- What happened?
- Where did it happen?
- Who was involved?
- What was said?
- What was unsaid?
- How did you feel?
- How did they feel?
- Where was the pinch point?
- Where was an unseen opportunity?

Journaling habits are different for each person and can include sketches, quotations and images glued in that help form a sense of awareness, of position, of problems, of possibilities. In the next section, having developed a habit of journaling, we demonstrate how the gathering of significant moments can help document a professional-personal educational journey.

Rivers of experience

Another tool for enabling reflexivity is called *rivers of experience*. This tool was developed and adapted from research with primary-age children, inviting them to reflect on their diverse creativities in music, and in the field of music teacher education. Pam developed the reflection tool 'Rivers of Musical Experience' in its first

Storying the journey to new spaces

iteration with children. For this exercise, professional musicians were instructed to annotate key turning points, critical incidents or significant episodes in their professional learning pathways, guided by the question: 'What are your rivers telling you about your learning pathways, career and education?' This tool could be used in any setting, for individual focused reflections or for group reflections. Through dialogue about the rivers of experience, insight into the themes and journeys both personal and professional can be gained. The reader can download blank copies of the rivers and further ideas in the series from the website unlockingresearch.org. In Figure 3.1, Rowan, a musician, describes key features of their journey to

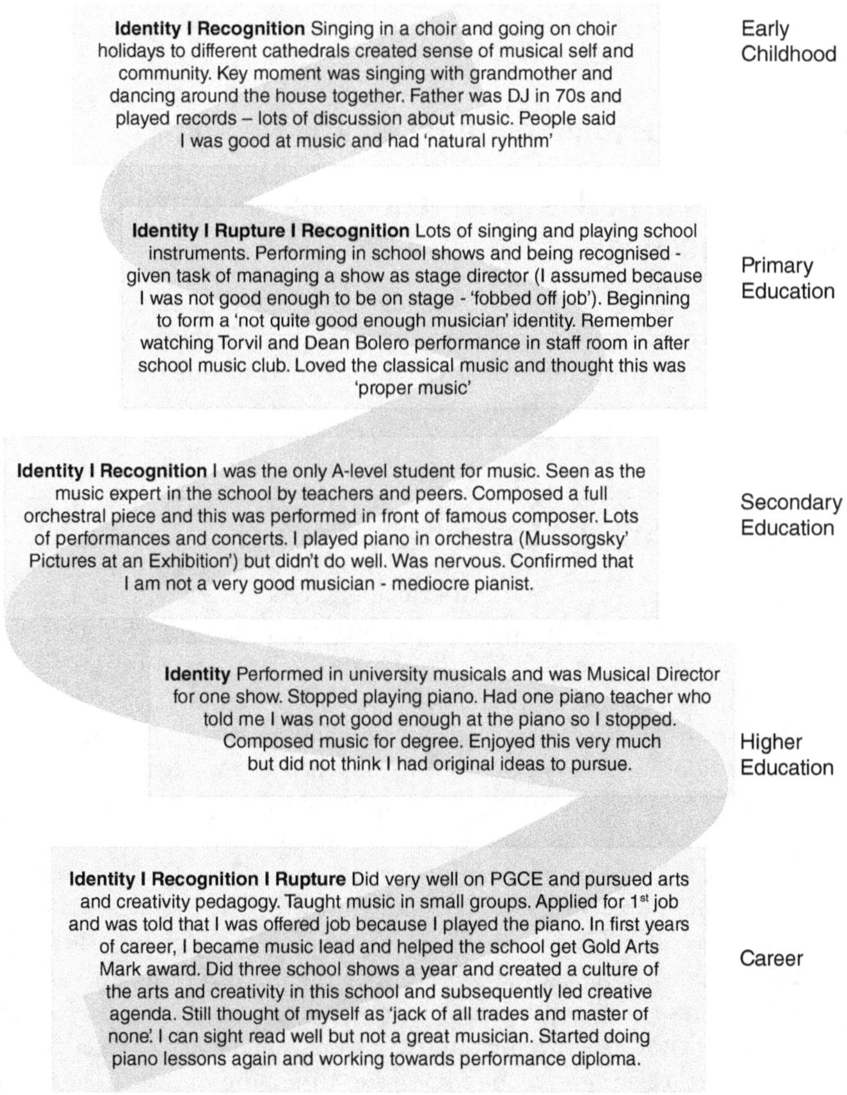

Identity I Recognition Singing in a choir and going on choir holidays to different cathedrals created sense of musical self and community. Key moment was singing with grandmother and dancing around the house together. Father was DJ in 70s and played records – lots of discussion about music. People said I was good at music and had 'natural ryhthm'

Early Childhood

Identity I Rupture I Recognition Lots of singing and playing school instruments. Performing in school shows and being recognised - given task of managing a show as stage director (I assumed because I was not good enough to be on stage - 'fobbed off job'). Beginning to form a 'not quite good enough musician' identity. Remember watching Torvil and Dean Bolero performance in staff room in after school music club. Loved the classical music and thought this was 'proper music'

Primary Education

Identity I Recognition I was the only A-level student for music. Seen as the music expert in the school by teachers and peers. Composed a full orchestral piece and this was performed in front of famous composer. Lots of performances and concerts. I played piano in orchestra (Mussorgsky' Pictures at an Exhibition') but didn't do well. Was nervous. Confirmed that I am not a very good musician - mediocre pianist.

Secondary Education

Identity Performed in university musicals and was Musical Director for one show. Stopped playing piano. Had one piano teacher who told me I was not good enough at the piano so I stopped. Composed music for degree. Enjoyed this very much but did not think I had original ideas to pursue.

Higher Education

Identity I Recognition I Rupture Did very well on PGCE and pursued arts and creativity pedagogy. Taught music in small groups. Applied for 1st job and was told that I was offered job because I played the piano. In first years of career, I became music lead and helped the school get Gold Arts Mark award. Did three school shows a year and created a culture of the arts and creativity in this school and subsequently led creative agenda. Still thought of myself as 'jack of all trades and master of none'. I can sight read well but not a great musician. Started doing piano lessons again and working towards performance diploma.

Career

Figure 3.1 Rowan's river of experience

51

becoming a professional musician. Rowan, as a performer-researcher-educator, stories their musical experiences during various phases of childhood, schooling and life after school. This shows an engagement in self-discovery, reflecting on the critical and intercultural incidents that influenced them, as acts of rupture in professional learning pathways, while narrating what matters.

Such reflexive tools signal new ideas about learning pathways and about teaching, but also illustrate how using words and imagery (of a river, for example) lays bare our thoughts that lead to thinking differently. As Maxine Greene reminds us, sometimes knowing how 'imagination breathes life into experience' (Greene, 1998, p. 22) is what enables us to turn over, around and upside down all that we take for granted – to 'lurch' as Greene would say, 'if only for a moment, out of the familiar and the taken-for-granted' (1998, p. 123) and question it all anew.

The doctoral study: intercultural creative learning

From personal to professional reflections: identifying a problem in practice

In this section, we document the development of a research study prompted by a professional experience that disrupted James's thinking. Box 2 starts with a moment between student and teacher that led to questioning and a sense that something was not quite right.

Box 2: A catalyst for James's research

A catalyst for my study arose during a conversation with a pupil called Shamira.[1] It was a Friday afternoon and I had just finished a whole-school singing assembly, during which we sang songs from many musical traditions: creative, engaging and intended to develop learning through the arts. Shamira came to speak with me after the singing and told me: 'Mr Biddulph, I'm not allowed to sing because it's against my culture . . . my Dad told me not to sing because we do not sing at home, it is *haram*'.[2]

I stood there, thinking what to say: all the children were engaged (weren't they?); I wasn't doing anything wrong (was I?); this was a National Curriculum objective, and I was teaching well – it was creative, challenging and fun (wasn't it?). Obviously, it was not against her culture (I thought); her family had misunderstood what UK schooling involved and I should speak with them to clear up *their* misunderstanding. But when I arrived at home, I realised how narrow my initial response had been; something did not feel right. I had homogenised a group of children in our school – making diversity orderly and structured. I was struck that exclusion can occur on

> many levels, sometimes without intention. I was taken aback about how little I knew about her life outside school, realising that 'there is not nearly enough practical discussion of ways classroom settings can be transformed so that the learning experience is inclusive' (hooks, 1994, p. 35).

From a personal reflection, James continued discussions with Pam, to define the possibilities of an academic study. Using the *rivers of experience* tool, he documented his professional journey thus far, which led him to identify two substantive aspects in which he was interested. It was from these reflexive insights that James eventually enrolled in a doctorate and began a research project that would try to make sense of creative learning from the diverse standpoints of children and, most importantly, from the standpoint in their family homes.

Researching creative learning: beyond school gates and through children's front doors

What follows in this section is James's synthesis of carefully gathered qualitative data, using arts-based techniques including drawings and photographs, as well as semi-structured interviews carried out informally during the process of being with the children in their family homes. The research was carried out over the course of 1 year and involved numerous visits to six children's family homes. These included times after school, at the weekend and during the school holidays. The ethical considerations and safeguarding of the research were considerable and all were documented and shared to ensure that both researcher and families were protected. Gaining access to the family homes involved lengthy and sensitive relationship-forming so that families had full control over access to their home, whether they wanted to withdraw and how long they wanted to continue. Every family welcomed James for the entirety of the research and were involved in reviewing the narratives and assumptions James made. The key research questions were:

> *What can we learn about creative learning from researching in ethnic minority immigrant children's homes?*
> *What is creative learning in ethnic minority immigrant children's homes; where and how does it manifest?* I was interested to explore what children do at home that evokes creative learning and to find out how creative learning arises, informed by family and context. To do this, I started by observing in the home, asking the children: how do you spend your time at home? Such an open-ended approach allowed for diverse responses to manifest and offer a broad 'way in' to researching in more detail what creative learning could be.
> *How do family ways of life influence the ways children's creative learning manifests at home?* This question was intended to explore the families' particular ways of life that influence how creative learning might manifest. I needed a

theoretical lens through which to make sense of the structures of family life and to expand understandings of the meaning of creative learning.

Rather than presenting his 'findings' as scientific data, James used *storying* as an appropriate qualitative and creative response. In so doing, the richness of experience could be presented to readers who had not had the privilege of doing the research with him, but through the narrative could walk part way to the children's front doors and begin to see what it might be like for them and what their creative learning might be. Before we introduce John, one of the children in the study, we emphasise the privilege and unique intercultural opportunity of connecting with people through research like this. In making relationships with each family, James learnt the importance of humility, of human struggle and celebration, of family and of the richness of human life. He learnt that creative learning was more nuanced and richly experienced and enacted than he had ever thought. And it was only by moving beyond the confines of the classroom and school gate that he was afforded glimpses of children's lives of creative learning in their own spaces.

Narrating the story of John's creative learning

> *They like Lego very much to play. Also, they like to draw many things. This room is often big mess and, er, papers everywhere, colours everywhere.* (Didi – The name the children called their father)

I knocked on the blue door. No answer. Again, I knocked and, again, no answer. Perhaps they had changed their minds, I thought. I wasn't sure whether they had fully understood, when I spoke to them on the telephone to arrange a visit. It was raining. I sat in my car and waited, watching students head for home from school, rushing energetically to their lives out of uniform, lessons, school, routines. My journal entry reflects the moment:

Journal entry 1: waiting for John – thinking about the methodological challenges

It's cold and wet and I am waiting in my car. They haven't arrived yet. Sitting here watching the children go home from school, I think . . . This is my research purpose: to learn more about children's *out-of-school* lives and their creative learning within *their homes* with family. But the distance between the students on the street and me in my car seems so vast and the assumption that I make that John, Maya and Sulaiman want to *be 'explored'* worries me. I feel daunted at the task at hand: the ethics so sensitive.

It was not long until a blue car parked behind me and out tumbled John's family: Rebecca (his older sister), Josiah (his younger brother) and Susan (the youngest).[3]

Then followed his father who beamed a warm welcome, shaking my hand (his two hands around my one outstretched hand) and telling me how pleased they were to see me. John's mother followed with shopping bags in hand and apologised for being late.

John lived in the least salubrious part of the district (according to local rumour about gangs and crime), an area where most houses were in a poor state of repair; they told me that they wanted to move out of this area soon. The streets were lined with large plastic bins, protruding bushes from concrete front gardens, crisp packets and other debris. It is a transient neighbourhood – people come and go and the sense of 'community', of people knowing one another, is difficult to find. I also experienced this in the street where I lived, which was only a short walk away from John's home. I didn't know my own neighbourhood. In their corridor, there were piles of leaflets stacked in boxes and versions of the Bible in Romanian and English – to be given to people in local shopping centres. The children rushed upstairs and returned, changed from their uniform into hand-knitted jumpers and slippers. They sat, children sitting on their hands, their father nodding his head, everyone smiling back at me. I smiled at them, paused and asked my first question, 'So, how do you spend your time when you get home?' Later, I documented the moment, writing:

Journal entry 2: articulating the intercultural experience of researching in homes

I knew then that this was a significant moment, our first exchanges at the interface of our different ways of thinking, understanding and experiences of living; the moment that Cixous says is the place where we are *tinted* and learn. The anticipation was palpable for me. My focus is on *capturing an understanding of the nature of creative learning*. What is it like? And what is it like at home? The theoretical framing will come later, as I build a picture of John, his family, his space(s), interactions, relationships, in these short/incomplete moments . . . my professional commitments, values and passions must be articulated here, must be seen and acknowledged so that my presence as researcher challenges me to reconsider what I think I see, to stop the potential and relentless practice of 'looking down' on other cultures/groups/parts of the school community. How else to build cohesion/community/understanding? Moving beyond front doors into other people's homes requires intercultural attitudes to explore, learn and start to change thinking.

There were some long pauses as we learnt what it meant for a teacher to be visiting a child's home and for them to understand what it meant to be hosting an English man, their previous teacher, in their 'front room'. I problematised the processes of the research design through these research experiences; the issue of presenting others without 'othering' was an important concern:

Journal entry 3: questions about representing 'the other' without 'othering'

As John's mother and older sister served tea, I felt both inspired and nervous: inspired by the opportunity of being in his home, knowing that this is an unusual experience for most teachers in the UK. I was nervous because the opportunity presented significant challenges, raising questions about how I should present John and his family authentically; how do I illustrate the physical, temporal and emotive aspects that '(in)form' their ways of life (acknowledging also that this would only ever be a facet of the whole because of the nature of a PhD thesis)? How do I narrate the lives of other people without 'othering' in a way that doesn't reinforce stereotypes or reaffirm the potential neo-colonial 'capturing', 'exploring' or 'discovering'? – even my use of the journey metaphor puts me in a possibly 'intrepid explorer' position (which feels uncomfortable).

We started talking about their journey from Romania to London, some 6 years ago. From what they said, it had been fraught with personal challenges, and through their narrative I came to understand how different their experience of being here in London was to my own. John's parents were born under the political landscape of a communist dictatorship, but had lived in the UK for a number of years, largely because they could not align their religious beliefs with this communist regime: 'I could not join the party so we couldn't do many things', said the father, 'we left to come here'. Then they returned to Romania after the end of the communist regime, but returned to the UK some years after with their young children.

Life circumstances had been challenging: one child had been very ill at birth, during which they (all six) had spent many months living in one room, and even during the period of my visits their father had a bad accident at work which resulted in him not working for some six months, putting financial pressure on the family. Despite such difficulties, the family's attitude to life, manifest in their talk and the ways they overcame these moments, was full of hope, linked with their evangelical Christian religious beliefs, I was told. One note in my journal recorded a conversation about culture, faith and tradition, which began building a picture of the influence of these beliefs on the family's dispositions:

Journal entry 4: John's family home as an evolving culture

John's father and I sat drinking tea and he explained his view of *culture* as different from *tradition* (his terminology). He talked of his past in Romania and he said that being in London meant that his children were 'changing', learning from others, experiencing the sense of being different as a minority group (with some negative national media reporting on the immigration of East Europeans). He told me that it was interesting being in 'multi-culture' but there were too many people and religions and 'strange ways'. He said his family life was changing, his home was 'always moving, moving on', with this sense of movement even evident in the dynamic use of spaces within John's home.

Together they had gravitated towards their 'own group', he said. Interestingly, this was *not* Romanian but instead a community largely of White British evangelical Christians. Being Christian was significant to understand their home culture/dispositions. The complexity of life seemed encapsulated in our discussion; being 'other/different' and/or 'same' related to my interest in the theories of Helene Cixous. How do I hear the parental voice(s), the cultural discourse that gives insight into their ways of doing things? I see how cultural valuing can be misread; how diversity, what is socially just, is misinterpreted; and the perpetuation of difference as romanticised, occidental, exotic, rose tinted. I thought I knew the children in my classes – and yet I feel despondent in realising that I've made so many mistakes.

So now . . . even more than creative learning . . . are questions of social justice, inclusion, equity, valuing, inextricably linked?

I spent most visits in the space they called the 'front room' and 'living'. It was full of large sofas, enough for them all to sit, a large TV, always switched off during my visits, and a large coffee table. Beneath the TV and stacked on the one bookshelf were board games, a box of Lego and unfinished knitting. There was a cardboard box that had been made into a pretend house in the corner of the room. This is where John seemed to live out his creative learning.

The journaling aesthetic seemed more accessible than a paper with a dense academic tone. Similarly, it reduced the distance between *researcher* from the *researched*, which in this study was vital to uphold an appropriate humane ethical approach. Moreover, the storying needed the researcher to pinpoint key moments to expand, problematise and respond to; in so doing, there is greater awareness of self and of other, and of the intercultural moments in between. Whilst not every teacher will be able to conduct such extended doctoral research, nor visit children in their homes necessarily, there are countless ways to engage with children to hear their stories of family, of family spaces and of experiences of life out of school. For example, inviting children to talk about their families, creating family board displays which expand throughout the year to include representations of the places they like to play, maps of the places they were born, collating questions that they ask or images of food they like to eat. Anything that helps bridge the experience of home and school is valuable. In so doing, we open ourselves to the possibilities that we know very little about the children in our care and that by thinking creatively about bringing their lives into school we can start to learn more.

Why intercultural creative learning matters

The research provides insights for storying and materialising inclusive spaces in primary schools – and for authoring new forms of intercultural creative learning:

for example, at the interface of children's cultural spaces of home and school. In James's study, three key findings emerged: that creative learning is *diverse*, that it is expressed in the *communality* of family living (and not in an individual way) and that it is considered a particular form of *family capital*.

Firstly, whereas in schools there was a sense of definitive meaning – where teachers talk about 'doing the creative curriculum' – at home creative learning was not a universalised concept or a particularly defined way of engaging. It was diverse because physical spaces are diverse. These spaces are used differently. How time is spent in these spaces is equally diverse – each with different real and symbolic meaning. Secondly, creative learning was expressed communally, in and through the ways communal spaces were used. Where it arose, creative learning resulted in the tendency to do things together, in the communality of each child's particular spaces at home. There seemed an ongoing adaptation in the ways the children engaged in activities at home, as the child habitus (or ways of life) encountered the family habitus. Finally, creative learning was valued differently in each child's case. As a form of family capital, it was valued differently by each member in each family home. It seemed that the children gained capital through the symbolic benefits of their activities in their physical, temporal and symbolic spaces. In John's case, this was revealed as a result of Romanian woodwork projects. These transactions involved different attributes such as self-determinedness, curiosity, resourcefulness, playfulness, and willingness to take risks and consider different possibilities, which were valued differently.

Bringing these three findings together, and building on the model of possibility thinking (Craft, Cremin, Burnard, Dragovic, & Chappell, 2013), a new model for creative learning in children's family homes was created.

The outer circle in Figure 3.2 shows how meaning (symbolic space) is made through the ways children spend their time in physical spaces at home. This created a sense of communal space (the next circle in). Within the communal space, the ways children and families engaged in and made sense of their individual and communal ways of life, and how they responded to 'spaces of uncertainty' (the times when children came across problems, confusions or mistakes) gave rise to creative learning. And creative learning was considered to include resourcefulness, playfulness, curiousness, being imaginative, being self-determined, risk taking and seeking out possibilities.

New points of departure

In this chapter, we have explored ways of developing reflexive practices through which practice is problematised and new questions are asked. As this story of one 'researcher-cum-educator-cum-researching professional' ends (for now), the hope is that the reader feels inspired to note, sketch, draw, respond, create and articulate their own professional story – to step back, reflect on and start new chapters with new learnings from this reflective analysis of practice. After all, the world is full of stories.

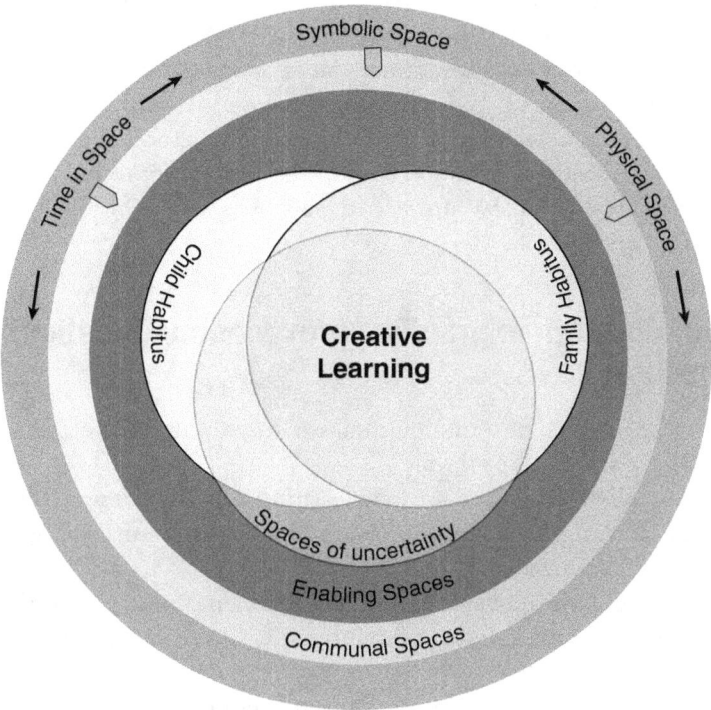

Figure 3.2 Intercultural creative learning from home model

As teachers, we need to work on the question of understanding, as a precursor to practice, lingering with the inner journeys, the performance of vulnerability and 'living the orange' (Cixous, 1994). This requires engaging in, and with, the unknowing and dissonance of interculturality and ways of thinking that may be far removed from one's 'comfort zone' or familiar cultural and/or professional contexts. It acknowledges the complexity of locations and identities in a global world.

These findings have implications for sculpting change in primary education through the co-creation of intercultural creative learning. We suggest that they will help primary education communities in a number of ways:

1 to inspire and invite children and educators to celebrate the immensity of difference encountered through storying;
2 to begin to think, live, feel, breathe and be ethical through intercultural practice;
3 to better understand how each of our life experiences reflect archetypes or cultural patterns that help situate our identities and how we can create personal meaning(s) together.

Storying the experiences of a school community requires institutional will to rethink what is meant by diversity. We have shown that engaging in a way that 'lives diversities' opens pathways of possibilities, to celebrate creative acts and to develop capacity to hear more voices. Such a shift in thinking about diversity begins to celebrate the plurality of creativities and the diversities of creative learning, and that creative learning must be understood as essentially intercultural. Intercultural creative learning relates to the propensity to be comfortable in spaces of uncertainty – to allow oneself to be tinted at the border crossing of cultural space (Cixous, 1994).

Unlocking research in practice: provocations for stimulating group discussion

1. How should we put 'interculturalism' to work to create a new era of cohesion and diversity in our school?
2. What will 'intercultural creative learning' as school design look like in practice?
3. What are/might be the storying times and communal spaces that matter most to us as a community?
4. How might we activate new participation and new partnerships with parents, working towards valuing how intercultural creative learning manifests in our school?
5. How can we engage with children to help them speak their creative learning from the diverse spaces in which they live?

Notes

1. Pseudonym used.
2. *Haram* is an Arabic word meaning sinful.
3. These are not their real names. Although they are from Romania, their original names are Biblical and so it was fitting that they chose similar Biblical names for their research personas.

References

Burnard, P. (2007). Provocations in creativity research. In L. Bresler (Ed.), *International handbook of research in arts education* (pp. 1175–1179). Dordrecht, the Netherlands: Springer.

Burnard, P., Kelly, E., & Biddulph, J. (2010). Mapping the creative journeying in practitioner research. In M. Khine and I. Saleh (Eds.), *Practitioner research: Teachers' investigations in classroom teaching* (pp. 1–15). Hauppauge, NY: Nova Science Publishers.

Cameron, J. (1993). *The artist way: A course in discovering and recovering your creative self*. London: Pan.

Cantle, T. (2012). *Interculturalism: The new era of cohesion and diversity*. Basingstoke: Palgrave Macmillan.

Cixous, H. (1994). To live the orange. In S. Sellers (Ed.), *The Helene Cixous reader* (pp. 81–92). New York: Routledge.

Craft, A., Cremin, T., Burnard, P., Dragovic, T., & Chappell, K. (2013). Possibility thinking: Culminative studies of an evidence-based concept driving creativity? *Education 3–13, 41*(5), 538–556.

Flutter, J. (2016). Fields and oceans: Helping professional doctorate students to orientate themselves and navigate through their practitioner research journeys. In P. Burnard, T. Dragovic, J. Flutter, & J. Alderton (Eds.), *Transformative doctoral research practices for professionals*. Rotterdam: Sense Publishers.

Gray, C., & Malins, J. (2004). *Visualising research: A guide to the research process in art and design*. Aldershot, England: Ashgate.

Greene, M. (1998). *Releasing the Imagination: Essays on education, the arts and social change* San Francisco: Jossey-Bass.

Hofvander Trulsson, Y., & Burnard, P. (2016). Insider, outsider or cultures in-between: Ethical and methodological consideration in intercultural arts research. In P. Burnard, E. Mackinlay, & K. Powell (Eds.), *The Routledge international handbook of intercultural arts research* (pp. 115–125). Abingdon, Oxon: Routledge.

hooks, B. (1994). *Teaching to transgress: Education as the practice of freedom*. London: Routledge.

Kelly, P. (2002). *Multiculturalism reconsidered*. Cambridge: Polity Press.

Modood, T. (2007). *Multiculturalism*. Cambridge: Polity Press.

Phillips, L. G., & Bunda, T. (2018). *Research through, with and as storying*. London and New York: Routledge.

Winstanley, J.-M., & Moule, L. (2021). Teachers as writers. In E. Hargreaves & L. Rolls (Eds.), *Unlocking research: Reimagining professional development in schools* (pp. 138–150). Abingdon, Oxon and New York: Routledge.

CHAPTER 4

Animating primary schools, inside and out: enlivening learning through meaningful memory-making

Elsa Lee and Sarah Stepney

This chapter is an outcome of a collaboration between an academic in the field of environmental sustainability education and a headteacher of a primary school. Elsa Lee writes as the academic in the environmental sustainability field while Sarah Stepney is a practicing teacher and co-headteacher at a school in Cambridge, UK: the Mayfield Primary School. We would like to stress that what we write about here is not the outcome of a research study, but is informed by decades of working in and with schools, and is spurred on by shared interests and the opportunity to better knowledge for both academic and practice purposes.

In writing this we adopt a first person collective approach, occasionally switching between our separate voices as academic and practitioner; but usually what we write expresses our shared, negotiated thinking, thus it is written collectively. Furthermore, we also represent the voices of the wider school community and the voices of the researchers we draw on, and that further consolidates our writing style in the 'editorial we', as this style is sometimes described.

Keeping with the aims of this book, we will explore the bidirectional relations between theory and practice through our co-author pairing of researcher and practitioner; seeking on the one hand to make academic research accessible and useful to practitioners through interweaving observations from practice with explanations from theory, and on the other to test the validity of educational theory through the eyes of a practicing teacher and school leader. We will be using *practice* to reveal how useful theory might be for classroom teachers; focusing on creating a rich description that might prompt readers, bringing up thoughts of their own practice and reflections on and of that. Through this chapter we reveal the co-authoring of memories that animates and enlivens learning *and* the school as a place, especially through engaging creatively with the outdoors.

The *theory* that we will be thinking with is a rather messy assortment of dimensions of posthumanism, new materialism, animacies and entanglements. The way these ideas are described by those sometimes seen as their originators (Gilles Deleuze and Felix Gautarri, Donna Haraway and Karen Barad, for example) is often deeply philosophical and can be daunting. With this in mind, we avoid providing detailed definitions, aiming to let their meaning emerge through the narrative of the chapter.

The authors of this chapter first met at the UK Government's House of Commons for a meeting of the Arts and Crafts in Education All Party Parliamentary Group. APPGs are an important means for the public to influence policy in the UK, providing a meeting place for members of the public and members of parliament to talk, regardless of party political affiliation. On this occasion, we were there because of our relationship with the arts-based charity, Cambridge Curiosity and Imagination (CCI[1]). Also present were two children from Mayfield Primary School, along with their parents and the school's other co-head. The children read out this list of wishes they had for all children at any school:

- Be free
- Imagine anything
- Have fun
- Know anyone can do it; there are no wrong answers
- Share and talk
- Not rush
- Try things out and experiment – make a mess
- See that art is everywhere
- Keep trying
- Move around, be comfortable
- Be brave and trust

The list grew out of the work the school had been doing with CCI, the aforementioned arts-based charity committed to getting children into the outdoors, using the arts as a means of developing their imaginative skills, amongst other purposes that have been published.[2] The children compiled this list during a day where art was used to reimagine a university department studio at the end of a 2-year project by CCI at Mayfield Primary School. The pertinence of this manifesto becomes evident during 1:1 conversations that children have with their teachers each term when the discussion often turns to outdoor learning and how individuals respond to their time outside. The overarching view from the children is that, when they are outside, they do not feel rushed, they do not feel watched and being able to move around helps them to develop their thinking. The children comment that they work better with their friends outside, and even those that are not their close friends! They comment that walking and talking with a partner without anyone looking over their shoulder is a freeing and positive experience, where they can explore ideas and come up with wrong answers and not worry. Teachers and children are able to draw on the experiences of being outdoors, and transfer these positive learning characteristics into the classroom, or indeed into any space they find themselves.

This manifesto and the description of its relevance in the school, when viewed through a posthumanist lens, reveals much about how a school can function in a relational way, to engage its children in learning that lasts a lifetime; learning that pops up over the lifetime of the person who experiences it in effective ways at moments of transition or points of inflection, or in quiet moments of introspection to be relived and re-actualised and reinterpreted or reformed on an almost daily basis. And this is the nub of our argument, that a posthumanist lens reveals schools as sites of memory-making (both intentionally as with classroom-based learning, or not, as with child-led break time rituals). These memories pop up over the child's lifetime and so they have a life-long impact. Posthumanism provides a basis for consciously making memories that can feed resilience, and a capacity for wonder, for example, alongside the existing intended consequences of remembering numbers and letters, for example.

Whatever our experience of schooling is, we have to accept that its impacts last a lifetime. How we are facilitated to engage with learning in schools (or at home, for those who are home-schooled) remains with us and returns to us across our lifespan in sometimes surprising and arresting ways, and it is for this reason (in part) that so much time and energy and financial resource is invested in getting it right. While the majority of this investment goes into the academic knowledge and understanding, intellectual and social skills, and (to a lesser extent) the spiritual and moral development of the children it is designed for, less attention is paid to the quality of the holistic experience of the child; although there is evidence of changing attitudes here. In England, the curriculum itself is becoming more holistic with renewed focus on the importance of the arts in the co-curriculum, and on the health and wellbeing of children and young people through, for example, the new and mandatory Relationships and Sex Education and Health Education curriculum. But what is still not given due attention is the hidden curriculum (Bilbao, Lucido, Iringan, & Javier, 2008; Crossman, 2020), which is seldom acknowledged (at either the policy or local school level). Yet it often leaves big impressions on children lives as they grow, or become with the creatures and places surrounding them. For example, what is it that children learn from rules that limit or permit movement around the school grounds and school buildings on the basis of risk? Do they learn that even places that are designed for them actually exclude them? Or do they learn how to take risks carefully, knowing that water mixes with soil, becoming slippery, because they have played in wet weather clothing on muddy ground in the rain outside the classroom? Do they remember the sense of an off-limits world; or do they remember the joy of being truly embedded and emplaced in their own place? And how do these different interpretations affect their ongoing becoming and growing?

Following this line of thinking, in this chapter we explore how animacy might be applied to schools. We will base our discussion on the school mentioned earlier, that works with outside agencies to develop their curriculum to be participatory, creative and inclusive. These agencies have supported creative, adventurous opportunities that underpin the development of embodied relationships with the school grounds and classrooms, and respectful relationships between adults and children. The agencies have also facilitated children and adults working together on developing how the school delivers the English National Curriculum and its development plan. Through the chapter we will reveal how this unfolds, but we will start by defining how we use the notion of animacy here and what this means for our description of animated school.

In our interpretation, all schools are animated (or enlivened) in some way or other. In this sense, the way a school is remembered and the meaning that the child (or adult) attaches to it depends on the experience the child has of it. To us, making meaning is how children see themselves in relation to the school, the memories they have of it, the kind of learning that happens when these sorts of memories are made. Meaning arises from the memories we make and re-make through our ongoing engagement with a place; meaning becomes part of our identity and therefore places become part of our identity. Place has been shown to be an important dimension of our identity (e.g. Ardoin, 2006; Kirkwood, McKinlay, & McVittie, 2013; Kudryavtsev, Stedman, & Krasny, 2012). Our identity is not fixed but constantly becoming, and so is constantly formed and reformed through the meaning we make out of the emplaced experiences we have. This process of ongoing meaning making, in turn, enlivens (or animates) places for us (Bodenhorn & Lee, forthcoming). Hence a school as a place rich in experiences for children is enlivened through the experiences that the child has here. The degree to which a child has the freedom to explore the physical limits of their mindful bodies and cognitive and social limits of their embodied minds through their material and relational engagements with the school, including both its physical and social dimensions, determines the kind of animation that the school takes on for the child. The school will reveal itself differently to each child that enters its gates because each child will bring a different set of experiences to bear on how they interpret their schooling.

In thinking of schools in this way we draw on the work of Karen Barad (e.g. 2007) and Donna Haraway (e.g. 2016) and many others[3] including previous work of the first author exploring children's connections to place (Bodenhorn & Lee, forthcoming). As we understand it, place (which might be a school or any other place) is conceptualised as much more than a physical location. It is a multidimensional, entangled phenomenon, with temporal, social, cultural, geographic, political, economic, psychological and biophysical dimensions and not just a purposed collection of buildings and their grounds.

We want to show that schools are places themselves, with complex and entangled identities; and that through enabling deep, relational knowledge of the school grounds and classrooms to develop using, for example, art and freedom of movement as a material, corporeal way to engage with the school grounds, schools can become intimately animated *for* children. Such conditions initiate development of intimacy that give a certain character to the enlivening or animation of lives and memories that is made real (or actualised) through the long-term engagement of children with place.

To make this work, first we accept that the way school is experienced by its human members, or how the school becomes animated for its members, is determined by the conditions for experiencing it that are generated by the interplay and interpenetration of its physical, social, cultural, political and other contexts. Then we can imagine that we can influence this animation or enlivening by consciously taking hold of its curriculum (both hidden and explicit) and intentionally designing it from an holistic point of view. In this way the school will be animated for the child as a place of meaningful memories that can underwrite how the child experiences the world as they grow. These memories can be a source of resilience and fortitude when shaped by experiences of overcoming challenges and navigating risks, for example. So a school animated in such a way leaves the child stronger with capabilities in place, ready to face the world daily and in future. Of course, we can never determine the actual experience that each member of the school has because each member will have a different interpretation based on the socioeconomic conditions of their home, for example, or the cultural dimensions of the country and communities in which they live, but, as we have long known and acted on through national and local policies, we can certainly influence what is experienced in this setting.

At Mayfield Primary School knowledge of the importance of the holistic experience that the children have (what we are here describing as the way the school becomes animated by and for its members) has led to a practice of working with approved outside agencies to help to deliver the National Curriculum creatively and participatively. Engaging children in not only creative and adventurous learning itself, but also in determining the shape of that learning, within the boundaries of the curriculum and other state-led policies.

Much of what we have been writing about so far has referred to posthumanist principles and thinking, and new materialism is tied up with this way of knowing the world. New materialism brings the material back into the forefront of discussions about knowledge and knowing, making the case that the material world and the thinking (or symbolic) world are inextricably entangled. Put simply we see new materialism as an attempt to bring together the world of symbols and the world of materials, and to show how meaning emerges in the intimate relations between thing-ness and think-ness, if you will. New materialism moves away from the idea that we make meaning in our internal but disembodied minds through the use of symbols like verbal or written language. It also rejects the notion that meaning is external: held within objects. Its aim is to show that the meaning we make of the world is created through our relational engagements with the world that we inhabit and it relies on quantum theory to achieve this (at least Karen Barad's version of it does).

By now it will have become clear that posthumanism and new materialism are heavily reliant on the concepts of materiality (how things can be experienced by the senses) and relationality (how things interact with each other). In describing (and thus analyzing) the practice at this school using these ideas, we aim to reveal the shape of the animacy that emerges here. In particular we will show the way that this school approaches materiality and relationality and temporality, and the potential this might have for generating a specific kind of animating of the lives of the school's members. For example, what is the impact of being able to immerse yourself into the place/school with all your senses, having time to do this at your own pace, and time to share this immersion with those around you on how you feel about your school and what you learn there? Returning to the manifesto from the school's children, the idea that 'art is everywhere' entails a deep and open way of looking at and knowing the world; a particular kind of intimacy: a way of inhabiting the world that is creative, conscious and observant. In turn the school becomes a place of adventure, curiosity and fantasy for its members.

The difficulty, of course, is that in doing so we will have to separate out these ideas from how they are experienced, and then we are doing the very thing that posthumanists warn against: we are untangling the inherently tangled. For posthumanist scholars the way a child or adult experiences a place such as a school can only really be understood through acceptance of experiences as entangled. However to describe that experience it will be useful to pull out some of its threads to see them separately, as they are entangled, and we ask that you bear with us if what we write does not make immediate sense; by the end, we hope that the narrative arc of our story will provide the impression we seek to convey: of a school animated by the foundational conditions intended to liberate the children and adults' relational, corporeal (or bodily), material intra-actions within it, through a creative adventurous approach to ensuring the curriculum targets are met.

So far in this chapter we have tried to develop a narrative that enables an understanding of animacy to evolve. Next we will focus on temporality, materiality and relationality, exemplifying each with experiences that members of the school we are writing from might have.

Materiality or recognising that our relationship to the physical world and how we engage with it impacts how we learn

At Mayfield Primary School children are given many opportunities for engaging with the school grounds. The school stipulates an afternoon outdoors every week for every class, called *out and about*. Whilst this takes different forms for different classes with different teachers, working on different parts of the curriculum, it is always a time for the children to explore the curricular imperatives through active, corporeal engagements with the school grounds. For example, children have access to a wide range of *bits and pieces*, these might be beads, pine cones, cotton reels, pegs, twigs, that are available outside in wooden trays, buckets and boxes. The children use these bits and pieces to create pictures that might explain their thinking to themselves and others; for example, creating the water cycle; for planning a story; for demonstrating a mathematical concept; or for simply producing patterns and pictures. This practical, hands-on (corporeal, material) approach encourages children to talk and to work collaboratively (relationally). It is also an approach that means that children can easily adapt their thinking without having to cross out in a book or use a rubber, thus giving them the freedom to make mistakes and learn from theirs and others' ideas.

The relationality of learning obvious in this description will be discussed in the next section. For materiality, this sort of activity makes meaning with a sensory element, the feel and look of the items enlivens the meaning, and this in turn animates the learning in a very different way to how ordering of images of materials in a textbook might do, for example. Giving learning meaning through this material, visceral experience has the potential of making it permanent and long term in a very different way to the kind of permanency that other (albeit also essential) ways of learning (like reading and writing) might afford.

Similarly, the commitment to being outside in any weather, to achieve whatever learning objective, gives that learning objective a different quality, a visceral, embodied sense with a potentially more deeply consolidated meaning that is differently animated for the learner. For example, younger children in the school look forward to their weekly *welly walks*. These walks, from their classroom to the *secret garden* (once called the conservation area, but now too well frequented to merit that name!), take children across the school grounds past the raised beds for gardening, through a cluster of trees and around the perimeter of the field. Along the way they stop and talk about what they see: what is the same as the last time they came and what is different? Before entering the *secret garden* they sit on logs and share hot chocolate, fruit and their experiences of their journey so far. They also talk about what they are looking forward to doing or seeing in the *secret garden* and remind each other of the things that they need to remember to keep themselves safe. A trolley of resources is taken along, amongst which is a large scrap book that belongs to all the children. If they choose to they can add to the scrapbook any pictures, writing and photographs that are produced during their visit. The connection to their surroundings is tangible. The children confidently navigate the terrain, climbing the trees, checking out the inhabitants of the pond, working and playing together, wherever their imaginations take them. There are no set expectations and no specific curriculum objectives to be hit. In reality the children are experiencing such a wide range of national curriculum objectives that there would be too many to count and record. This description of the way the children use the school grounds as a learning resource is replete with material engagement. Of particular interest is the importance of movement and mobility.

Here the way that the children move through the terrain demonstrates an easy familiarity with the matter that makes up their surroundings. But mobility also influences the quality of learning that takes place. Recent work on walking (see Shane O'Mara, 2019, for example) identifies how the brain is more alert when the body is in motion, which might influence how much of the learning during these sessions becomes part of the child's mindscape, to pop up and be relived in later years.

Also worth noting here from a posthumanist perspective is the reliance on noticing what is the same and what is different. Karen Barad talks about the importance of 'difference' to help us to understand the world, and here it appears to be serving the same purpose (2007). These children are learning about the world through their observations about what has changed when they revisit a place over an extended period of time and are learning a great deal from this that can be applied to their curriculum work.

Another example of material engagement with the school grounds is the freedom these children have to climb trees, up to a risk-assessed height. This freedom to test the physical limits of the body and to learn how to manage the fear entailed in this activity brings potential for a new kind of animation to the space, coupled with the kind of intimate knowledge of a tree that can only come from being held in its branches, or skinning your knee on its trunk. Getting to know your school grounds through your body – a visceral, embodied, corporeal, mobilised knowledge of the grounds, animates the space to create a positive relational engagement with it (for most) and it is reasonable to presume that this positive affect will overflow into the classroom.

Relationality or recognising the positive impact for everyone when teaching and learning is truly collaborative and built on relationships

Talking here about relationality as one entangled dimension of the impact of climbing trees leads us to our next example of this school's practice. Relationality here refers to how human members are connected to each other through their shared activities and experiences, but it also refers to the way the members of the school relate to the physical space (as in the earlier example of a child climbing a tree, where the tree becomes something special to the child, a part of that child's identity perhaps, because of the encounter between the two). Essentially it is about the relationships that form in and with the space, but it is not just about communication in those relationships, as the example of the bits and pieces activity earlier points to. It is also about sharing experiences and a shared understanding that develops through that.

Another example of an activity that gives learning here a relational dimension is collaborative rug writing, an activity that children can be seen undertaking during *out and about* sessions. Each child, with a friend or two, takes their *out and about* books (these are A3 sketchbooks with solid covers) and a rug and finds a space to sit. Together they write stories. One child will scribe whilst together they come up with ideas. This is a very liberating experience for children who struggle to write independently, but more often than not have wonderfully creative ideas. As a headteacher I can imagine many reading this and being skeptical about the success of this activity, as I would have been at the start of our journey. But it is important to bear in mind that getting to this point is just that, a journey; and handing over freedom to a class of children can be a scary step to take, but we at Mayfield have found over and over again that we have been surprised by the children's response to being outside of the four walls of their classrooms. They feel less anxious, less judged and more supported by one another. Outside the classroom the adults become learners alongside the children, and the children enjoy this honesty that we never stop learning, something that they sometimes fail to recognise in the classroom. Central to the success of this approach is the relationality that emerges in this description, between children, between children and adults, and between the children and the place that they are working in.

This relational sense of co-learning is embedded further through an approach called 'Spirals of Enquiry' that is used at Mayfield. Spirals is essentially about listening to our learners and responding authentically to what we hear through our ever-adaptive teaching practice. Each term the children have a 30-minute 1:1 session with their class teacher. During this time they are asked to name two people in school who believe they will be successful, and are encouraged to discuss their learning in terms of what is going well and what they are finding challenging. The key to the success of these conversations is in the changes that teachers make to their classroom practice in order to support the children's learning. When children see these changes happening they recognise that they do have influence over the adults who teach them, and that their reflections on their learning do bring about change. They begin to see themselves as authorities on their own learning and this influences how the school space is animated for them. The relations between the child and the adult here have an impact on both the adult and the child. The relationality of this approach has far-reaching consequences for the becoming of those involved, as well as for how the school is known and remembered; how the school is animated.

Temporality, or building connections between the past, present and future through creative memory-making

Another important dimension of posthumanism is time, and our experience of it. We have alluded to this already in our description of how meaningful experiences in school can flash up throughout our lives and be relived in new ways shaped by the times in which we revisit them. In recognising this, posthumanism moves away from a linear, hierarchical definition of time, towards a more disrupted, experiential understanding of time that might *drag* or *fly*, depending on the activity that is being undertaken, or the emotional state of the humans involved. In this regard, CCI who work with this school on their arts-based practice, are influenced by the Reggio Emilia[4] approach to slowliness, and this is evident in the kinds of activities that they do with the children and the way they value the children's pace of learning.

The children's manifesto outlined earlier in this chapter identifies 'Not rush' as one wish for schools. This expression in the negative hones us in to the meaningfulness of this statement. It can be interpreted as being about moving slowly when moving around the school grounds or as an admonition to change the way we, as adults, live our daily lives. It might be as much a comment on modern, fast-paced living as it may be a plea to take the time in school to develop visceral, embodied knowledge of what the curriculum aims to teach.

An exemplification of the impact of the children's wish is evident in the experience of one year group who were regularly visiting the secret garden. At the very start of our journey with *out and about*, the teacher of this class planned a range of activities for the children to do whilst they were in the secret garden. It very quickly became apparent that the children were gaining much more by being allowed to explore and connect with their environment each week, rather than being constrained by specific questions from the teacher. Like the welly walk, it became apparent that it was enough just to ask, 'what is the same, what is different' and then share together what the children had discovered. In doing so we noticed the enthusiasm gained by the children of wanting to find out more about what they had noticed. Providing resources for the children, without being overly prescriptive as to how they are used, and giving them time to explore freely encourages further investigation and creative thinking. An example is the use of mirrors. Provided with small rectangular mirrors, children created the most incredible art installations, and along the way learnt about light refraction, symmetry and the power of looking even more closely at your surroundings. This attention to the children's wish not to rush has not ended up in wasted time, as one might fear, but has enabled time to be used wisely with the potential for rich learning and deep engagement.

Another way in which the work at this school chimes with how posthumanists discuss temporality relates to meaning making. The time gifted the children to be outside potentiates deeper relationship with their surroundings. The grounds are no longer just about time out of the classroom for breaks, but they have become a place to learn and grow. They have become a resource for the children's imagination, influencing how they write stories and the kind of visual art they produce, as with the mirror art described earlier. This in turn has the capacity to influence the meaningfulness of the school to each member, potentiating a strongly positive affective engagement that might then spill over into a sense of enthusiasm for learning both inside and outside the classroom, which may in turn be carried out of the school gates into homes and communities and forward into the future lives of the children. Thus we see that a school intentionally animated to engage the embodied imagination through visceral, slowed-down exploration of the curriculum-in-place may potentiate a lifetime of meaning making through reliving childhood memories in new contexts. This re-actualisation of experiences is an important element of Barad's work that holds that time is not simply and exclusively linear and regularised as the clocks and schedules we live by dictate. The way we experience events and make memories anew, repeatedly, reshapes how we think of time.

To illustrate, one of us, the first author explains: I have a particular memory of how I would spend break or what you might know as recess at school. At the age of 6, a friend and I could be found running up and down a small hill holding hands; every break, every day. I remember the feel of her hand, and the sense of rising joy as we sped up down the hill and the occasional tears when we fell over at the bottom, soothed away by a friendly hug together. I relived that experience recently when one of my children joyfully careened down a slope, tumbling down at the bottom. The experience "flashed up" as Barad would say (Barad, 2007). Then I relived it when I told my child about it. In the reliving of this experience I was squashing linearised time; bringing the past into the present. That memory, relational, material and embodied as it is, is stronger for me than any single moment at a desk in an ordered, hierarchical classroom. This is not to say that order and hierarchy indoors is unnecessary; far from it! Rather, we would like to suggest that when order and hierarchy are interspersed with child-led, free and playful moments in spaces where boundaries are more flexible, permeable and permissive, then both become animated, by the other (for example, a biology lesson on tree morphology becomes animated by the corporeal experience of climbing in its branches and the memories that experience creates; whilst a walk in the woods becomes animated by curriculum knowledge of what goes on below the ground in the unseen realms amongst the trees' roots and rhizomes and mycorrhizas) and what emerges is a differently animated, and arguably more meaningful kind of learning.

Some conclusions for rethinking practice

In our understanding, all learning is animated by how it is generated, but learning that is animated in a way meaningful to children through being knowledgeable about the child and the child's place has the potential to be stickier (Bodenhorn & Lee, forthcoming), than learning that relies solely on static, desk-based activities.

Recognising this, that engaging outside agencies with these principles of creative adventuring, letting children lead and genuinely participate makes learning sticky, has had significant effects on teachers at Mayfield, as observed by the school's leadership team. A lovely example of children leading their learning is that of planning a story. For years we have been slaves to the *story mountain* scaffold, showing children one way of planning a story. But at Mayfield you can see classes planning their stories outside, encouraged to choose how they do this – use the bits and pieces, act out the plan, draw the plan, write the plan, tell a friend the plan, or simply just write – because that is what some of us like to do.

It has to be acknowledged that to get to the stage we are at has taken time. It has taken bravery on the part of the teachers, and a commitment by us as headteachers to give teachers permission to go *off curriculum* for one afternoon a week in spite of the pressure that we feel to complete a packed national curriculum. Teachers report frequently that at the start of the journey they felt anxious and out of control, not having four walls to contain their class. The ability to know what every child is doing is taken away, and instead a much greater level of trust has to be given over to the children; and so their manifesto becomes manifest.

We have tried to build towards a sense of a school where the body is allowed the freedom to explore, adventure, create, participate and lead within reasonable constraints; a school that provides the space for this sort of memory-making becomes highly meaningful for its students. We have endeavoured to convey the way in which the kind of corporeal experience that being free to climb trees or have fun connects individuals to a place; a place that is engaging, a place that is loved and a place where time becomes precious and valued.

Any school is animated by its constituent parts (including the humans, the buildings, the state policies and so on) and the way they interact. In many schools this happens as part of the hidden curriculum in a haphazard way. Taking hold of that process of animation and intentionally guiding it can have far-reaching consequences for changing practice, but it might also reveal the very rich and varied experiences already occurring, and might then simply consolidate and enhance existing practice.

Accepting that a school will be animated differently to different people, regardless of what we as educators do, we can then work on depth of engagement and the joy and depth of learning through considering the entanglement of material, corporeal, relational and temporal elements at play, and making them visible. Whilst none of this is new, experiential learning has long been recognised as impactful and important (see Kolb's learning cycle and designing classrooms for learning, (see Reggio Emilia, for example: Lenz Taguchi, 2010) the posthumanist lens shines new light and provides a coordinating framework from which to consider them.

In thinking about all of these ideas we might also make connections to the science of learning that is gaining traction as a new dimension in teacher education programmes in England. Researchers based at the University of Bristol provide free online resources at www.scienceoflearning.org, putting forward an engage, build, consolidate model, based on neuroscientific studies of how the brain learns. What role might the arts and the outdoors play here? And how does a posthuman framing of the arts and the outdoors fare under the scrutiny of the science of learning? If being outside with all of its relational and material affordances elicits a positive emotional response that engages children who might otherwise not have shown interest, and if the outdoors provides a space for new knowledge introduced in the classroom to be applied in different ways through material and relational media, thus consolidating learning and making it permanent, then the approach that Mayfield Primary School takes stands up to this scrutiny in the short term at least, but only time will tell for how long its impacts last.

The provocations that follow may spur educators to put these conclusions into conversation with their own practice.

Unlocking research in practice: provocations for group discussion

1. Identify five of the most memorable experiences you have had with children at your school. Why do you remember them? What makes them meaningful to you? Do you think the children would identify the same ones? What do you think this says about your hidden curriculum? How can you incorporate this meaningfulness into daily practice, in positive ways?
2. What would having a weekly *out and about* afternoon look like in your school? How might this help to achieve your curriculum targets? How might this enrich learning? What barriers are there to this in your school? How might you overcome them?
3. How can you connect your discussions arising from Question 1 and 2 earlier to the science of learning?

Notes

1. https://www.cambridgecandi.org.uk
2. https://www.cambridgecandi.org.uk/product/artscapers-being-and-becoming-creative (Aycliffe, Sapsed, Sayers, & Whitley, 2020)
3. Coole and Frost's (2010) edited volume is a good place to start reading about these issues because it is grounded in practice that is relatable to education.
4. https://www.reggiochildren.it/en/reggio-emilia-approach/

References

Ardoin, N. M. (2006). Toward an interdisciplinary understanding of place: Lessons for environmental education. *Canadian Journal of Environmental Education, 11*, 112–126.

Aycliffe, P., Sapsed, R., Sayers, E., & Whitley, D. (2020). *Artscapers: Being and becoming creative*. Cambridge: Cambridge Curiosity and Imagination.

Barad, K. M. (2007). *Meeting the universe halfway: Quantum physics and the entanglement of matter and meaning*. Durham: Duke University Press.

Bilbao, P. P., Lucido, P. I., Iringan, T. C., & Javier, B. R. (2008). *Curriculum development*. Philippines: Lorimar Publishing, Inc.

Bodenhorn, B., & Lee, E. (forthcoming). Animating place for children: A comparative analysis. *Anthropology and Education Quarterly*.

Coole, D. H., & Frost, S. (Eds.). (2010). *New materialisms: Ontology, agency, and politics*. Durham and London: Duke University Press.

Crossman, A. (2020, August 26). *What is hidden curriculum?* ThoughtCo. Retrieved from https://www.thoughtco.com/hidden-curriculum-3026346

Haraway, D. J. (2016). *Staying with the trouble: Making kin in the Chthulucene.* Durham: Duke University Press.

Kirkwood, S., McKinlay, A., & McVittie, C. (2013). The mutually constitutive relationship between place and identity: The role of place-identity in discourse on asylum seekers and refugees: Place-identity, asylum seekers and refugees. *Journal of Community & Applied Social Psychology, 23*(6), 453–465. https://doi.org/10.1002/casp.2141

Kudryavtsev, A., Stedman, R. C., & Krasny, M. E. (2012). Sense of place in environmental education. *Environmental Education Research, 18*(2), 229–250.

O'Mara, S. M. (2019). *In praise of walking: The new science of how we walk and why it's good for us.* London: Bodley Head.

Taguchi, H. L. (2010). *Going beyond the theory/practice divide in early childhood education: Introducing an intra-active pedagogy.* London: Routledge.

CHAPTER 5

Posthumanist creative ecologies in primary education

Anne Harris

Introduction

This essay puts the case that new approaches to creative education using some core principles of posthumanist theory offer a dynamic key to transforming primary education toward more creative, and more ecologically-sustainable, knowledge-building and embodied creative collaborating. The co-authored, co-creative structure of this book mirrors new movements in creative approaches to education research, including a recognition of the ways in which humans can usefully 'collaborate' with non-human others, and suggests practical ways in which new creativities and posthumanist theory point toward future primary education possibilities that build awareness of and respect for all non-human components of primary students' education. The collaborative structure and community ethos invite readers into a range of encounters with what I'm calling 'posthumanist creativities' in order to collaboratively play and reimagine primary education futures that focus on creative environments, ecologies and practices. Dismantling the boundaries between 'academics' and 'teachers', as this volume does, helps reconfigure the language about creativity away from a relentlessly human-centred focus to include non-human collaborators such as the built environment, animals, plant life, sandboxes and other sites of and partners in serious play.

This chapter, like the others in this volume, helps tell a story of how primary education is opening up to new ways of thinking, being and doing as teachers, artists and researchers across diverse contexts. They honour multiple ways of knowing and becoming. Going forward from the current pandemic circumstances and into the coming constraints and possibilities it has engendered requires new ways of thinking about expertise, pedagogies and learning contexts. Primary teachers, teaching assistants and school leaders are perfectly positioned to highlight the diverse knowledges and always-already present collaborative approaches that exist in primary school contexts.

Posthumanising creative ecologies

By advancing a 'creative ecologies' (Harris, 2016, 2018) model, I have argued that a more holistic, relational and systemic approach can be more powerful than individual or siloed approaches, whether those be in teaching, learning or environment-focused aspects. In a creative ecologies approach, multiple creativities productively co-inform and co-create all aspects of the practices, people and places involved. And this does not just address educational contexts either. This model can be applied to any environment which seeks to become more creative through a relational and cross-pollinating approach (Sawyer, 2019; Amabile, 2018), including those who seek innovation in the ways in which creativity is applied, considered or fostered in sociocultural ways in classrooms.

Late twentieth-century creativity discourses in education remained, for the most part, limited by singular and individual humanist notions of creativity, such as teaching creative thinking or creative pedagogies (Cremin, 2018). Some innovations toward more transdisciplinary creativities, including as framed through the lens of STEAM (Burnard & Colucci-Gray, 2020), have helped diversify understandings and appreciation of multiplicities of creativities in education contexts. More recently, creativity's appearances in national curricula are characterised by combining with notions like critical thinking and innovation, which inevitably prioritises innovation or critical thinking over the creativity component, and too often suggests they are interchangeable (CCSS, n.d.; ACARA, n.d.), although South Korea continues to lead in targeting multiple aspects of creativity in both primary and secondary education (NCEE, n.d.). They all share a focus on written, 'academic' subjects rather than experiential and exploratory activities, which all creativity research agrees is required for growing creative risk-taking and enjoyment. The twenty-first century and its dual provocations of rapid development of artificial intelligence and machine learning, alongside the accelerator of COVID-19, has produced an opportunity for seriously reconsidering the ways, places, relationships and processes which we have traditionally considered 'good education'. It is time for something new.

Posthumanist theory offers what some are calling a paradigm-shifting move toward thinking with nature in ways that can embed sustainability and eco-awareness in a new generation from early years. By adopting posthumanism's core beliefs of decentring the human from its pre-eminent position in the hierarchy of planetary beings, matter and needs, primary education has the opportunity to rethink practice through a lens of making-with, becoming-with and experiencing-with, rather than 'teaching' or 'learning' as separate activities occurring in subjective and or geo-political siloes and separations.

While posthumanist theory has expanded into multiple disciplines since the start of the twenty-first century (Braidotti, 2013), others have applied this lens to early childhood and primary education contexts and investigations (Chappell, 2018; Hackett, MacLure, & Pahl, 2020). In particular, Kerry Chappell (2018) has extended her work with Anna Craft to theorise a notion of posthumanising creativity, in which she critiques the humanist focus of her earlier work. She acknowledges that, with the passage of time, and the deepening of an 'emergent ethical' understanding of ecological sustainability, a recognition of the non-human contributors to creative ecological sustainability (think animals, plants, ecosystems) with whom we collaborate is required (2018, p. 286).

The five domains of creative ecology in educational contexts

I start with my model for an ecological approach to fostering creativity, which I have been developing over the past decade (Harris, 2018). A creative ecological approach to creative education in primary contexts can be broken down into the five domains that comprise this model, a model that can be used in any context: policies, processes, products, partnerships and place/physical environments (see Figure 5.1). Together they make up an entire 'ecology' or ecosystem. Attention to these elements allows actors (learners, users, workers and non-human collaborators)

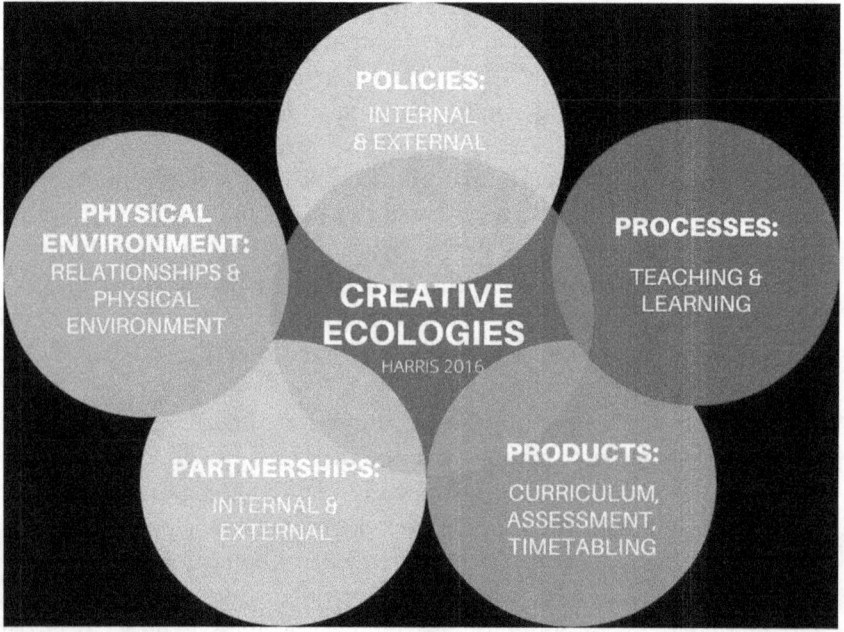

Figure 5.1 Creative ecologies model (adapted from Harris, 2016)

to cross-pollinate and work collectively to enhance the creativity of the whole environment rather than breaking it down into individual (and sometimes not coordinated) elements. The model's five elements are all not only interrelated and overlapping (in the model and in life), but require focused attention in order to build an integrated creative ecology that is sustainable. These five elements, comprising the ecosystem of creative potential, are all always-already in process, and interacting to facilitate or inhibit creative events and experiences.

Teresa Amabile (2018) asks how we might incorporate individual psychological and cognitive understandings of creativity (of which there is a large body of research) with the organisational, collective and socio-cultural. Such enquiries can be productively linked with education contexts, but also go beyond. For the purposes of this book, let us look at the five P's of this model, as they apply to primary education contexts.

Places/physical environments

Posthumanism, especially in early childhood and primary education, sees learning as an encounter between young children and environments, non-human actors (actants) and others (Malone, 2017), through which the human and more-than-human might come together to productively advance what we know about innovative education. There are theoretical turf wars between 'posthumanist' and 'anti-humanist' and other subcategories of these siloes, but the most important thing to remember is that an expansion of teaching, learning and researching in this area can benefit all stakeholders in so many positive ways! It is time to put aside shades of difference and celebrate innovation in a creative, relational way.

For creative ecologies, the place element is so important. It is a kind of element that is easily ignored, is considered passive, and is only (traditionally) seen to support the work of human actors who seek to foster creativity. What if the non-human actors drove our efforts toward more creatively and sustainably engaging with the planet? What if, as in Indigenous place-making accounts and practices, nature encounter comes first, before story, self and culture? Some scholars, including Margaret Somerville, have applied key aspects of posthumanist theory to education practices, specifically with young children (Somerville, 2017; Hackett et al., 2020). In particular, Somerville turns to the concepts of 'intra-action', 'common worlds' and 'thinking through Country', the latter of which brings together 'Indigenous and western nature/culture approaches' (Somerville, 2017, p. 20). For Somerville and others, education scholars are called to dismantle the nature-culture binary that has until now defined the work of subject and knowledge construction. Instead, she argues, it is time to 'move beyond the binary constructions that underpin the belief that the human species can be understood as separate from nature or the environment' (p. 18). Braidotti has argued that advancing a sustainable, equitable and creative programme of radical social change in late capitalism requires us to move beyond individualism and invest in 'the pursuit of collective projects aimed at the affirmation of hope, rooted in the ordinary micro-practices of everyday life' (Braidotti, 2013, p. 192). Similarly, an ecological approach toward creative change in primary schools (and elsewhere) is committed to collectivism and offers an anti-human-centred and anti-individualist model.

Processes

Processes is an important element in the creative ecologies model, partly because it has for so long been forced into the background. Process-oriented education has been, at different times in history, more and less valued. But what can we make of process-oriented models of creativity education today, as standardisation reaches global scales? Posthumanism offers one approach, in attending to all learning and becoming as an 'intra-active' event in which all actants are co-creating one another, where human subjects are co-produced with non-human collaborators. In primary school settings, there are endless examples of this kind of approach, from immersion in nature materials in the classroom, to outdoor immersive activities in which the students co-create with natural materials. Animals, too, play a larger role in learning in the primary years than perhaps any other stage of formal education. Following Somerville, it is crucial to start with all processes of co-creation as interdependent and with none taking precedence over others; in primary contexts, these creative ecological processes might be playful, restful, curious, material, tactile and more.

Products

Products have long been the focus of creativity in education, as in all other areas of enquiry. While this model regards products and productivity as important, it also acknowledges the importance of process ability in the new twenty-first-century work and living contexts. It considers interpersonal (or relational) creativity to be pre-eminent in the new workforce. Citizens now want and deserve to be affirmed in work that can be personally fulfilling as well as productive.

One of the great attractions of posthumanism for education more generally, and primary education specifically, is its ability to directly confront the valorisation of products as central to learning. The tension between 'products' and 'processes' is as old as education but, through a posthumanist lens, the potentially-always-already creative 'products' of primary education can become the co-making of self, toys, tools, events, materials, time, air, tears, laughter, emotions and anything else that contributes always or briefly to a learning encounter. Somerville draws on 'common worlds' theory to address the 'political and ethical imperative' of living more sustainably, which 'involves a shift from a focus on human-human social relationships to consider heterogeneous relations between a whole host of living beings, non-living, and living forces' (2017, p. 22). The static notion of 'product' dissolves like sand in the surf, and the truth of living learning with/in the child takes on new depth.

Partnerships

In such a neoliberal environment as our emergent post-COVID world requires, it is understandable to ask questions about the ways in which creativity is being advanced, valued and fostered. They are not easy to answer. This chapter suggests a way forward in which creative individuals combine with creative environments, as well as creative practices, within an ethics of co-creation and care, to lead ways forward for both creative individuals and creative assemblages. The possibilities of creative more-than-human actants is exciting and energising. How might primary educators work together toward advancing a posthumanist creative primary ecology in which all participants are equally valued and equally agentic? What posthumanism offers to creative primary education is a possibility of partnering (entangling) at every level with not only human others, but more-than-human others and selves. This invites encounters with inanimate objects that have agency, and being active partners in the child's learning and the creative learning/becoming of the objects. The same can be said for natural and artificial materials and attention to their lives and stories. Posthumanism demands we abandon the old siloes of human, material and physical worlds and see them all as co-creative. In such a world view, everything in the primary student's environment, both internally and externally, can be considered partners in creative learning.

Policies

In some ways it is clear that policy considerations should come last but, at the same time, a volume like this one, which seeks to level hierarchical and disciplinary differences, asks readers to consider how to move beyond disciplinary and sector-identified politics in order to strengthen creativity growth in diverse contexts. One of the ways in which creativity or creative/cultural industries has been able to move ahead is through attending to the national-level economic policy concerns of creative and cultural workforces. If education sectors can continue to build bridges with economic entities (like Creative Australia, Creative Victoria), we might see the kinds of cross-disciplinary interests being advanced that have grown so well in the UK and US.

While perhaps less visibly than in secondary contexts, primary school contexts and practices can also be considered sites of tension between the 'outcome' focus of creative activity, and the 'relational or process' approach. The chapters in this volume attest to the diversity and commitment of teachers, school leaders and researchers to keep both in sight. Using the creative ecologies model, educators and scholars can address all five of the foci individually and collectively, which addresses the range of experiential, relational and outcome-focused needs that are present in primary contexts.

The primary educators and their collaborators in this volume, like so many of our peers, continue to work toward innovative responses to the ongoing contractions of space, time and funding that so negatively impact primary education. These chapters, like the creative ecologies model, offer a counter-narrative to the pervasive commodification of creativity (Harris, 2016), highlighting the ways in which whole-system approaches including non-human actors can enhance the requirements of national curricula and policies. Recognising that primary education contexts already provide a rich ecology of multiple creative elements allows for more sustainable approaches, collaborations and frameworks for re-imagining twenty-first century education as relational and creative communities. The chapters in this volume show how non-human elements, including architecture, gardens and other outdoor communal spaces, classrooms and even weather, co-create creative learning experiences with children and teachers that themselves can be embodied and embedded in bodies more sustainably. By taking seriously posthumanist ideas like 'decentring the human' in primary education curriculum, pedagogies and learning contexts, endless opportunities for respectful, relational and sustainable creative learning can occur.

A creative ecological approach to primary education can also address the urgent need for schools and teacher education programmes to rapidly improve their approaches to preparing students for secondary school next steps, threading a more integrated, progressive and effective 'education lifespan' that is not so rigidly siloed into early childhood, primary, secondary and tertiary chunks. As Whitehead (1929) encouraged us nearly 100 years ago, there is no need to reduce creativities to 'what humans do', but rather we can allow our natural creative impulses, skills and pleasures to return us to more holistic education approaches which can add multiple values simultaneously, through rich and embodied experiences, consciously co-bodying with non-human others.

Applying creative ecologies beyond educational contexts

Readers might (understandably) be tempted to conceptualise this model as one focused on education contexts only. That would be a mistake. Why? There is nothing at all wrong with models that are exclusively education-focused. However, in this book there is dynamic attention to the ways in which education contexts and beyond-education contexts work in tandem to expand the educational possibilities of twenty-first-century learning, and to respond to evolving changes, predominantly machine learning and the coronavirus pandemic.

But why would it be a weakness to lean on education-only models? The kinds of creativity (and other) models for capacitation need to go beyond discipline-specific models – that is, they need to address the contemporary cross-disciplinary and cross-sectoral needs to build a successful life. What does it take? It certainly requires the kind of creative capacities that go beyond 'creative and critical thinking' skills and capacities.

Why? Well one (and perhaps the most prominent) reason is because educational contexts in many ways are *not* different from work, social and home contexts. It is not a neoliberal argument to say that primary and secondary success in classrooms should articulate into more direct post-secondary classroom goals than just 'you were a good student'. The goals of primary, secondary and post-secondary contexts must be joined more effectively, a goal articulated so compellingly by the authors in this volume.

The creative ecologies model (Harris, 2016, 2018) is effective for building creativity and creative cultures in any context, and – like other kinds of ecologies – takes into account the whole environment and all elements, both human and non-human. Creatively dynamic primary education, like other formal education contexts, requires strong practice-based and reflective collaboration amongst all players, and all five elements of the creative ecology. With these kinds of commitments, an integrated, sustainable primary education can embody the shift of focus from creative capacities or skills to growing creative sustainable communities and ecosystems, far beyond primary or other formal education classrooms and life-wide.

So how might using the creative ecology be useful in work, home or play contexts? With the increase across all sectors in working from home, it is more important than ever to attend to the atmospheric and non-human aspects of one's environment. Partnerships are crucial for all engagements in increasingly globally mobile, digitally informed, twenty-first-century cultures of work and play. This model can assist in addressing the kind of internal (familial, local) partnerships that enhance wellbeing and feelings of connection; it can also help look deeply at the kind of 'external' (work, geopolitical, friendship and work-focused collaborative) partnerships we all or cultivate in COVID and post-COVID lives. The global pandemic has also highlighted the ways in which attending to our relationships to physical environments has changed for the better as well as in challenging ways. Increased time spent with nature, with local service providers, with less long-distance travel, has significantly impacted the ways in which learners at any age are thinking, doing, making and collaborating. The creative ecology model can be used with great effect in any setting, whether formal or informal, work, educational or social.

Building creative relational ecologies

Co-authoring is the structure of this volume, but it models an important approach to primary teaching and learning practices, as well as creative co-living. By recognising that the contributors here bring diverse but equally important contributions of lived experience, knowledges, multidisciplinary practices and ethics, readers of this book will see the strength and benefits demonstrated by this co-creative approach.

This text, like good teaching and research, takes readers on a journey through innovative 'research-informed practice', drawing from projects originally conducted both in the UK and elsewhere. The idea of research-informed practice, or cross-sectoral applied research, also sometimes known as participatory action research, has already shown its many strengths. But in the wide-ranging precarity and economic contractions of this pandemic time, a book like this is invaluable in reminding educators, researchers, students and policy makers of the value of (and indeed the urgent need of) collaborating across the 'education lifespan' (Harris, 2016). By telling collaborative stories about what practitioners in these various contexts know as good practice, a powerful multi-perspective narrative emerges that speaks in the diverse ways required to diverse stakeholders and audiences. Policy makers, for example, can see the connections between classroom teachers, teacher educators, primary-age researchers and higher education training. This multiplicity is crucial to ensuring rich primary education into the future.

By adopting an additional posthumanist dimension to the creativities storied in this volume, it is possible to simultaneously consider how cities, environments, neighbourhoods, classrooms, ecosystems and various learning sites all contribute to the experience and efficacy of the learning and teaching that is being planned and rolled out in rapidly changing geopolitical sites. A text of this kind expertly demonstrates not only in content but also in process how partnerships between educators and academics can become an invaluable part of transforming primary education in innovative, relational and sustainable ways.

One aspect of primary education that has long held the attention of those education-focused researchers is the embodied, affective nature of the encounters within such contexts. Unlike secondary education, primary education is naturally collaborative, material-focused and experiential. The essays in this book attest to the relational, embodied nature of the work and the need to incorporate emotion, affect and empathy in the ways in which young learners and their adults come together. One opportunity here is that the integrated (transdisciplinary) nature of the work in primary education contexts, and the greater focus on process over product in secondary education, provides an opportunity to consider assessment and learning encounters that are more focused on experience than outcome for twenty-first-century education innovation.

Instead of singing the same old song, how might we turn to posthuman (or more-than-human) collaborators in primary contexts to build relationships with the environment, limited resources, and animals and inanimates with whom we co-exist, rather than trying to overcome them in some way? It can be hard to shift mindsets in this way when relentless cycles of human-centred creativity assessment and ranking threaten to reduce creativities education to the same narrow 'skills and capacities' as other subjects or ways of learning. One example of this persistent (and increasingly global) standardised testing and comparison is the incoming PISA test on creativity and critical thinking, delayed due to COVID-19 but still scheduled for the first test in 2021, with the and first results shared in 2022. Seventy-nine countries currently take part in the PISA tests which measure maths, science and reading, but several of these have declined to take part in the incoming creative thinking test. Why? Creativity is, for the Department of Education in England and Wales, not part of the core curriculum and so testing in this area is considered by some to be not the best use of resources. Creativity scholar Bill Lucas, who has been instrumental in the formulation of the test, has seen the decision as representing a false binary between 'core' subjects and creativity. There is another binary implicit here though: why must creativity (or any subject/area of enquiry) be measured and compared in order for it to be valued in the place and practices of educational contexts? The proposition itself is anachronistically human-centred and out of step with what we know about children's wellbeing, or about building satisfying adult lives. How can we encourage a shift in mindsets or advocate for complementary relationships with creativity education rather than succumb to large-scale standardised testing like this? By imagining primary schools (or other ecologies) as ecosystems in which all bodies are necessary to the system's survival and long-term thriving, the old distinction between humans and all 'others' begins to break down. The focus shifts to a relational environment that cannot survive without its diverse and equally valued components.

Conclusion

Returning once more to Somerville's attention to the three components of posthumanism that resonate so strongly with primary education contexts ('intra-action', 'common worlds' and 'thinking through Country'), we start to see the creative ecologies model as an instantiation or material example of how to enact these values. Attending to primary school contexts as ongoing events (intra-actions) in which students are interactively co-creating themselves with other human, non-human, environmental and emotional objects and movements allows teachers, parents and others to make room for student-led enquiry in all five realms of creative ecology. The common worlds approach incorporates what Chappell (2018) has explored as an ethics of posthumanist creativity in which care, stewardship and wellbeing of all are cross-implicated and at the forefront of enquiry. Lastly, as Indigenous knowledges and Somerville's articulation of 'thinking with Country' show, the possibilities for a posthumanist approach to primary education offer

> Hope [as] a way of dreaming up possible futures . . . it is a powerful motivating force grounded not only in projects that aim at reconstructing the social imaginary, but also in the political economy of desires, affects and creativity that underscore it.
> (Braidotti, 2013, p. 192)

The chapters in this book offer breadcrumbs down a path of discovery of that ethos, toward a brighter future of co-creation and hope.

Unlocking research in practice: provocations for group discussion

1. How should we help our students to become more curious and attentive to the 'non-human' elements in their learning environments?
2. How will exploring creative collaborations with non-human partners help our students build respect for other forms of life?
3. What are some strategies that students already use when playing that we can bring into our formal learning activities to help build these awarenesses and practices?
4. How might we model collaboration with non-human others for our students in our teaching practices?
5. How can we help shift our own and our students' mindsets toward the non-human world?

References

Amabile, T. M. (2018). *Creativity in context: Update to the social psychology of creativity*. London, UK: Routledge.

Australian Curriculum, Assessment and Reporting Authority (ACARA). (n.d.). *Australian curriculum*. Retrieved from https://www.australiancurriculum.edu.au/

Braidotti, R. (2013). *The posthuman*. Hoboken, NJ: John Wiley & Sons.

Burnard, P., & Colucci-Gray, L. (2020). *Why science and art creativities matter:(Re-) configuring STEAM for future-making education*. Rotterdam, the Netherlands: Brill-i-Sense.

Chappell, K. (2018). From wise humanising creativity to (posthumanising) creativity. In K. Snepvangers, P. Thomson, & A. Harris (Eds.), *Creativity policy, partnerships and practice in education* (pp. 279–306). Camden, London: Palgrave Macmillan.

Common Core State Standards Initiative (CCSS). (n.d.). Retrieved from http://www.corestandards.org/

Cremin, T. (Ed.). (2018). *Creativity and creative pedagogies in the early and primary years*. London, UK: Routledge.

Hackett, A., MacLure, M., & Pahl, K. (2020). Literacy and language as material practices: Re-thinking social inequality in young children's literacies. *Journal of Early Childhood Literacy*. Advance online publication. https://doi.org/10.1177/1468798420904909

Harris, A. (2016). *Creativity and education*. Camden, London: Palgrave Macmillan.

Harris, A. (2018). Creative agency/creative ecologies. In K. Snepvangers, P. Thomson, & A. Harris (Eds.), *Creativity policy, partnerships and practice in education* (pp. 65–87). Camden, London: Palgrave Macmillan.

Malone, K. (2017). Ecological posthumanist theorising: Grappling with child-dog-bodies. In K. Malone, S. Truong, & T. Gray (Ed.), *Reimagining sustainability in precarious times* (pp. 161–172). New York: Springer.

National Centre for Education and the Economy (NCEE). (n.d.). *South Korea learning systems*. Retrieved from https://ncee.org/what-we-do/center-on-international-education-benchmarking/top-performing-countries/south-korea-overview/south-korea-instructional-systems/

Sawyer, K. (2019). *The creative classroom: Innovative teaching for 21st-century learners*. New York: Teachers College Press.

Somerville, M. (2017). The Anthropocene's call to educational research. In K. Malone, S. Truong, & T. Gray (Eds.), *Reimagining sustainability in precarious times* (pp. 17–28). New York: Springer.

Whitehead, A. N. (1929). *Process and reality: An essay in cosmology. Gifford Lectures delivered in the University of Edinburgh during the session 1927–1928*. Camden, London: Palgrave Macmillan.

PART

Sculpting primary curriculum change

Chapters in this part re-think practice in primary education for 'the unknown future'. It features examples of teaching and learning as non-dualistic models of curriculum and pedagogy where the translation of creativities is mutually informative and triggers radical change.

CHAPTER

Innovating change through creativities curricula

Michelle Loughrey and Richard Gerver

Creativity, change and innovation

For many years the education discourse has articulated and heard repeated calls for curriculum change in schools. In recent times, the international health crisis of the coronavirus pandemic in 2020–21, the global economic crisis of 2007–08, major global environmental issues, growing socio-economic divides and the resulting polarisation in geo-politics have all amplified this need for change in education and the curriculum. Creativity is frequently identified as a cornerstone of the future of education for cultural, civic and economic reasons. For the purposes of this chapter, and indeed this book, it is vital that we do not see the term creativity in its generic sense, or as a simple silver bullet that can heal or solve everything. It is deeper and more nuanced than that.

In 1998 the National Advisory Committee on Creative and Cultural Education (NACCCE) was established by the Department for Education and Employment (currently Department for Education) and the Department for Culture, Media and Sport. Its report, *All our futures: Creativity, culture and education* (NACCCE, 1999), called for a national strategy for creative and cultural education. One of its key recommendations was that 'the importance of creative and cultural education is explicitly recognised and provided for in schools' policies for the whole curriculum, and in government policy for the National Curriculum' (NACCCE, 1999, p. 192).

More than 10 years later, the Cambridge Primary Review (Alexander et al., 2010), in proposing a new curriculum framework, identified 'Arts and Creativity' (Alexander et al., 2010, p. 267) as one of eight domains of learning, and argued for a curriculum that is more creative, flexible, outwardly focused and developmentally appropriate; as well as more teacher driven and pupil focused (Alexander et al., 2010).

Another 10 years have passed and still debate continues about the primary school curriculum and the need for fundamental change in primary education. In Part 2 of this book, we explore how unlocking research has informed and advanced primary education practice, resulting in diverse creativities, such as interdisciplinary creativity, wellbeing creativity and primary creativities, bringing about transformational change to primary education, and creating future-making[1] school/classroom-based practices. In this chapter we look specifically at primary school curricula and explore the role of the primary curriculum in sculpting change, asking what kinds of creativities this involves and what authorings/co-authorings of change are emerging.

Futurelab, an independent research organisation, became part of the National Foundation for Education Research (NFER[2]), an independent centre of education research, development and insights in the UK, in 2012. In 2008, Futurelab published a handbook, *Promoting transformative innovation in schools*, to 'prompt debate around the nature and purpose of innovation in schools and to share approaches and tools that may promote innovative practice in schools' (Sutch, Rudd, & Facer, 2008, p. 2). In its introduction, the authors explain the intrinsic link between innovation and creativity:

> when we talk about the need for innovation, we mean the sort of transformative innovation that challenges our assumptions about how we do things. We mean developing creative approaches to problems, by asking questions about the status quo, about accepted practice and about the prevailing 'logic' that permeates the system. As Hargreaves (2000) argues, 'you cannot have innovation without creativity', and creativity is not simply about incremental improvement, it is also a process which breaks down existing patterns of mind and develops new ways of doing and seeing things.
>
> (Sutch et al., 2008, p. 5)

This mindset of seeking to think, know and act differently is central to this chapter, as we aim to explore ways of sculpting, authoring and co-authoring change in the curriculum and the challenges associated with this endeavour. This should not be regarded as 'another initiative' to sit on top of or alongside existing practice, but as a methodology that interrogates what we do and how we do it, and then, in turn, catalyses change, evolution and meaningful developments that lead to a curriculum that is richer and more appropriate to the world our children will be inheriting from us.

Complementing Futurelab's *Promoting transformative innovation in schools* handbook, a review commissioned by BECTA (British Educational Communications and Technology Agency, which closed in 2011) in 2009 explored 'the challenges of promoting and supporting innovation' (Kirkland & Such, 2009, p. 2). In this literature review the authors, Kirkland and Such, identified seven overarching themes which influence education innovation:

- innovation, i.e. the introduction of something new that supports a change
- informal social and support structures, i.e. the social environment which plays an important role in the success of innovations

- formal environment, i.e. the organisational infrastructure of the school
- risk aversion: a key factor that inhibits the ability to innovate and as such has implications for the extent to which any educational setting has the appropriate enabling conditions for innovation
- shared vision, i.e. the starting point of all efforts to transfer practice and take it to scale
- leadership, i.e. the impact of leadership on the motivation to innovate
- change management, i.e. change management strategies (Kirkland & Such, 2009, pp. 15–39)

What this research highlights is the importance of context on a human, rather than an intellectual, level. These influences help to explain why in many schools, it could be argued, discussions about education and curriculum innovation invariably focus on or come back to ideas about how to refine existing systems or curricula, in order to make them more efficient or 'more creative'. In this chapter many of these influences permeate our exploration of how future makers and organisational culture cultivate a multiplicity of creativities which overcome potential barriers to facilitating meaningful engagement in the development of transformational change.

The creative curriculum or creativities curricula?

We begin by challenging the often heard phrase: 'we do the creative curriculum'. What is the creative curriculum? This is a key and challenging question because, at the heart of it, we must ask ourselves: what does creativity mean or what does it mean to be creative? Creativity is an interesting and challenging term with various definitions and different meanings to different people. It is culturally bound. It is context bound. It is bound in meaning-making in communities that are richly diverse.

We suggest that one of the difficulties of talking about 'the creative curriculum' is that it is regarded as something finite. In discussions about curriculum and curriculum design, educators might find themselves in conversations which seek to pinpoint what the finished creative curriculum looks like: what the model is, what the content is. With a definite article, the concept of change and diversities in curricula is denied. Instead, we suggest that new language should be used to challenge the concept of a curriculum as being a finite, static model with fixed content, and to explore what it might mean to be, to enact, to live, to embody and to experience *creativities curricula*.

This is not to devalue the creative curriculum/creativity in the curriculum (terms which are often used interchangeably) or to suggest that these are not relevant; indeed, when we were headteachers, both of us would have described the curricula in our schools as 'creative', and we are champions of the importance of creativity being at the heart of children's learning and at the heart of the curriculum/curriculum practice. It could be argued that it is diverse creativities which in fact underpin and facilitate the delivery of *a* creative curriculum. We use the term *creativities curricula* because innovating curriculum change requires us to think more deeply than a superficial consideration of curriculum content and to think beyond how to make an existing curriculum more creative, tweaking and refining what we have always done, and meeting the outcomes we have always needed to meet.

We suggest that creativities-forming curricula:

- create a sustainable approach to designing a future-making and future-proof curriculum that is developmental, evolving and responsive to the ever-changing needs of children and, more importantly, the society into which children will be moving; a curriculum that is not predetermined;
- (re)empower educators to respond intuitively and creatively to the needs of the children in the class/their school, so that educators feel confident that they can do this autonomously;
- open up the narratives of/on new creativities that catalyse the imagination in changing learning and teaching;
- unlock the possibilities of a wide range of curriculum aspirations such as diversity education and wellbeing education, which are themselves part of the multiplicity of creativities which underpin primary education.

This aims to achieve a curriculum that is more fluid and flexible, and open and imaginative to consider what is actually possible.

Opening up a discussion that provokes and inspires reflections on what we actually need in or from a curriculum is important because how curriculum design relates to our aims is profoundly important. How do we design a curriculum to meet the identified need(s) we have in mind; what are our aims and purposes; how will these aims be fulfilled (including pedagogical aspects); how can this be achieved and what role do creativities play in realising this?[3]

In order to unpick what this could mean in reality we need to create systems where the profession and the people around the profession are skilled and empowered to advance a developmental, evolving and responsive curriculum. So the first key question is: what role can educators and children play in (co-)authoring a curriculum that goes beyond preparation for the future and yet is actually future making?

Creativities curricula: innovators as future makers

Educators as future makers

Is it the educator's role to know everything? This is not to challenge educators' professionalism, but rather it attempts to explore what that professionalism could or should look like. It could be argued that an educator's real skill – their professional ability and capacity – lies in being able to translate complex concepts and knowledge into tangible forms that children can understand and activate.

Mark Priestley and Constantinos Xenofontos from the University of Stirling in Scotland argue that 'effective curriculum making has to be underpinned by developed conceptual understanding by the curriculum makers' (2021, p. 3). They suggest that 'if we are serious about enabling teachers to become effective curriculum makers, then we need to not only raise their professional capacity – we also need to address their cultural and structural working conditions' (2021, p. 8).

If part of our responsibility as educators, a core part of our moral purpose, is to enable children to respond actively, humanely and with imagination to the challenges of their futures, then by definition it is impossible for educators to know everything. Therefore, an important role for educators, including leaders, in creativities curricula is to create a process of curriculum co-design that steps and bridges across a whole range of people and organisations.

What if every educator had regular access to creative experiences outside education? Creative experiences fire the creative process, which allows educators to use their professionalism in a wider context, with greater understanding, to create a broader offer (Sefton-Green, 2011). If we are asking educators to innovate curriculum change, then their creativity and imagination needs to be stimulated by exposure to new experiences. The more limited your experiences are in life, the less you are able to think outside the box. Matthew Syed, former England number 1 table tennis player now speaker in the field of high performance, identifies a 'powerful interaction' that is created when creativity manifests as 'technical innovation'.

In stage one, experts engage in purposeful practice and, as a consequence, develop new techniques. In stage 2, other individuals corral these innovations to increase the efficacy of practice, leading to new innovations in stage 3, and so on (Syed, 2010 p. 93).

Box 6.1: Reflection from Michelle

One of the most profound experiences in my very early career was when I was offered the opportunity to work alongside the cast and production team of two Cameron Mackintosh musicals in the West End of London: *Cats* and *Les Misérables*. I was incredibly fortunate to spend time with several other educators learning about, amongst other things, set and costume design, theatrical make-up and the workings of a theatre. The aim of the project was to create a multi- and transdisciplinary learning and teaching resource, which was shared with primary and secondary schools across the local authority. It was an unforgettable experience, not least because I was chosen by the make-up team at *Cats* to be transformed in to a Jellicle cat and rode the tube back to East London in full make-up!

Afterwards, when I was developing materials for the teaching resource and planning for learning back in my own classroom, my lessons, and the curriculum, were enriched by my experiences. I had seen abstract learning outcomes put to work in a professional context. Being able to contextualise learning for children (and myself) in the context of a theatre production bought it to life and gave it meaning. Children love stories and I had plenty to share. Most of the children had never been to the theatre and I can vividly remember the day we took 90 Year 5 children to the West End of London to see *Cats*.

The learning that came from this experience not only influenced what I taught and how I taught it. It installed a deep sense of the importance of collaboration. I learned from drawing on the knowledge, skills and experiences of a diverse range of personnel working in theatres. Developing an appreciation of the challenges involved in other sectors and organisations was an important part of my professional development.

As seen in Michelle's reflection in Box 6.1, making connections with diverse organisations and with people outside education can enrich professional development and training beyond that which enables educators to become more efficient in specific curriculum, subject areas or pedagogical practice. Through creative partnerships, for example with sports and arts organisations, museums, science laboratories, technology companies and so on, educators can broaden their knowledge and understanding of what is going on in the world around them, not just in their local communities or within their local employers, but in a more global sense.

Another example of this is described by Richard in Box 6.2.

Box 6.2: Reflection from Richard

Alienus non diutius is Latin for alone no longer. It is written above the entry to the Pixar Studios campus. It is a place committed to collaboration and the belief that ideas can come from anyone, at any time. It is an organisation that also knows that new ideas need to be catalysed by new experiences. Some years ago, I was fortunate enough to visit the campus. It is where I found out about their university. Every employee every week goes off to study an area of personal interest. There are two simple caveats: whatever people choose must not be job related and must be accredited. My favourite example was the story of one of the kitchen staff who went off and learned to pilot a hot air balloon. When he came back, a creative

> director was so inspired by his story that she asked him to work with her team on developing the concept into a script idea. His key observation from his experience had been that when he took his first solo flight he had felt free for the first time in his life. His insights must have been inspirational – the script idea became the film *Up*!
>
> I have always believed that as educators, and indeed as children, it is vital that we keep stimulating our creativity through new experiences. They do not have to be grandiose, but they do need to be regular. It is impossible to be creative when you do the same things with the same people every day; it too often leads to recycling the same thinking. As educators we owe it to ourselves and our students to keep broadening our world view, our experiences and our imaginations. It is also vital that we share our thinking and those experiences with others because new experiences and collaboration are the alchemy that can lead to the gold at the end of the creative rainbow.

What if working inclusively with musicians, artists, scientists, sportspersons and technologists equated to working differently to realise the purpose and aims of creativities curricula? What could the possibilities be? What could be the impact on children's cultural capital[4], their aesthetic appreciation, their capacity for self-expression?

Providing opportunities for educators to engage in creative experiences can extend their professional capacity, connect them with professionals beyond the world of education, and develop their knowledge and understanding of the breadth and value of working beyond the prescribed curriculum. This contributes to new ways of thinking and knowing about developing and creating education, which in turn can bring about new curricular ideas and designs. This can prompt thinking about creativities curricula, for example by considering:

- What are the skills and dispositions needed for children to become responsible citizens of the world?
- What are the implications of educators becoming committed to new creativities curricula suiting their specific context and community?

Many primary schools in the UK are already involved with businesses, charities and organisations in their local community. One of the ways that primary schools can broaden the range of authorings of creativities curricula is by educators (not just pupils) spending time in/with these organisations, co-creating what children need in and from their school's curriculum and community practices, and noticing how this can have positive social/societal impact.

The Final Report and Recommendations of the Cambridge Primary Review (Alexander et al., 2010) identified 'The local component, or the community curriculum' (pp. 273–275) to sit alongside 'The national component, or the national curriculum' (pp. 272–273) as part of developing a new curriculum framework. In a presentation to the Westminster Education Forum in May 2011, Professor Robin Alexander, Director of the Cambridge Primary Review Trust, described the advantages of this approach:

> *To the national curriculum, and responding to demographic diversity, cultural plurality and individual differences, is added a 'community curriculum', with the proportions roughly 70/30 national/community. Time is freed up not only for schools to exercise their own judgement about curriculum and pedagogy, but also to encourage them to work together and to work with their local communities to ensure that the curriculum responds to local needs and local opportunities, as well as giving children a national entitlement.*
>
> (Robin Alexander, 2011)

If we can think differently about training and development, then educators can use their professional expertise to start to translate their creative experiences, built through creative partnerships, into teaching and learning strategies.[5] This, combined with a philosophical view and pedagogical expertise we develop as professionals, mixed with the practical experience we gain as practitioners, develops a greater sense of putting philosophy *into* practice. The role of the educator is not to know everything; the educator's professional expertise and genius lie in translating those abstract concepts into teaching and learning strategies, to ask better questions, and to enable diverse innovations and opportunities to co-exist with what we already know.

Children as future makers

Other fundamental partners in developing a culture of co-authoring and co-design are children. The work of Jean Rudduck and Julia Flutter (2004) on pupil voice and engaging pupils in evaluating and improving their school shows that, when we listen to children talking about their experiences in their worlds of school, we can learn how to improve this and how we do it. Despite this body of research, children as partners in future-making is still an underdeveloped concept in practice.

It could be argued that the questions children ask in early years' classrooms are the ones PhD candidates should be writing about. Children ask these questions because their curiosity about the world incites their questioning, and this is part of a cognitive/cultural/social process that equips them with what they may need in adulthood.

- What would happen if the Earth's core went cold?
- Why do teachers make us read old stories?
- How do ripples form and why do they spread out across the water?
- Could dinosaurs evolve back into existence?
- Why are our top eyelashes longer than our bottom eyelashes?

These are just some of the 390+ questions from children featured on the Curious Kids section of the website The Conversation.[6] The Conversation, which originated in Australia, launched in the UK in May 2013. Children can upload their questions to the website for experts from academic and research departments from universities across the UK to answer.

Children need to have opportunities, as do educators, to ask 'big' questions, hypothesise, challenge and make connections. What if we built the space for children to philosophise, debate and research the answers to these questions through creativities curricula?

If we want to genuinely engage children as co-authors in and of their learning, we (may) first need to challenge our perceptions of children's capacity to do this. We need to reflect on how we can and should give children autonomy, so that their understanding of the world and their place in it helps them to feel safe, reassured and empowered about their future.

In her research on leading school change in partnership with pupils, Kaye Johnson explored 'ways of enabling primary school children to become co-researchers and co-participants in transforming schools' (2004, p. 2). In her report *Children's voices: Pupil leadership in primary schools* (2004), Johnson reflects on her own advocacy of children's participation in schools:

> My thinking draws heavily on the emerging body of literature that re-positions even young children as competent, active agents who demonstrate considerable insight into, and control over, their daily lives. In reconceptualising children as thinking, feeling and active participants in life, I also draw on moral arguments that recognise the entitlements of children to a fair say in their own affairs.
>
> (p. 7)

To develop processes which result in pupils as partners in future-making creativities curricula, the following questions could be explored:

- What opportunities do we offer in schools for children to collaborate with educators to articulate their hopes, dreams, aspirations and fears?
- Are 'pupil voice' activities an act of consultation, or information gathering, where their voice is heard but children are powerless to act or effect meaningful change?
- Or are there other more meaningful forms of engagement where children and educators become partners – co-authors in matters that are important to them – to bring about transformational change?

So how do creativities curricula empower children to contribute to future-making discourse?

Early Excellence[7] offers an example of where children and their voices have been central to curriculum innovation. Through a series of blogs about 'The impact of a child-centred Curriculum in KS1',[8] a school details an initiative which set out to put 'children and their development at the heart' of a 'child-led, play-based' curriculum. This involved developing an enabling environment[9] and exploring 'Plan, Do, Review'.[10] In their most recent blog (October 2020),[11] school staff note the impact their responsive curriculum is having on the children, which includes: 'increased levels of engagement', 'improved interpersonal and social skills', and children who are 'far more confident and willing to take appropriate risks'.

Through developing a culture of co-design and by educators, pupils and communities engaging in the co-authoring of the curriculum, it can be seen that creativities curricula foster a collaborative approach. It is very difficult to be creative on your own. Consider an orchestra: the orchestra does not make music solely based on the creativity of the composer, the conductor or the first violin. The creative process comes from the combined skill, experience and understanding of all of the orchestra's members, which results in its exquisite sound. So what are the conditions and opportunities that are needed to innovate change through creativities curricula?

Creativities curricula: a culture of innovation and change

Creativities curricula are not just about building creative processes. Creativities curricula also foster, and indeed necessitate, a culture of innovation. We have suggested that creativities curricula are about designing a future-making and future-proof curriculum that is developmental, evolving and responsive to the ever-changing needs of children; one that (re)empowers educators to respond intuitively and creatively to the needs of the children in their class/school and opens up narratives of/on new creativities. Therefore, inherently, creativities curricula also require demonstrable enactments of new ways of thinking, knowing and acting in order for transformational, future-making changes in policy and practice to transpire.

As educators it is sometimes helpful to remind ourselves that we learn nothing new by getting something right or doing what we have always done; isn't this what we teach our pupils? In order to affect transformational change in our schools, in our education system and in the communities we serve, we must be prepared to push ourselves out of our comfort zone. Exposure to new experiences and new ways of thinking, knowing and acting are just as important for the CEO of a multi-academy trust as they are for a child in their first year of school. Unlocking research, the principle upon which this series of books is founded, is about creating a culture of questions, not answers, finding possibilities and asking ourselves: what if . . .? If the purpose of research is to challenge what we think, what we know and what we do, then when engaging with research we must ask ourselves: am I researching to defend my point of view or am I researching to understand something new or different? This is an important distinction. We effect change from the realisation that we do not know or cannot do something, from taking risks and from making mistakes. At these crucial points we must not walk away or form judgements about each other; this is the pivotal space where creativity, innovation and change are happening.

A culture of assumed excellence

At the beginning of this chapter, we noted research which identified influences in education innovation. Most, if not all, the influences identified concern the impact of organisational culture on the capacity for creativity, innovation and change to flourish.

Broadly speaking, it can be argued that there are essentially two types of organisations in the world: those built on a culture of assumed incompetence and those built on a culture of assumed excellence (Gerver, 2019). The larger and more traditional group (including some schools) have developed organisational cultures that are predicated on the beliefs of industrialism and the work of Frederick Winslow Taylor (1911), who was one of the founding minds of the industrial model. Simply put, the principle of industrialisation was to focus on efficiency because focusing on efficiency increased productivity; by increasing productivity you improve profitability, and if profit is put back into improving efficiency, the perfect cyclical model for industrial development is created.

Foundationally and culturally, these organisations are built on an assumption of incompetence – a culture where individuals only need to be efficient and to do what they are told to do. Performance is managed by making sure that everyone complies with a process, based on a belief that people will only do their best and be at their most efficient if they are managed. This fosters a culture of compliance and, as is human nature, results in a focus on the things that people are told are going to be important for their self-preservation (i.e. to keep their job, receive a pay rise, etc.). Another effect of this type of culture is that people can become dependent on their managers. They defer to the next level up to tell them what to do and how to do it. If there is a problem that they could potentially solve, people defer to more senior personnel to ensure the problem is solved either by their manager or as their manager would like. This can lead to frustration when there does not seem to be capacity within an organisation to come up with something new, creative or innovative; a situation which arises because the culture has never been built that way.

What role can creativities curricula play in evolving an alternative culture? What are the implications for leaders and leadership training and development relating to building ethos and culture?

In an increasing number of organisations, and in some schools, cultures are being reimagined, resulting in the emergence of a culture of assumed excellence (Gerver, 2013). In this culture there is a powerful belief in the talent and ability of people in the organisation to do extraordinary things, where gifted persons are recruited and conditions are created for them to flourish, such as experiences which stimulate their creativity. When individuals and teams come together, it is without a fixed agenda or outcome in mind for a discussion that focuses on what projects and ideas can be turned into reality. It is not that management structures do not exist: rather than getting people to prove their capability and then allowing freedom to innovate and be creative, the culture of these organisations gives them freedom first and then manages based on the fruits of that freedom.

An Organisation for Economic Co-operation and Development report published in 2015, *Schooling redesigned: Towards innovative learning systems*, identified seven conditions for education system redesign:

- reducing standardisation, fostering innovation, broadening institutions
- appropriate accountability and metrics for twenty-first-century learning
- promoting learning leadership, trust and learning agency
- widespread collaborative expert professionalism
- ubiquitous professional learning
- connectivity and extensive digital infrastructure
- flourishing cultures of networking and partnership
- powerful knowledge systems and cultures of evaluation (OECD, 2015, pp. 25–28)

These conditions are an integral part of developing a culture in which courage, trust, motivation and professional autonomy exist in an organisation, where psychological security is nurtured, so that creativities curricula can thrive. A culture predicated on the assumption of excellence creates an environment in which creativity, innovation and change can thrive.

What if every educator worked and every child learned in a school or classroom that fostered these conditions, a culture of assumed excellence? What could the possibilities be?

A culture of risk taking

If we want educators, pupils, schools and communities (in their broadest sense) to engage with creativities curricula, then this will involve not just thinking differently, knowing differently, and building a culture in which creativity innovation and change can thrive. It will also involve finding new and other ways of performing or acting. Each of these enactments brings a level of intellectual and emotional risk taking. Many of the chapters in this volume illustrate how this degree of risk taking can bring about innovation and change in primary curricula (for example see Chapter 7 by Hickey-Moody, Cook and Portelli and Chapter 8 by Fenyvesi, Brownell, Sinnemäki and Lavicza).

Part of being a highly skilled educator is being instinctive. To enact this, educators need to work in a culture where they feel trusted, supported and secure to be instinctive and act on those instincts. The curriculum in England, associated regulatory frameworks (for example, Ofsted[12]) and the public scrutiny of school performance data (for example, league tables), are often seen as being so prescriptive and so high stakes that educators are increasingly worried about experimenting and trying anything new.

What if every educator (and every child) felt trusted, supported and secure to take a risk, to try something new? What alternate curricula or pedagogic possibilities could emerge?

Moving away from a culture of dependence (on the familiar, the tried and tested) to one of collaboration and interdependence, we can (re)empower educators, pupils and communities to feel secure in practice, experimentation and development. However, this is not without its challenges. Stepping into an organisational culture that fosters a high degree of professional autonomy, such as in the example of a culture of assumed excellence, can be terrifying, especially if you are not used to working in such an environment. Because of the increased levels of autonomy in organisations that foster this way of working, there is unlikely to be a 'standardised' way of doing things, which in itself can be disconcerting if one is used to a more 'corporate' approach. Rather than being less accountable, perversely one is more accountable, so the quality of what one delivers is higher because the expectation is higher. This level of professional autonomy can be overwhelming; nevertheless, what this autonomy allows is no limitations to focus because of the absence of arbitrary targets to prove one's worth.

This has implications for how we think about initial teacher education and training, the induction of staff into our organisations and the ways in which we support each other to be accountable. What do we need to include, as part of our induction processes, to support staff to thrive in a culture of assumed excellence? How can we think differently about accountability frameworks so that these become enabling and encourage the creativity and professional risk taking we know can bring about transformational change?

If we are successful in doing this, we can capitalise on some of these influences on innovation identified at the start of this chapter. Educators (and pupils) working in a culture where they can take risks, be bold and innovate, because they feel trusted, supported and safe, will be able to perform meaningful, transformative change. Think of the possibilities . . .

Conclusion

Creativities curricula concern what we teach (future-making creativities curricula); where we teach (the culture we create in our schools and classrooms for creativities curricula to flourish); why we teach (reflexivity, modification and adaptation within creativities curricula) and how we teach (engagement with new creativities that catalyse new thinking about learning and teaching). As this is a model that is cyclical, never finite, without regular re-engagement with these elements and curricular reconfiguration the curriculum quickly becomes irrelevant. This is certainly a challenge given the immense level of change in schools.

Change is exhausting when it is imposed on schools, or on educators, because there is a feeling of lack of control. Creativities curricula create change that schools and educators lead and own. This is the kind of change that is sustainable, rather than exhausting, because it is driven by the community and the professionals within it. Rather than lurching from one set of imposed principles to another, change feels sustaining, sustainable and developmental. It is proactive rather than reactive. Educators are not inherently averse to change and development. Being more creative and more research driven, in its holistic sense, empowers us to take control of the change agenda for ourselves (Gerver, 2013).

There will inevitably be important conversations about the challenges of creativities curricula – for example time, funding, resources – but it is important not to get stuck in conversations about those challenges. The invitation for creative leadership (see Crawford et al., this volume) is to identify what the parameters are and how to overcome those obstacles. Creativity and the creative process is the ability to problem solve, to professionally engage in a challenge and find a solution to it.

Building on the principles of developing a culture of assumed excellence, creating safe and brave spaces for intellectual and emotional risk taking and reclaiming ownership of the change agenda reinforces that educators are professional, highly skilled experts. Through creativities curricula, educators further develop their understanding of their own unique context, their capabilities and their professional personality. This will enable them to create, amongst other things, a personalised library full of creative learning and teaching strategies and techniques which will make an important difference to curricula, pedagogy and to children.

Innovating change through creativities curricula is not grandiose but granular. It is about incremental shifts in thinking, behaviours and action. It is not a finite process but evolutionary and should grow as we grow, as do the children in our classrooms and in our schools. By expanding children's horizons, experiences and opportunities through creativities curricula, we can fire children's imaginations and feed those capacities for longer and at an enhanced rate. If we commit to this, then we can help children to dream and develop aspirations, no matter what their background or personal context. Children can see the world as open, filled with opportunities, with things to do and places to go. They can start to contextualise their place in the world and their value to it.

Creativities, like learning and life, are messy; the best comes from having a go, taking a risk. Remember, great educators are not perfect; just like children, they play, they explore and they learn. The important thing is to galvanise our confidence to take the first steps and to encourage and support each other to continue the journey.

Unlocking research in practice: provocations for group discussion

1. If creativities curricula are evolving and responsive to the ever-changing needs of children and the society into which children will be moving, should every school have a different curriculum? What are the benefits of this? What are the challenges of this?
2. What research/experiences would you like to have access to, outside education, that would be of value and how could you make this come about?
3. What if every child learnt in a culture of assumed excellence? What would this look like? Does that sound like your classroom/school? What are the implications of this? What will you do as a result of this reflection?
4. How can consultation between staff and pupils be meaningfully amplified in your school?
5. What are the barriers to innovation and change in your school/classroom? Which creativities can you activate to overcome these?

Notes

1. By future-making we suggest a future-making education as 'a widening out of possibilities for appraising and attending to our presence and our purpose in the world' (Burnard & Loughrey, this volume).
2. See https://www.nfer.ac.uk/
3. See the first book in the *Unlocking Research* series: Biddulph, J. & Flutter, J. (Eds.). (2021). *Inspiring primary curriculum design*. Routledge.
4. A term introduced by Pierre Bourdieu to refer to the symbols, ideas, tastes, and preferences that can be strategically used as resources in social action (From *The Dictionary of Sociology* https://www.oxfordreference.com/view/10.1093/oi/authority.20110803095652799). The term 'cultural capital' can be thought of as legitimised knowledge which allows parents and children to secure advantages from the educational process. Cultural capital can be embodied in dispositions (habitus) of the mind and body, objectified in cultural goods (such as books or musical instruments) and institutionalised through educational qualifications (Bourdieu, 1986).
5. See the second book in the *Unlocking Research* series: Hargreaves, E., & Rolls, L. (Eds.) (2021). *Reimagining professional development in schools*. Routledge.
6. See https://theconversation.com/uk/topics/curious-kids-36782
7. See https://earlyexcellence.com/
8. See https://earlyexcellence.com/latest-news/press-articles/play-based-curriculum-in-key-stage-1/
9. See https://earlyexcellence.com/latest-news/press-articles/developing-an-enabling-environment-ks1/
10. See https://earlyexcellence.com/latest-news/press-articles/continuous-provision-in-ks1/
11. See https://earlyexcellence.com/latest-news/press-articles/child-centred-play-based-curriculum/
12. See https://www.gov.uk/government/organisations/ofsted

References

Alexander, R. (2011, May 10). *Priorities for a primary curriculum*. Presentation to the Westminster Education Forum, London. Retrieved from http://robinalexander.org.uk/wp-content/uploads/2019/12/Priorities-for-a-primary-curriculum-Westminster-Forum.pdf

Alexander, R. et al. (2010). *Children, their world, their education: Final report and recommendations of the Cambridge Primary Review*. London and New York: Routledge.

Bourdieu, P. (1986). The forms of capital. In J. Richardson (Ed.), *Handbook of theory and research for the sociology of education* (pp. 241–258). New York: Greenwood.

Gerver, R. (2013). *Change: Learn to love it, learn to lead it*. London: Penguin.

Gerver, R. (2019). *Education: A manifesto for change*. London: Bloomsbury.

Hargreaves, D. (2000, November 22). *Towards education for innovation*. Presentation at the Institute of Education, London.

Johnson, K. (2004). *Children's voices: Pupil leadership in primary schools*. National College for School Leadership. https://dera.ioe.ac.uk/5067/1/randd-pupil-lship-johnson.pdf

Kirkland, K., & Such, D. (2009). *Overcoming the barriers to educational innovation: A literature review*. Futurelab. Retrieved from https://www.nfer.ac.uk/publications/futl61/futl61.pdf

National Advisory Committee on Creative and Cultural Education. (1999). *All our futures: Creativity, culture and education*. London: DFEE.

Organisation for Economic Co-operation and Development (OECD). (2015). *Schooling redesigned: Towards innovative learning systems*. OECD Publishing. https://doi.org/10.1787/9789264245914-en

Priestley, M., & Xenofontos, C. (2021). Curriculum making: Key concepts and practices. In J. Biddulph & J. Flutter (Eds.), *Inspiring primary curriculum design* (pp. 1–13). Abingdon, Oxon and New York: Routledge.

Rudduck, J., & Flutter, J. (2004). *Consulting pupils: What's in it for schools?* London and New York: Routledge.

Sefton-Green, J., Thomson, P., Jones, K., & Bresler, L. (Eds.). (2011). *The Routledge handbook of creative learning*. Oxon: Routledge.

Sutch, D., Rudd, T., & Facer, K. (2008). *Promoting transformative innovation in schools: A Futurelab handbook*. Futurelab. Retrieved from https://www.nfer.ac.uk/publications/FUTL20/FUTL20.pdf

Syed, M. (2010). *Bounce: The myth of talent and the power of practice*. London: Harper Collins.

Taylor, F. W. (1911). *The principles of scientific management*. New York, London: Harper and Brothers.

CHAPTER 7

The creative pedagogue: enacting affective pathways for interdisciplinary embodied creativity in primary education

Anna Hickey-Moody, Peter J. Cook and Nathan Portelli

This chapter has grown through dialogue about creative pedagogies across the primary curriculum. The concept of the *creative pedagogue* traverses subjects, spaces and classes. It is an idea through which we express the creative synthesis of curriculum into embodied learning experiences for primary aged students. The creative pedagogue understands learning as embodied, experiential, unconscious, affective. *Embodied expertise* is central to the creative pedagogue, which in the context of this chapter we define as knowing and feeling through the body. Children often learn without thinking that they are learning – they sense and intuit knowledge as they pick up patterns, numbers, information. In developing embodied expertise in creative education, the primary school teacher on our authorship team, Nathan Portelli, has been inspired by specific educational strategies such as *The Learning Pit*,[1] *Talk Moves*[2] and yarning circles with indigenous communities. We focus on two case studies from Nathan's classroom, firstly a creative and embodied approach to mathematics education and, secondly, reconciliation yarning circles and indigenous gardening.

Exploring these examples through the concepts of *affect* and *habit*, with contextual definitions appearing in the next section of this chapter, we develop a robust model of creative pedagogical practice derived from Nathan's experience of cross-curriculum primary education, brought together with Hickey-Moody and

Cook's experiences of arts-based research in the primary classroom. Our model presents the educator as someone who embraces creativity as a pivotal component of their pedagogy, enabled systemically by a school environment that allows for a diversity of approaches. In examining an educator at the centre of the creative learning ecology, we investigate innovation as a starting point. We offer a practical philosophy, or ethos of practice, along with some pedagogical methods, for primary teachers wanting to practice more creatively.

Embodied creativity

Embodied creativity supports an interdisciplinary approach to teaching and learning that is located primarily in the body. Reframing all core teaching and learning in the primary years to enact embodied creativity is especially important when working with children from lower socio-economic status, and culturally and linguistically diverse families because it opens a range of expressive pathways other than the English language. Additionally this approach futureproofs pedagogical needs for the classrooms that are yet to be known. Children and adults from low socio-economic families often have difficult experiences with institutional education. This can lead to negative habits in relation to schooling (Hickey-Moody & Harwood 2018), which prevents access to and uptake of education. We think about teaching and learning through a shared understanding of the concepts of *affect* and *habit*. These concepts are intertwined with the acquisition of all forms of knowledge, skills and competencies. The dictionary definition of affect is to "touch the feelings of; move emotionally, as in 'he was visibly affected by the tragedy'" (Lexico, Affect, n.d.). A habit is "a settled or regular tendency or practice, especially one that is hard to give up" (Lexico, Habit, n.d.). In building on these terms, we acknowledge that both terms have a philosophical grounding, and have been subject to long-standing debates in and across fields of educational sciences, media studies, anthropology and psychology. We offer a selective introduction to these histories in what is to follow.

All educational experiences work through creating positive or negative affects. These affects are primarily non-verbal and often pre-cognitive, which means they are feelings and confused ideas before they are intellectual endeavours. Indeed, the nature of an emotional response may prohibit an intellectual endeavour. As a concept, affect helps us to understand that certain mixtures of people and contexts involved in education can be either detrimental or positive for learners. Some teachers or schools create "sad affect" in their students. Spinoza views bodies as modes that respond to affective encounters through increasing and/or decreasing their capacity to act:

> When it [a body] encounters another mode, it can happen that this other mode is 'good' for it, that is, it enters into composition with it, or on the contrary decomposes it and is 'bad' for it. In the first case, the existing mode passes to greater perfection;

in the second case, to a lesser perfection. Accordingly, it will be said that its power of acting or force of existing increases or diminishes, since the power of the other mode is added to it, or on the contrary is withdrawn from it, immobilized and restraining it (IV, 18 dem). The passage to a greater perfection, or the increase of the power of acting, is called an affect, or feeling, of joy; the passage to a lesser perfection of the diminution of the power of acting is called sadness.

(in Deleuze, 1988, p. 50)

As suggested by the earlier quotes, French philosopher Gilles Deleuze builds on Spinoza's work on affect, and calls us to think through the debilitating impacts of sad affect as a mourning *of something one does not have*. He explains that "out of sadness is born a desire, which is hate. This desire is linked to other desires, other passions: antipathy, derision, contempt, envy, anger and so on" (Deleuze, 1992, p. 243). The first stage in changing sad affects caused by education is to accept and acknowledge the fact that school systems often treat disadvantaged communities in racist, classist and problematic ways (Harris, 2016).

Habit is a partner concept to "affect", and habit helps us to understand the ways bodies relate to educational systems and experiences. For example, children often fall out of the habit of reading as they enter puberty and begin to develop more comprehensive social lives. Affect, or more specifically, lack of affective attachment, is the reason why children stop reading at this stage. They become affectively entangled with mediascapes and social worlds in ways that make the significance of written worlds seem less appealing. Other habits such as school attendance and homework completion are affectively regulated: they occur when the students are connected to them and they feel significant. Educationalist John Dewey's (1859–1952) psychological and pedagogical take on "habit" is also embodied and context-specific. His conceptualisation rationalises the reasons for personal traits, such as an individual's passivity and activity, or the extension and contraction of the body and mind. For Dewey, like for Spinoza, habits are both individual and social. Spinoza calls social habits "associational pathways" (Hickey-Moody & Harwood, 2018). In a similar turn of phrase to Spinoza's "associational pathways", Dewey (1922) claims that "we cannot change habit directly: that notion is magic. But we can change it indirectly by modifying conditions, by an intelligent selecting and weighting of the objects which engage attention and which influence the fulfilment of desires" (p. 20). Teachers working in lower socio-economic status, and culturally and linguistically diverse contexts in Australia, or in similar international contexts, have to work to reframe educational habits that have developed over the course of generations. The bridge between theory that was first published in 1677 and today's practices is the belief that a change of conditions and supports is needed for a positive *affective habit modification*. For primary educators this means that when children have "bad habits", or if they want a child to have a new habit, teachers need to begin by creating a positive emotional entanglement with the issue. Children need to want to learn, and see the importance of learning, before they can be expected to modify habits. Cultivating this positive affective attachment is the first job of the primary teacher. All creativity is embodied. We use the term embodied creativity to foreground the role of the body in learning and teaching, and specifically in cultivating affective attachments and modifying habits. Teachers need to begin with the body and the emotional landscape of learning in order to create positive affective attachments to learning.

Autoethnography of creative pedagogy

Our acknowledgement of an educator's experience as being notable and potentially transformative for others aligns with some central concepts that underpin autoethnography. As a methodology, autoethnography aims to represent the personal as a possibility for broader cultural understanding and application (Holman Jones, 2005). Derived from the various parts of the term itself, this approach to research explores a personal (*auto*) experience to better understand a cultural (*ethno*) phenomenon, through analysis and representation (*graphy*). When researchers work with *autoethnography*, they engage in retrospective reflection to find highlights that are culturally significant for themself and others. The moments move beyond that of an autobiography and are analysed through other conventions (Adams & Holman Jones, 2008; Wall, 2008). For example, a primary teacher choosing to approach research from an autoethnographic perspective would consider their own experiences as a vehicle to communicate concepts to students.

Exploring our ways of knowing is a practice that has long been considered important for autoethnographers, and is inextricably linked to ways of *learning* and, conversely, to ways of *teaching*. More so, investigating ways of knowing challenges the potential of binaries between teachers and learners as a power differential (Barr, 2019). For example all teachers will have some experience of struggling to learn, and the affective disinvestment that accompanies this experience. Similarly they will have passions and interests. The orientations, connections and habits – both good and bad – that are developed through this experience provide resources to draw upon when working to engage students who are not connected to curriculum tasks. When autoethnographic concepts are explored in the classroom there can be a social equalising that affords the teacher opportunities to learn as much as the learner. For example, teachers might draw on their learning journeys as a resource for their students in order to show that everyone has to rework negative learning habits at some stage of their learning journey – even teachers. The classroom is only one part of the fieldwork that might be analysed, given the robust planning and networking that occurs on a daily basis for teachers. The reflections on previous lessons and observations of students and classroom culture help to define the expectations of the entire school community. Storytelling is a feature of autoethnography (Leavy, 2016). Experiences are recounted through the eyes of the key participant, open for interpretation against enforced social parameters that serve as analytical borders. As with learning, autoethnography comprises agreed understandings and expectations. Lessons are usually prepared in advance and with enough detail to provide structure, but equally enough leeway to allow for open-ended opportunities. Within the structure, learners are given permission to explore and experience their own responses to the lesson (Alexander, 2013). These experiences are interconnected as data events and able to be understood theoretically depending on the context of the inquiry. One such example of an autoethnographer in practice is presented here as a creative pedagogue.

Introducing a creative pedagogue

Nathan Portelli graduated in 2016 from Southern Cross University, Gold Coast, Australia. While completing his teaching degree, he was employed full time as a teacher's aide in special education. Working in this capacity provided valuable insight into the ways schools, teachers and learners co-exist within the systemic ecology. Additionally, Nathan was a semi-professional football (Rugby League) player. Upon completing his studies, Nathan moved back to the far north coast of New South Wales to teach full-time in the coastal Kororo Public School. As a teacher, Nathan has taught several grade levels and also coordinated whole school wellbeing, social skills and technology programmes using LEGO robotics.[3] Nathan now assumes the role of practicum supervisor within the school, offering support and guidance to pre-service teachers.

As a reflective educator, Nathan regularly considers new approaches to teaching concepts. The pattern of planning and implementation is considered and builds upon the concept for *Backward Design* (Wiggins, Wiggins, & McTighe, 2005), whereby desired results are first drafted, followed by potential evidence, and then the development of related learning activities. This process echoes many creative practices. It is these creative approaches that are invoked to work directly on students' affective habit. Nathan explains his approach to teaching by saying:

> *When approaching an idea I always begin with . . . strong foundations, this can take the longest amount of time, however if this is done correctly the project has a strong base. I begin with why am I undertaking this endeavour? How will I achieve the aim? Who is this going to affect and who can be engaged to support the process?*

Nathan's emphasis on building strong foundations reflects his appreciation of the longevity of the educational process and how it maintains a focus on the sequential and iterative stages. Strong foundations are key to educating primary-age children across the gamut of learning disciplines and cross-curriculum priorities. Nathan continues through saying:

> *Following on from the foundations and frame, I try to move forward to the protective outside (bricks and roofing). How can I make this better? Can I involve a different teaching strategy? Is there an outside agency that can support? How can I further support all students in engaging in this project? Develop a strong understanding of the whole*

> *student who you are going to be involved with – what makes them tick? I try to speak with family, current teachers, prior teachers and make an effort to break the ice before the project even begins.*

What becomes evident in understanding Nathan's approach is his strong capacity to reflect. As a practitioner, this becomes a form of self-evaluation, however, the constant consideration of how to better understand the children in his class is commendable. Australian teachers are required to demonstrate their understanding in/outside the classroom developmentally throughout their careers (Australian Institute for Teaching and School Leadership, nd). In particular, Nathan's creative pedagogical approach relies heavily on Standard 1 "Know students and how they learn". The standard requires teachers to appreciate physical, social and intellectual characteristics, alongside their linguistic, cultural, religious and socio-economic backgrounds. Additionally, one aspect of this standard discusses specific teaching strategies for indigenous students, and more broadly, how to differentiate the learning experience for all students. Inherently, creativity brings together seemingly disparate concepts and differentiation may benefit all students by, for example, incorporating sound and movement to reinforce mathematical concepts, embracing varied learning styles.

Nathan spends equal time considering students, as he does designing and facilitating the process of learning. Focussing into the detail of the learner and the experience is akin to a process of creativity that often requires the overview to be realised through detail.

> *The next step is the tiny decorations that only the trained eye can appreciate. You have created a house and that is great, you can live and survive. But in all I do, I am always searching for "what will children remember"? I find this the most enjoyable component of my job because it is the detail that children appreciate. And they can only be discovered by truly understanding and knowing the student. Quite often it is little things like taking the time to walk with a child and provide them with feedback on something you picked up on that they thought no one would ever notice. It could be that you brought everyone a 1-dollar paddlepop after a hard day's work.*

Apart from the evidence of robust planning, Nathan intrinsically understands that his work is deeply relational. It is essential for the teacher to develop effective relationships with students and to establish trust within the learning environment. It is the transformative connections that he needs to make with all of his class that enables his creative practice to occur. Alongside these processes are ever-present reflective moments that enhance and improve, tweak and refine. And the inevitability of those processes, or a subsequently connected process, needing to begin again.

> *Following on from this strong foundation for learning and eye for detail that are the foundation of learning relationships are the "home renovations" in learning that change*

learner's habits. After you have lived in your house or engaged in the project for a certain amount of time What do you reflect on? What would you change, How would you change it? Why would you change it? The whole process begins again. . .

Nathan's practice is best understood through the detail of his ever-present thought-plans and blueprints. To this end, we focus on two case studies from Nathan's classroom, considered here as autoethnographic vignettes.

Vignette 1: a creative and embodied approach to mathematics education

The first vignette demonstrates a creative approach to mathematics through the use of colour and place value systems. In Australia, mathematics is a core subject where children and young people develop essential skills and knowledge in numeracy and complex applications of mathematical concepts and principles (Australian Curriculum, n.d.b). Of significance is understanding place value systems, which provides the relative position of a digit by its position (place) in the number. For example, a single number (1, 2, 3, etc.) appears as the rightmost digit, the tens (14, 26, etc.) are the second right, and hundreds (344, 789, etc.) the third right (New South Wales Education Standards Authority, 2012). This system establishes a critical understanding of the value of numbers and becomes the base for multiplication and more complex numerical concepts, including algebra.

Use of colour, equated to each of the places in this scenario, provides access to visual learners alongside the numerical scaffolding that proves beneficial as more complex mathematical concepts are explored. This use of colour and pattern develops *habits* that are the basis for numeracy and, later in life, financial literacy. Nathan explains:

When approaching my mathematics teaching, I developed a strategy that incorporated colour. I identified children's understanding of the place value system as an extremely important lynch pin in their understanding of mathematics in general. In order to better support the establishment of students' understanding of place value, I utilised a visual scaffold. This visual scaffold was the identification of ones (1) with the colour yellow, tens with the colour green and hundreds with the colour blue. The important component of this was that I incorporated it within all things mathematics: if I was using MAB blocks as a teaching resource, they were spray painted with the corresponding colours; if I was writing numbers on the board, I would ensure that they were highlighted in green, yellow and blue with the class discussing each time with students as to why this was happening. Eventually it went from the point of me explicitly teaching the system to students reminding me of the system and, most importantly, why it was like that. "The 7 needs to be green and it is not a 7 anymore. It is 70 because it is a ten". This continuous giving and taking of information around place value consistently supported students' understanding of the concept and supported their habitual development of numeracy.

Nathan continues, explaining that,

> *as learning continued to progress through to addition and subtraction, students were able to use their more informed understanding of place value and the colour system to now understand addition and subtractions strategies with greater success. An example of this is teaching students jump strategy. When given the problem 12 + 14, they will have an understanding that both of the numerals one are actually green, which means they are a 10 and that is their value, while the 2 and the 4 are yellow which means they are 1's. With this knowledge students can place the largest number 14 (which they will be able to identify as the largest through their improved knowledge of place value) on the visual representation tool of a number line. The use of colours now helps with the jump strategy as students can draw the tens jumps larger and in green. Following from this, they can use the ones jumps smaller and in yellow. This provides visual representations and support for students, and they begin to transfer this capability to a mental strategy.*

Nathan works with colour, repetition, memory and dialogue in cementing affective pathways of numeracy that become established as habits. He explains that as the children's numeracy habits become increasingly established, he removes the affective scaffolds that are key to their initial adoption:

> *As students progress through the year, I begin to take away the visual scaffold of colours as their achievement progresses. I ensure that students do not become reliant on this and that they understand the colours are just a tool.*

Nathan describes the impact of this approach to be palpable. It is not necessarily demonstrated by students as excitable, but more noticed as a personal achievement of understanding, a quiet connection that is obvious because "their eyes light up". This is especially significant for visual learners in the room as it fits their style of learning. Nathan notes that many more young people arrive at their schooling years needing to learn visually. It is something that is becoming more inherent within their pre-school culture. Children have often been exposed to multi-sensory games and television shows that provide high-quality engaging visual effects. Engaging with children, acknowledging their current comfort zone, is a key to pedagogical success.

In Nathan's experience, it is rare for a student to show reluctance to this approach of learning. More likely, students may be confused by the concept. At this point, Nathan engages strategies for differentiation groups, where students may strategically come together for distinct purposes and to revise at requisite levels. This subsequent strategy is employed with the caveat that the class is always inclusive irrespective of the individual's capacity or unique learning plan. The success of this approach is mostly seen in the resurgence of cognitive understanding. When it is time for the scaffolding to be withdrawn, it becomes a slow transition. The colours are discussed less frequently and replaced more often with the numbers without aid. Nathan considers as a point of interest that it could be research-worthy to explore if his students still employ the colour strategy long after the scaffolding has gone, or if it is purely a transitory process of learning. This vignette demonstrates the relationship between affect and habit, as the affective pathways built through colour, repetition, memory and dialogue serve as the foundation for habits that remain even when the affective scaffolding is removed. Teachers can use any strategies of differentiation they find useful, and may want to invite the children to choose these as a way of involving them (e.g. sound, movement, colour).

Vignette 2: developing reconciliation yarning circles through indigenous gardening

The Australian curriculum comprises subjects such as mathematics, science for primary and is then supported through cross-curriculum priorities. The relevant priority for this vignette is Aboriginal and Torres Strait Islander histories and cultures, which aims to ensure that Aboriginal and Torres Strait Islander identities and knowledges are present within the curriculum (Australian Curriculum, n.d.a). Within the state framework of New South Wales, the Aboriginal education policy states that it aims to better educate Aboriginal students while better educating all students about Aboriginality (New South Wales Department of Education, 2012). These policy imperatives make mandatory the need to incorporate indigenous knowledge as part of the primary curriculum. The deep connection to the earth and storying around indigenous knowledge lends itself to practical scenarios. The following vignette explored eloquently provides the opportunity to both better understand indigeneity and localised issues as well as an alternate lens to an understanding of science, humanities and social sciences. Nathan explains his approach to teaching this subject, saying:

> In teaching Science and Human Society and Its Environment, across a number of stages, I identified that there was an opportunity for quality resources to be created to support all students' understanding of indigenous customs and traditions. This included interactions with food, animals and other people, and how they were used to live for thousands of years. Instead of taking the conventional route of creating a traditional teaching resource such as a PowerPoint that is constructed by teachers for students, I reflected on the fact that the most powerful form of teaching is where teachers establish an environment in which students can facilitate the learning of their peers. It was through this idea and discussion with other teachers that I decided to establish a Stage 2 and 3 indigenous cultural groups with the aim of rejuvenating our indigenous garden and creating digital resources to be accessed by all students. The aim was for all information to be taught by student's peers, who were existing members of the cultural group.

Nathan continues, explaining that,

> Prior to venturing on this journey I ensured that I personally had investigated protocols around delivering local indigenous knowledge. I sought out prominent members of the

local Indigenous community including elders and Aboriginal Education Officers within local public schools. Additionally, I became an active member of the local Aboriginal Education Consultative Group (AECG) in order to discuss my own ideas and to stay connected with the local indigenous community.

The next step in the process was to hold discussions with teachers involved in initially creating the indigenous garden at the school many years ago. How was it designed? What was the initial purpose? Who was involved? In developing an understanding of this, it can then be communicated to the students involved.

The next process was to investigate information on the amount of indigenous students at the school and make contact with them to inform them of the group and its objectives. One clear component to this communication was informing students that I would be going through the learning pit with them and quite often they would be teaching me; they loved this and it really excited them. In this component I also ensured that families of students were informed of the journey they would be going on and welcomed their involvement, input and knowledge openly.

The fun stuff! Once groups were established, students spent the first few lessons working in the garden, restoring it. This included weeding, mulching and replanting. It was through this process that students established a sense of belonging to the garden and the plants. They were now invested in the project and from here I welcomed members of the community to share knowledge on the plants in the garden.

Now that students had a vested interest, I split lessons into half practical in the garden and half theory working through Google Classroom to research and construct information slides on two specific plants, Lemon Myrtle and the Grass Plant. One of the most important pieces of feedback that I received from students in reflection at the end of lessons was that they loved coming to indigenous groups because they got to miss out on doing English and Human Society and Its Environment, as they much preferred learning about the plants. My response to this really shifted their thought process as I revealed to them that they had been doing English – they had been reading information, comprehending it, constructing sentences, editing their work, critically evaluating ideas and publishing texts. Along with that they had also been engaging in history and geography through learning about the plants and their uses.

Next, students engaged in creating Lemon Myrtle biscuits; again they were required to use a broad variety of practical literacy and numeracy skills to follow the procedure correctly. Following this came the most important component of the activity. The indigenous students became leaders and facilitators of learning. Students were able to teach a Year 6 class divided into small groups how to create the cookies while communicating information around the plant and its uses for indigenous people.

Currently students are continuing to develop educational resources to share with the school community, and partnerships with local high schools have been established where older students can support students within our groups with their knowledge and transition processes can also be established for Year 6 students.

The use of the indigenous garden to understand science, history and geography was met with excitement by all involved. Firstly, the indigenous students were overwhelmed by the positive approach to understanding indigeneity and how this was being passed on to non-indigenous students. The indigenous students felt that their culture was being recognised in a really healthy way, which in turn validated them as members of the school community. Non-indigenous students described their genuine interest in the knowledge being communicated and the practical base of its delivery. The most significant component of the activity is that the learning was delivered by peers. This powerful disruption of the regular teacher-learner mode established strength of both the content and positively promoted the indigenous students who role modelled the connection to country. This affective connection to country, established through repetitive acts of being in and on the land, is what anchored the children's attachments to place and their emotional investment in this outdoors classroom and learning experience.

Students who initially appeared withdrawn from the activities were nurtured into involvement through teacher's intervention. It was soon after this was role modelled that the peer mentors adopted that practice as well. The success of the activity was most noted by the pride of the indigenous students who were validated by the experience and ably presented their cultural significance. Excitement, respect and acceptance were key characteristics for all students involved in the experience.[4]

Feeling learning, changing thinking

The affective pathways to learning presented earlier take different forms: colour, place, repetition, discussion; but they both lead to student connectedness and positive learning habits. The classroom environment is essential for the effective communication of the curriculum. Relational expectations and reminders indicate the place of learning is inclusive. Nathan's classroom is not limited to a room, but defined more accurately as where the learning exists. There is consistent evidence of the care for the learning environment from Nathan's planning and from his focus on where and how the children will best understand the concepts being explored. The experiences that Nathan choreographs approach knowing through making experiences that connect the children affectively to positive learning pathways and outcomes. This drives the decisions on what environment is the best fit, and how all children can be accommodated irrespective of their stage of development. This planning is vital in understanding and transforming the patterns and habits that need to be explored. Habit, in this instance, is embodied and reflects Hickey-Moody and Harwood's (2018) ideas on the contextual notion of learning. The indigenous garden described in Nathan's vignette exemplifies the way that Dewey (1922) and indeed Deleuze (1988) aspire for a modification of conditions, to enable effective learning.

Once the environment is established, the pedagogical relationships can emerge. The relationships between Nathan and the content is essential as his understanding of the class and, more significantly, the individual children and their learning style, relative level of ability and learning goals. Nathan explains this within the metaphor of the detailed decorations in the learning house build. The detail of individuals is part of what makes the learning transformative. It is this rework of habit that relies heavily on the relationship between all aspects of the ecology of learning outlined by Harris (2016). The relationship involves the teacher and the learner, and in the case of the indigenous garden vignette, a strong connection to the local community. Of note is the power of the differential groups that Nathan relies upon as a pedagogical strategy. The need to revisit concepts for some children is reinforced throughout the activities and becomes a cornerstone of the peer-to-peer learning established to address inclusivity. At the core of this concern are the affective nature of learning and the learner. The understanding of the inevitability of concepts being confused journeying to enlightenment echoes Spinoza's early discussions, also taken up in Hickey-Moody (2013).

Implementing creative pedagogical approaches requires an in-depth knowledge of content and emotional investment in teaching and learning. Nathan's processes evidence the basis of creative pedagogy as ongoing and iterative. In the example of the indigenous garden vignette, apart from considering the students' relationship to the content, Nathan embarks on his own professional learning and networking with key personnel including local indigenous elders and staff who supported the establishment of the garden. This practice or habit has become essential in establishing solid connections with indigenous knowledge along with addressing negative influences that Harris (2016) describes as contributing to the creative ecology in schools.

Positioning and selecting the content within the scope of children's context provides a working bridge to learning. As Nathan explains, children arrive at school from a highly sensorial digital life. These platforms engage through consistent and changing visual imagery in rapid time. As such, understanding children and their context required understanding affect, including further Deleuze's (1992) concept of sad affect. Often, contexts reduce rather than grow children's capacities to act. Building an affective bridge from current to future context is a viable solution to the negative impacts of sad affect and engages children in content that is positively satisfying.

Changes to patterns of learning are key to the augmentation of affective habit. An example of this can be found in Nathan challenging children to explore the mathematical concept of place value through colour. Colour is prioritised for children to qualify the numerical positioning, allowing for greater accessibility, especially for visual learners. Altering approaches to include all styles of learning ultimately aligns with the pre-cognitive and often non-verbal affective conditions noted by Deleuze (1988). Similarly, appreciating the validation that indigenous students feel as a result of locating cross-curriculum priorities amongst previously siloed curriculum knowledges presents examples of how affect can be practically implemented.

Amending habit, as proposed by Hickey-Moody and Harwood (2018), emerges from (re)considering individual and collective patterns. Developing strategies that challenge these patterns are found in Nathan's approach to place value. Initially, it appears that the activity is about colour, and then numbers, and eventually the colour aspect subsides to return to the understanding of numerical place value. The changes are indirect, positive and encouraged for all levels of learning, and differences are acknowledged as part of the process.

The practice of redressing negative impacts associated with sad affect (Deleuze, 1992) can be found in Nathan's work in the indigenous garden. The notion of peer-to-peer learning is an example of how the practice of pedagogy is fluid between teachers and learners and, as such, embodies new information. When indigenous students are offered the opportunity to communicate their new and existing knowledge to non-indigenous students, this changes sad affect and creates positive affect, moving towards establishing positive practices of habit. Students develop their own resources for learning and extending on their school community to work with neighbouring high schools. Moving learning from the self to the community and then to a broader community exemplifies the transformative impact of positive affective habits. Modifying the surrounding conditions rather than changing habit directly is aligned with the aspirations considered by Dewey (1922). Establishing a positive embodied learning experience, in the way Nathan approaches these activities, works towards (re)framing the negative school connection that many young people have, especially those designated as low socio-economic status (Hickey-Moody & Harwood 2018).

As a reflective teacher, Nathan needs to consider what evidence can be considered as a change in student thinking and doing. Nathan notes that in the indigenous garden activity, children were initially unaware of the depths of learning taking place. Nor were they cognizant of the interdisciplinarity involved in the activity. When highlighting to children, their response was positive and connected their learning with changes in thinking. They understood that the tasks they had undertaken were vehicles for discovery and that learning could be embodied beyond conventional classrooms and approaches. As the colour-based scaffolding was withdrawn on the place value experience, children connected the cognitive processes of the mathematical process. They were able to appreciate the heightened understanding of the concept. Those who needed to could revert to the colour approach for revision. All children were included in the changes of thinking, both individually and as a collective. While nurtured by this creative approach to pedagogy, children benefited from an innovative understanding of learning that ultimately embedded the ideals of Spinoza (Hickey-Moody, 2013). The building involved in these experiences is based on understanding and celebrating difference and being a reflective educator that engages in amending both teacher and learner affect.

Affective pathways

In exploring Nathan's *affective pathway* approach to crafting positing numeracy habits and connections to country, we see a reworking of habits of disconnection to learning contexts and the development of emotional investments in learning. Nathan offers one of many possible examples of how teaching disadvantaged students is about changing patterns (Harwood, Hickey-Moody, McMahon, & O'Shea, 2016). The most important strategy for connecting with children is to be interested in their worlds and let them lead the discussion. Arts-based and play-based activities provide excellent opportunities for children to share their worlds with teachers, providing opportunities for the teachers to connect and draw children into other curriculum-based spaces. Building on this example, then, we want to offer some suggestions of what makes a creative pedagogue.[5]

Constant reflection of alternate approaches for delivery, both pedagogical and cross-curricular.

The example of Nathan's teaching shows interdisciplinary curriculum and reflexive approaches to interdisciplinary curriculum delivery. To be a creative teacher one has to be brave enough to fail and to acknowledge when things are not working and re-making new strategies for learning. Interdisciplinary curriculum is often best taught through project-based learning, which creates a broad spectrum of ways for learners to engage.

Being a lifelong learner- always professionally developing. Being prepared to be a learner with the children.

This quality extends the first point: critical reflection on practice cannot be underestimated. Further, creating opportunities for children's agency to teach adults can be a means for developing effective and responsive pedagogies. Capillary power shows that children teach their teachers how they can learn, if only their teachers can listen.

Understanding and embracing difference as an activator to disrupt habit.

Difference is always a productive force that can teach new ways to do things, can gesture towards new pedagogies and show up the limits of existing teaching methods. Negative affective attachments to schools and learning experiences need to be understood as systemically, culturally and socially produced and as able to be re-shaped through appropriate affective pedagogies (Hickey-Moody, 2013).

Unlocking research in practice: provocations and prompts

1. What do the children in your classroom teach you about how they learn best?
2. How can *interdisciplinarity embodied creativity* be explored in project-based learning?
3. How can *negative habits and attachments to schooling* teach you to teach differently?
4. What *affective pathways* to positive learning habits are you building with your students?

Acknowledgements

We would like to acknowledge the traditional owners of the unceded lands on which we work. Decolonisation is an ongoing process.

Hickey-Moody's work is supported by the *Australian Research Council* (ARC) Future Fellowship FT160100293.

Notes

1 See for example, https://www.youtube.com/watch?v=KwsmicqjyFg
2 *Talk Moves* is a strategy for scaffolding complex ideas into meaningful sections. Further information is available at this link: www.educationgov/Talk Moves
3 See for example, https://education.lego.com/en-au/
4 See *Arts-Based Methods for Research with Children* https://www.palgrave.com/gp/book/9783030680596
5 Those interested in the theoretical perspectives developed here might like to read: Hickey Moody, Anna. 2013. "Affect as Method: Feelings, Aesthetics and Affective Pedagogy". In: Rebecca Coleman and Jessica Ringrose, eds. *Deleuze and Research Methodologies*. Edinburgh, UK: Edinburgh University Press, pp. 79–95.

References

Adams, T. E., & Holman Jones, S. (2008). Autoethnography is queer. In Norman K. Denzin, Yvonna S. Lincoln, & Linda T. Smith (Eds.), *Handbook of critical and indigenous methodologies* (pp. 373–390). Thousand Oaks, CA: SAGE.

Alexander, B. K. (2013). Teaching autoethnography and autoethnographic pedagogy. In *Handbook of autoethnography* (pp. 538–556). Abingdon, London: Routledge.

Australian Curriculum. (n.d.a). *Aboriginal and Torres Strait Islander histories and cultures*. Retrieved from https://www.australiancurriculum.edu.au/f-10-curriculum/cross-curriculum-priorities/aboriginal-and-torres-strait-islander-histories-and-cultures/

Australian Curriculum. (n.d.b). *Mathematics rationale*. Retrieved from https://www.australiancurriculum.edu.au/f-10-curriculum/mathematics/rationale/

Australian Institute for Teaching and School Leadership. (n.d.). *Understand the teacher standards*. Melbourne, Australia: AITSL. Retrieved from https://www.aitsl.edu.au/teach/standards/understand-the-teacher-standards

Barr, M. (2019). Autoethnography as Pedagogy: Writing the "I" in IR. *Qualitative Inquiry*, 25(9–10), 1106–1114.

Deleuze, G. (1988). *Spinoza: Practical philosophy* (R. Hurley, Trans.). San Francisco, CA: City Lights Books. Original work published 1988.

Deleuze, G. (1992). *Expressionism in philosophy: Spinoza* (M. Joughin, Trans.). New York: Zone. Original work published 1990.

Dewey, J. (1922). Habits as social functions. In *Human nature and conduct: An introduction to social psychology* (pp. 14–23). New York: Random House, Modern Library.

Harris, A. (2016). *Creative ecologies: Fostering creativity in secondary schools*. Retrieved December 12, 2019, from http://creativeresearchhub.com

Harwood, V., Hickey-Moody, A., McMahon, S., & O'Shea, S. (2016). *The politics of widening participation and university access for young people. Making educational futures*. Abingdon-on-Thames, UK: Taylor & Francis.

Hickey-Moody, A. (2013). Affect as method: Feelings, aesthetics and affective pedagogy. In R. Coleman & J. Ringrose (Eds.), *Deleuze and research methodologies* (pp. 79–95). Edinburgh, UK: Edinburgh University Press.

Hickey-Moody, A., & Harwood, V. (2018). Technologies of orientation: Pathways, futures. In L. Grealy, C. Driscoll, & A. Hickey-Moody (Eds.), *Youth, technology, governance, experience* (pp. 158–174). Abingdon, UK: Routledge.

Holman Jones, S. (2005). Autoethnography: Making the personal political. In Norman K. Denzin & Yvonna S. Lincoln (Eds.), *Handbook of qualitative research* (pp. 763–791). Thousand Oaks, CA: SAGE.

Leavy, P. (2016). *Fiction as research practice: Short stories, novellas, and novels* (Vol. 11). Abingdon, UK: Routledge.

Lexico (n.d.a). Habit. In *Lexico.com dictionary*. Retrieved March 2, 2020, from https://www.lexico.com/definition/habit.

Lexico (n.d.b). Affect. In *Lexico.com dictionary*. Retrieved March 2, 2020, from https://www.lexico.com/definition/affect

New South Wales Department of Education. (2012). *Aboriginal education policy*. Retrieved from https://policies.education.nsw.gov.au/policy-library/policies/aboriginal-education-and-training-policy

New South Wales Education Standards Authority. (2012). *Mathematics K- 10 syllabus*. Retrieved from https://www.australiancurriculum.edu.au/f-10-curriculum/mathematics/rationale/

Wall, S. (2008). Easier said than done: Writing an autoethnography. *International Journal of Qualitative Methods*, 7(1), 38–53.

Wiggins, G., Wiggins, G. P., & McTighe, J. (2005). *Understanding by design*. Alexandria, VA and London, UK: ASCD.

CHAPTER

8

Activating creativities by emphasising health and wellbeing: a holistic pedagogical practice from Finland

Kristóf Fenyvesi, Christopher S. Brownell, Jukka Sinnemäki and Zsolt Lavicza

Introduction

This chapter describes a creative and innovative pedagogical approach that has been developed within the Finnish education system. This approach focuses on the co-authoring and development of primary school learners' wellbeing, including physical and mental health. We describe this approach using a series of short narratives that centre on the everyday classroom practice of one Finnish teacher, Jukka Sinnemäki. The examples concentrate on the sculpting of the learning process and the environment, and weave together a developmental narrative to highlight the importance of the slow and careful emergence of a classroom learning community that emphasises safety, respect and concern for its members. We describe how the students and their teacher have transformed their school environment to reflect their individual and collective needs, skills, emotional capacities and values. The goal of this creative process is to maximise each of the students' full potential and support them in finding motivation and joy in learning and life; in short, to flourish. The examples will show how, over a 20-year career, Sinnemäki left traditional school hierarchies behind to focus on sculpting a thriving children's community of learners including their physical capacities, personalities and identities.

Sinnemäki has developed 'KnowNow Key', a curricular approach, an innovative piece of technology and an analytic method based on fostering holistic wellbeing and child-centred pedagogy. This innovation fuses participatory pedagogy with big datasets collected via wrist-watch-like fitness trackers that provide the wearer with bio-feedback data. The aim of this method is to inform students of the benefits and consequences of their choices regarding physical activity, nutrition and several other factors. We will end by showing ways in which the holistic pedagogical model meets the goals of multidisciplinary learning, especially within a STEAM framework. This will be illustrated through examples of collaboration and research with the Experience Workshop STEAM Network, a Finland-based organisation for education innovation, that carried out several projects with Sinnemäki's students.

In this chapter, we will introduce the story of the teacher Jukka Sinnemäki, and his journey of activating his own creativities as a practitioner and innovator, while providing a sketch of his pedagogical philosophy. This is a portrait of an uncommon approach to the practice of teaching. We encourage everyone (teachers, administrators and policy makers) to consider how you might turn classrooms into places that prioritise human flourishing and wellbeing over compliance and proficiency. We will situate this philosophy in the context of the current Finnish National Core Curriculum for Basic Education (FNCC) (FNAE, 2016), arguing that this holistic philosophy of educating students with the ultimate goal of their wellbeing has grown out of the same emphasis within the FNCC. Our intent is to share some of the story of Jukka Sinnemäki's genesis as a teacher, curriculum designer, professional development provider and educational technology designer. We will look inside his classroom and listen to him and his students as they describe their wellbeing-centred, innovative learning environment, what it is like using his pedagogical approach to holistic learning and the STEAM projects developed recently in their creative learning space.

Jukka Sinnemäki (b. 1975) was a student in Finland's schools, and is now a teacher at the Jyväskylä Christian School in Central Finland. With a Master's in Education and Philosophy and a Principal Preparation Certificate, he has also completed a degree in product development. His everyday experiences as a teacher and his background in educational leadership provided him with the background to organise his pedagogical ideas into an innovative system and launch his 'edtech' (educational technology) start-up based on the idea of merging creative learning with a holistic pedagogy focused on wellbeing and related values.

Sinnemäki's multifaceted educational achievements have garnered him several national and global awards. Among these he was a top 50 finalist in 2018 at the Global Teacher Prize, which is often regarded as the Nobel Prize for Education. Then, in 2019, he received the Global Teacher Award in New Delhi, India; and was selected by RoundGlass as one of the world's most progressive thinkers and doers in the field of learning from the key discipline that focuses on wellbeing. With 20 years of experience in education, his roles have included being a teacher in several Finnish schools and principal of the Jyväskylä Christian School. A self-ascribed 'risk taker', his motto is 'Learning happens when you see the unseen in every child'.

After almost two decades in his teaching career, Sinnemäki, growing out of his own discontent with his practice, shifted his focus to what he could do to unlock a larger variety of creative potentials in his students – isn't it always the case that questioning and dissonance breeds innovation and progress? Sinnemäki experimented in his own practice. Listening to his students he took on fitness challenges with them; connecting with them in this way helped bridge the gap between teacher and student. Soon he was adding more challenges and all of his experience brought to focus just how important it is to situate student learning within a variety of real-life processes. He began to collect various forms of data from these experiences. Conducting interviews of children and parents, associating these with academic achievement. Logging health-related data via a variety of digital fitness tracking devices and along the way seeking and receiving feedback from colleagues. Recently he has entered into a doctoral programme in education research to further his research skills, so as to gather evidence to enhance our understanding of what are the causes of the success of this method.

Sinnemäki seeks to assure his students that they are seen, heard and valued for being themselves. He attempts this through creating a sense of belonging to the community, and offering praise for doing praiseworthy things. In this he strives to ensure that his students' identities are developing without fear and with minimal stress in a safe environment. In short, he seeks to foster a place where they belong to an active and creative community. The overall goal is that each student has a series of moments where their previously unseen potentials are recognised and achieved and they then 'become themselves', while not feeling the need to become copies or imitators of someone else. 'Students becoming themselves' is interpreted here in Paulo Freire's sense, which also introduces the metaphor of sculpting with reservations, based on *We make the road by walking: Conversations on education and social change* (Horton & Freire, 1990, p. 181):

> The other mistake is to crush freedom and to exacerbate the authority of the teacher. Then you no longer have freedom but now you have authoritarianism, and then the teacher is the one who teaches. The teacher is the one who knows. The teacher is the one who guides. The teacher is the one who does everything. And the students, precisely because the students must be shaped, just expose their bodies and their souls to the hands of the teacher, as if the students were clay for the artist, to be molded. The teacher is of course an artist, but being an artist does not mean that he or she can make the profile, can shape the students. What the educator does in teaching is to make it possible for the students to become themselves. And in doing that, he or she lives the experience of relating democratically as authority with the freedom of the students.

One of Sinnemäki's remarkable contributions as a teacher was supporting students to increase their self-awareness by reflecting on the crucial role in the learning process of a person's lifestyle, various aspects of their mental and physical balance, sleep, nutrition, sports activities, friends, family, social contacts and so on. Thus, when it comes to learning, one should not forget these aspects as one designs learning experiences and goals. This is one of the main reasons he created the programme: to help students to gain self-awareness through pedagogy- and technology-supported, holistic self-reflection and to enhance their wellbeing through learning. The programme also supports teachers' and parents' awareness of health and wellbeing in order to help them to positively focus on their impact on children's lifestyles.

Sinnemäki believes that the teacher needs to possess the following skills, values and characteristics to make a difference:

- *Transparency*: just like their students, teachers are encouraged to be themselves. Teachers should not feel the need to act like they know it all in front of their students. They should tolerate mistakes, including their own, and reveal themselves as vulnerable human beings.
- *Passion*: to run the extra mile together with the students and to be ready to recognise the unseen in each student.
- *Humility:* to be open, not to be confined to just one version of their world, to be able to listen to new ideas, and take suggestions even from those that reflect different views.
- *Adventurousness:* when children are wanting to be bold, or to take the risk to try a new way to solve a problem, or to be open to a new idea. Adventurousness is also seen in teachers who do not always approach a subject in the same way, or who experiment with new learning environments.
- *Persistence*: is necessary to cultivate the culture of not giving up and can be seen when children want to stay in school even when the school day is over.
- *Patience*: is an essential quality to value the qualities of each student, to give them enough time to grow, and to accept that learning takes a lifetime to complete.

By focusing on the whole schooling experience through a strong focus on activating and leveraging interpersonal relationships, Sinnemäki fulfils complex requirements coming from the Finnish National Curriculum. On the other hand he inventively puts into practice the creation of safe, caring and responsive schools. Accomplished according to the principles of 'values pedagogy' (Lovat, Dally, Clement, & Toomey, 2011). Values pedagogy aims to actualise both the individual student and the broader school ecology by setting the 'new paradigm of learning' on nurturing students holistic wellbeing. Further, it is focused on developing skills and increasing knowledge. In the values pedagogy's framework, the sense of wellbeing encourages and impels students to strive to reach their full potential. It directs teachers' attention to 'explicitly teaching values and scaffolding children's social and emotional development while, at the same time, requiring positive modelling by teachers and the creation of safe, caring and responsive schools' (Lovat et al., 2011, p. 67).

Jukka Sinnemäki's pedagogy for holistic wellbeing

Sinnemäki's pedagogy is centralised around the slow and careful sculpting of the learning process, both for the individual and at the community level. The process can be described as collective competence development, emphasising the collaborative and creative improvement of a healthy learning environment. The result is the slow and careful emergence of a learning community that emphasises safety, respect, health and wellbeing along with concern for its members. Within a safe environment, children dare to show their feelings and emotions, and fulfil their needs for physical activity, which creates a necessary foundation for balanced development. From this process transformation is possible; the transformation of the individual student and of the nature of the learning community as a whole. Each of the members find themselves situated within and instrumental in the creation of an environment wherein they can flourish.

In 2018 Sinnemäki and his students installed treadmills, climbing walls and pull-up bars in their classroom. The process has continued with several other types of sports equipment and interactive devices, e.g. interactive video walls in 2020 (see Figure 8.1 and Figure 8.2). The equipment was a prize for the students' achievement of several challenges, including more physical activity during their time spent in the school. This material change helped the emotional and mental transformation and supported everybody in leaving the traditional school hierarchies behind.

A focus on sculpting a thriving children's community of learners across physical capacities, personalities and identities can achieve another level of child-centred pedagogy. Connecting innovative pedagogy and technology motivated Sinnemäki to create KnowNow Key, a pedagogical programme including curriculum and a device (see Figure 8.3) for the holistic improvement of learning communities' wellbeing. The combination of physical activity, data-collecting 'wearable' sensors and biofeedback provides positive reinforcement and accurate assessment of the consequences of choices students make regarding their behaviour. Through embodying learning experiences students can develop new perspectives on their own wellbeing, which gives them the opportunity to learn to control the inputs into their physical-mental balance. This can lead to them being in optimal condition even in the face of great challenges.

For learning to be useful and meaningful, in the spirit of WHO's (2020) recommendations for health-promoting schools, it should be viewed as a comprehensive and holistic process. By that, Sinnemäki means teaching the importance of sufficient and regular amounts of physical activity, recovery, recreation, sleep and healthy food as a basis for learning. Likewise, the pupils need positive encounters, encouragement, friends, motivational teaching and guidance, and the circle is completed by support at home.

As attested by research, increasing physical activity on school days has many positive effects (Moilanen, Äyrämö, & Kankaanranta, 2018). Nowadays, the

Figure 8.1 A primary-level classroom space in Sinnemäki's school before the student-driven health and wellbeing transformation process started. Photo: Jukka Sinnemäki

Figure 8.2 Sinnemäki's classroom space in Jyväskylä Christian School after the student-driven health and wellbeing transformation process took place. Photo: Jukka Sinnemäki

school-aged child's life is full of various stimuli that cause difficulties in relaxing and diminished focus on tasks that require prolonged attention. Likewise, the constant bombardment of external stimuli also weakens creativity and self-actualisation. Therefore, one of a school's critical functions is to encourage children to practise tasks and skills that improve general and executive cognitive functioning. This requires a holistic pedagogical model that meets the goals of multidisciplinary learning.

According to Sinnemäki's pedagogical philosophy, transformation starts with an understanding of the students' needs. Before including any extra devices in the classroom, it is essential to build a relationship and trust with each of the students.

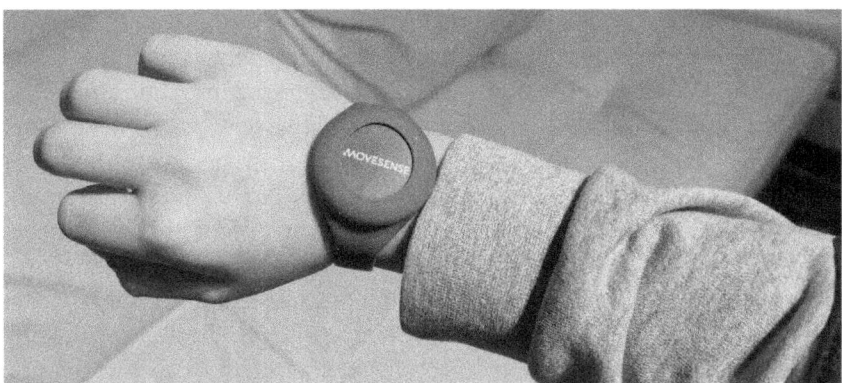

Figure 8.3 The KnowNow Key Device. Photo: Jukka Sinnemäki

This relational development period can take months for a new group, and it is a continuous process. It requires prioritising human development over subject-based studies, a careful and respectful engagement in the students' everyday life and activities, openly showing interest in the things students like and dislike, their questions and opinions, and actively providing security and encouragement at both the individual and community levels. To accomplish this, Sinnemäki received encouragement and trust from his pupils' parents along with a great measure of autonomy from within the school structure itself.

Development of primary school students' physical and mental wellbeing according to the Finnish National Core Curriculum for Basic Education

Jukka Sinnemäki favours describing his pedagogical approach as 'holistic', which the Cambridge Dictionary (2020) defines as 'dealing with or treating the whole of something or someone and not just a part'. The concept is commonly used in several fields, including medicine, philosophy, and even mindfulness and gastronomy, and holistic approaches in education and pedagogy also have a long history. However, to map Sinnemäki's pedagogical holism, we do not need sophisticated methods for networked thinking or reviewing the most complex and integrative pedagogical theorists. It is enough to follow the current Finnish National Core Curriculum for Basic Education (FNAE, 2016).

'Holistic' is an often-used term to summarise the essence of Finnish education. Holistic as an adjective appears repeatedly as a conceptual leitmotiv within the FNCC, carrying a variety of meanings and roles, and inspiring new interpretations and contexts in the everyday world of education in Finland. Holistic, integrated instruction, along with multisensory, phenomenon-based methods to support the development of transversal competencies, including multiliteracy, are delineated throughout the FNCC. There are several passages on holistic support and holistic development in various contexts, even holistic rehabilitation (to provide educational support in a particular situation, such as when a student requires medical treatment or is in quarantine at home). Nevertheless, the term 'holistic' appears most frequently to describe holistic wellbeing. Holistic wellbeing and holistic growth are complex concepts that characterise the Finnish curriculum on all levels, including policy, content, pedagogical methods, educational leadership and implementation.

The FNCC's strong ties to holistic educational ideas, including students' holistic wellbeing, suggest FNCC's firm commitment to values pedagogy rather than instrumentalist approaches to learning (Lovat, Toomey, & Clement, 2010). Quality teaching for students' holistic wellbeing prioritises students' social and emotional needs and society's betterment, instead of focusing mainly on standardisation, according to industry needs (Lovat et al., 2011). Authentic pedagogy fosters 'educational imagination' and further creativities, such as artistry in teaching and learning (Lovat, 2020).

The reasons for this apparent and necessarily broad focus on holistic wellbeing in the FNCC can be explained by recognising the overall impact that Finland's establishment as a Nordic welfare state had on its educational policy. In the 1980s, Finland's socio-economic and cultural transformation could not have been successful without thematising the elaborated notion and various dimensions of wellbeing in all educational contexts. As part of the same process, radical decentralisation, which gave the lead to local authorities, schools and teachers, has linked pedagogical holism to fundamental democratic values. This involved increased participation and deeper collaboration at the level of implemented pedagogical methodologies and trending educational leadership styles. Between 1985 and 1988 the school inspection system was abolished, and local authorities gained autonomy to create local curricula, which enabled unique expressions of the curriculum, including Sinnemäki's original interpretation of holistic wellbeing, among the other key concepts of the FNCC.

Two complete chapters of the FNCC are devoted entirely to the introduction of holistic wellbeing in the Finnish educational context. Chapter 5 of the FNCC (FNAE, 2016, pp. 36–48.) focuses on 'Organisation of schoolwork aiming to promote learning and wellbeing', and Chapter 8 concentrates on 'Pupil welfare' (FNAE, 2016, pp. 81–89). There are several sub-chapters organised around the key topics in the context of holistic wellbeing. Holistic wellbeing provides the framework for ensuring safety, physical and mental health, meeting basic needs, and individual and community care across all levels of Finnish basic education. Holistic wellbeing and pupil welfare also serve as the background and a goal for building trust, shared responsibility, improving participation, agency, inclusion, the joint reflection of school and home values, and promoting sustainable lifestyles.

As a broad pedagogical perception of the different aspects of health and human advancement, the Finnish approach to holistic wellbeing and pupil welfare cannot be separated from the enactment of the FNCC in local curricula. This is supported by the fact that the main components of holistic wellbeing and pupil welfare are introduced in the FNCC as issues that are subject to local decision making (see FNAE, 2016, pp. 46–48, 86–89). Finnish school governance is based on teacher autonomy, and decentralised and prosocial leadership, with extensive degrees of freedom and full transparency. These all foster an environment ripe for creative adaptation such as this narrative of Jukka Sinnemäki's pedagogical development and philosophy of the classroom environment.

In accordance with the FNCC, Sinnemäki's core value is supporting the learning community as the heart of the school culture. According to this interpretation, the bases of the learning community are shared leadership, dialogue, cooperation and participation. The learning community is peaceful and empowering; it relies on self-evaluation and communication with parents and other partners. It promotes physical and emotional wellbeing (FNAE, 2016, p. 28).

The establishment of wellbeing and safety in everyday school life is another important principle in Finnish schools, and it is emphasised by Sinnemäki too. The school's structures and practices are supposed to create preconditions for learning, equality, flexibility, versatility, accessibility, predictability, fairness, trustworthiness and the rejection of discrimination (FNAE, 2016, p. 28).

The interaction and versatile working approach involve active learning. Learning in Finnish schools is meant to be based on a diversity of learning styles, creative work, play, movement and experiences. The free access to the exceptionally rich equipment in Sinnemäki's classroom invites students to do creative exercises whenever they need it. FNCC recommends re-connecting in-school and out-of-school learning, and encouraging project- and module-based education, multisensory learning and interaction with working life (FNAE, 2016, pp. 28–29). As our concrete examples will show, all of these options are integrated in Sinnemäki's everyday pedagogical practice.

From the perspective of Anne Harris's (2016) model of creative ecologies in education (details of which are featured in Chapter 4), it is important to recognise that Sinnemäki's school, similarly to other Finnish schools, in order to provide space for more creativity, is moving away from centralised leadership towards networked structures. Finnish teachers are aware of the challenges of such a creative ecological transition and make several pragmatic and 'everyday' recommendations on interaction and negotiations between their school's various participants, including pupils, teachers, special educators, caregivers, administrative staff, social workers, service providers and labour market actors. This is among the requirements to fulfil FNCC's complex goals and respond to today's difficult challenges when it comes to health and sustainability.

The fact that creativity is among the most often mentioned 'cross-cutting' topics serves to validate creative schooling as a welcome perspectival change in Finnish education. The processes, partnerships, policies, products and the physical and emotional environment are all integral to discussions related to creativity. The theme of creativity appears in FNCC nearly 100 times in multiple configurations, contexts and roles. FNCC, as a policy document, promotes the implementation of creative factors to reinforce the education system's ecological coherence.

This affirms both the descriptive and transformational capacity of Harris's model of creative ecologies in education and Burnard's concept of multiple, diverse creativities (Burnard et al., 2017).

Just as it is implemented in multiple ways in Sinnemäki's students' STEAM projects, creativity has multiple functions in the FNCC too. Sinnemäki's pedagogical innovation has helped to develop this highly complex creative conceptual network on the topic of wellbeing and health.

We cannot complete this brief introduction of how the FNCC supports Jukka Sinnemäki's holistic wellbeing-based pedagogical portfolio without mentioning two key concepts which open new perspectives in our discussion of the field of educational leadership. Prosociality and collective competence development are indispensable to Sinnemäki's implementation of a holistic pedagogy. A prosocial attitude and collective competence development are two closely related concepts that seem to be characteristic of Sinnemäki's holistic practice and Finnish basic education in general.

From recent studies (Yada, 2020) it seems that *prosociality* (the willingness, behaviours and values for benefiting others, irrespectively of positional roles [Yada, 2020, p. 24]) and *collective competence* (the group's ability to work together, and additional aspects, including values and attitudes, how to use tools, and relationships with others [Ibid. p. 45]) have a lot to offer in diverse classroom practices, the teacher-student relationship, everyday creativity in the educational context (Szabó, Fenyvesi, Soundararaj, & Kangasvieri, 2019) and pedagogical innovation. According to recent interpretations in educational leadership studies, prosociality concerns motivation, behaviour and experience to help others (Yada, 2020). It can be reflected in multiple ways, as Figure 8.4 shows. The various actions, attitudes and behaviours represented in the diagram are characteristic of Sinnemäki's own practice as well. Hand in hand with collective competence development, we can recognise these components as the motivators and enablers of Sinnemäki's

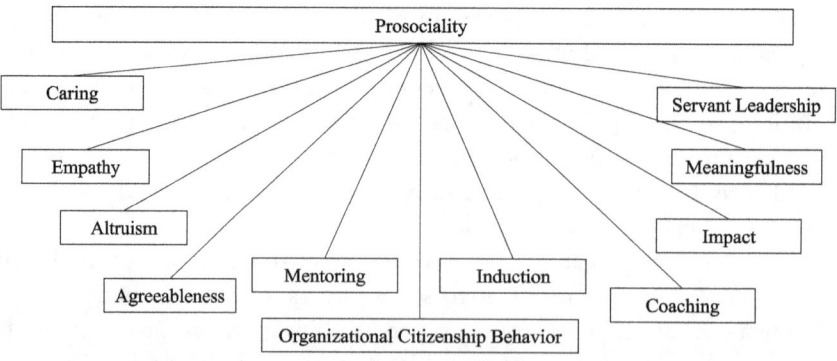

Figure 8.4 Conceptual model of prosocial elements in educational leadership (Source: Yada & Jäppinen, 2019, p. 981)

pedagogical innovations. We illustrate their functioning in the next section using examples taken from Sinnemäki and his class's recent and ongoing projects.

Projects for the everyday promotion of holistic wellbeing

Following the significant growth of international interest and also the technological development of Finnish education, several educational export companies and influential Finnish edtech start-ups have appeared in both the national and the global markets. In sizable multidisciplinary research and development networks, private sector actors are creating services together with researchers, practitioners and teachers in a practice that has become known as the 'Finnish solution' (Niemi, Multisilta., Lipponen, & Vivitsou, 2014). Considering the overall emerging entrepreneurial spirit in Finnish education, teachers in Finland are often regarded as innovators and developers. As part of their master's degree, Finnish teachers are also qualified in educational research. Behind several Finnish edtech companies, there are experienced teachers who have created the solution. Edupreneurship capacities in Finland mainly lie in teachers' autonomy and flexibility in the school organisation, and independence in selecting or creating the learning topics, and teaching materials and tools (Linna & Laaksonen, 2018).

This process of teachers transforming into 'edupreneurs'[1] is among the many reasons that Jukka Sinnemäki's professional and entrepreneurial development was positively received among students, colleagues and parents in his school. His efforts were recognised and valued both at the interpersonal and the organisational level. Sinnemäki found support for his innovative ideas for several reasons, including (1) the elaboration and implementation of his own experimental pedagogical methodology based on holistic wellbeing and STEAM; (2) a radical physical and mental transformation of the learning environment based on the needs and wishes of his students; and (3) participating in cutting-edge educational innovation research projects and creating his own edtech start-up (see: www.KnowNow.fi).

In the next section, we will show how, as a result of his 20-year pedagogical experience, Sinnemäki expanded and in some cases surpassed the traditional Finnish school hierarchies to focus on sculpting a thriving children's community of learners who are developing their physical capacities, personalities, identities and multiple creativities.

Transformation of the learning environment to accommodate various creativities based on health and holistic wellbeing

As a primary school teacher, Jukka Sinnemäki is usually the head teacher of a class. He works as the teacher of the same group, generally until the group finishes their sixth grade. Like most Finnish primary school classrooms, Sinnemäki's classroom looks unique, reflecting the class community's specific needs and wishes. The learning environment is the result of a collaborative and creative sculpting process. This creative sculpting process is inspired by the class community's history on the one hand and by a carefully planned, shared creative vision of the learning space on the other. The creative and collaborative interpretation of the Finnish National Core Curriculum's guidelines – such as 'the holistic wellbeing of the school community and each pupil is taken into account in the development of learning environments' (FNAE, 2016, p. 31) – is unfolding slowly as a full-time activity over several years in which all students participate. Sinnemäki's role as a teacher is to creatively facilitate the collective sculpting process, to support the students in negotiating ideas and expressing wishes, and to be a creative coach for the community and a curator of the environmental sculpting process. The goal is to co-create an innovative learning environment, which is, in the spirit of the FNCC, 'safe and healthy and promote healthy growth and development as indicated by the pupils' age and capabilities' (FNAE, 2016, p. 33), where 'learning is supported by a peaceful and friendly working atmosphere and a calm, peaceful mood' (p. 33).

By making use of his 'edupreneurial' spirit, his research-based and professionally developed knowledge, and the learning community's shared creative vision of holistic wellbeing, Sinnemäki has successfully supported his students to realise an atypical learning environment. They started without any special equipment in the classroom, but now after undertaking this joint journey, which has engaged students' creative activities, innovations, interests, curiosity, passion and enthusiasm for expressing themselves, they have radically transformed the classroom. They creatively transformed the classroom space by combining the physical components of a modern classroom with an impressive selection of sports equipment, available at all times to fulfil students' physical needs. The transformed classroom provides a 'possibility space' (Burnard et al., 2017) for exploring, experiencing and developing multiple creativities, with a great emphasis on health and wellbeing. Students, teachers and visitors can move during and between various tasks, release stress, or celebrate the completion of an assessment or an educational achievement with different sports exercises. A video (KnowNow, 2019) illustrates the environment and the multiple, diverse creative activities that this environment inspires in the students.

The classroom includes treadmills, indoor skiing machines and a green wall to make the study space healthier and more comfortable by providing better indoor air. According to the producer, the green wall improves cognitive performance and halts fatigue. In addition to the health challenges, Sinnemäki has actively organised his class and the parents to join cleaning programmes, which was rewarded by sponsorship grants, which supported the realisation of the unique interior.

The impressive amount of useful sports equipment in the classroom was collected and 'earned' by the students by organising various health campaigns in their school and beyond. These health campaigns were based on students setting challenges for each other, their teachers, and the whole school community. For example, the students organised a chin-up challenge. As a result, the class's collective total repetitions of chin-ups increased from 50 to 300. Accordingly, a well-known Finnish sports equipment distributor donated fitness equipment of the pupils' choice. However, an even more significant reward was the fact that this challenge increased the entire school's motivation and that it reduced conflict, thus improving the classroom and the whole-school atmosphere. A significant positive impact was also perceived related to solidarity, working hard to achieve results, and developing social skills. The transformation of the single classroom (see Figure 8.2) later initiated a school-level transformation of the whole learning environment. Currently, the school's shared spaces, where the students spend their free time when they are not outdoors during recess, are also fully equipped with various training equipment and technology (see Figure 8.5).

To fulfil the sponsors' expectations and reward the students' significant achievements with publicity and positive feedback, Sinnemäki organised social media campaigns to make their joint efforts highly visible. The video that he created and shared on social media (KnowNow, 2019) set the record as the most viewed social media post ever created in Finland with 7 million views, over 55,000 shares, and tens of thousands of comments. In addition to creating edupreneurial capital, this became an unforgettable story for the students, who worked hard for the results and appeared in the video.

In addition to physical wellbeing, the creative sculpting of mental wellbeing also had some entrepreneurial components but pointed toward various creative community values. The idea of Tea Thursdays was intended to encourage students to read more. Sinnemäki's class had a fruitful collaboration with a local tea shop. The students could sell tea in their school. Through this project, the students earned money for their class and learned several details about how tea is produced, packaged and sold. This collaboration provided creative insights to the students on how to become an entrepreneur and as a multidisciplinary learning project

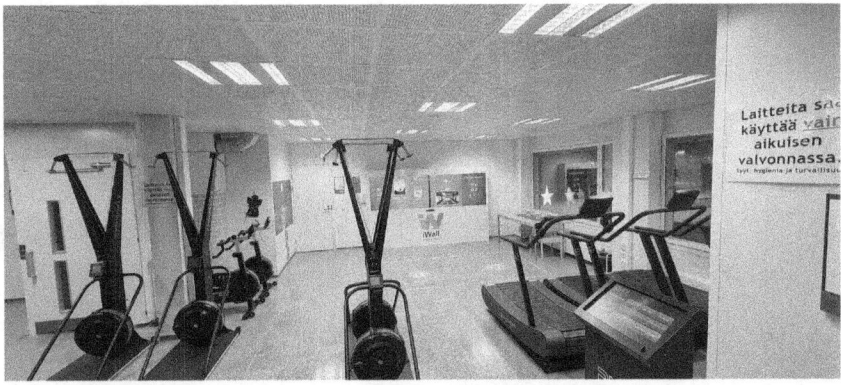

Figure 8.5 Jyväskylä Christian School's Open Lobby Area with free-to-use sports equipment and interactive technology. Photo: Jukka Sinnemäki

integrating several subjects for complex skill development. Many components of this project quickly became part of the class culture and routines. Before lessons, students prepared different kinds of teas while they looked for comfortable places to read books. These comfortable places were often on the top of the sports equipment (see Figure 8.6) and some students combined reading with repetitive movements, like slow walking on the treadmill in a peripatetic manner. The students loved these occasions and many of them enjoyed the benefits of reading books for the first time, being able to relax and calm down.

The class co-authored a practice they call 'Tea Thursdays' wherein they agree to silent learning periods focused on reading a book of their own choosing. These occasions have increased enthusiasm for reading, along with creating excellent recreation and relaxation times. As you can see in Figure 8.6, these silent periods do not necessarily take place with the children in strictly organised (adult-oriented) arrangements. Students have options, negotiate them with each other and the teacher, and then engage in the extended reading times.

Cooperation with different out-of-school actors like sports equipment distributors, real estate investors and local small businesses has dramatically diversified and enriched the school days. These projects contributed to the holistic wellbeing concept from different perspectives. Additionally, increased attention was invested into the wishes, innovations and various creativities of each child. The children responded by doing tasks more patiently, persistently and with better goal-oriented mindsets, within a supportive atmosphere, which invited all to activate the mind and the body at the same time.

This act of transformation would not have happened if the children had not been intrinsically motivated. Therefore, bringing about change and transformation requires a particular form of learning, not merely teachers telling children what to do, or what is wrong and what is right. According to Sinnemäki's experience,

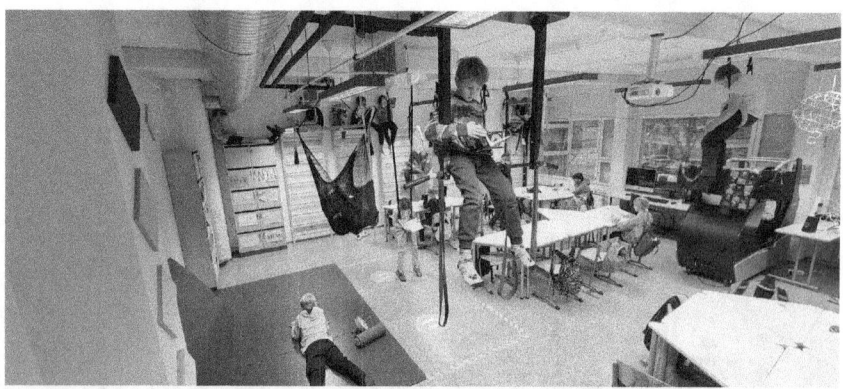

Figure 8.6 A 'Tea Thursday' reading time in Sinnemäki's class. Photo: Jukka Sinnemäki

cultivating this motivation requires three ingredients that foster various kinds of creativities:

- *Autonomy*: the right to be in control of one's own choices. Individuals need experiences to lead or guide their learning.
- *Competence*: children are allowed to use their areas of expertise and strengths that provide an experience of success and capability.
- *Relatedness*: the surrounding community and relationships provide an overall supporting structure and momentum, fuelling motivation and learning.

The 'KnowNow Key' solution for improving health and wellbeing in everyday learning

Sinnemäki has developed 'KnowNow Key' (KNK: http://knownow.fi/en/), an innovative curriculum, analytic method and technology to enhance the implementation of his holistic wellbeing pedagogy. Sinnemäki's related edtech start-up aims to inform members of the learning community, including students, teachers and parents, about the benefits and implications for wellbeing, of their choices regarding physical activity, nutrition and several other factors.

The infusion of an edtech solution brings a focus on the practical introduction and scalable implementation of pedagogy for holistic wellbeing on five levels:

1 to enhance learning
2 to strengthen educational leadership
3 as a critical component in an innovative learning environment
4 to activate embodied creativities for learning
5 to promote health awareness.

He seeks accessible and measurable insights into how the learning community members feel about their physical and mental condition. 'Are they ready to learn and optimise the management of their life?' 'What are the influencing factors behind that?' For students, this focus offers feedback regarding personal decisions related to learning and wellbeing. For teachers, the device and available analysis serves as an entry point to implement the pedagogy of holistic wellbeing and a method for collecting evidence of the phases of implementation. This theory provides a framework for holistic wellbeing in practice, and gives teachers and school principals access to information in real time, so that they can make the right pedagogical decisions. Educational leaders can better follow the pedagogy of holistic wellbeing both for the individual student and at the classroom level. Providing novel and actionable information to parents about their children's holistic wellbeing in school and during their free time is a key outcome. It also enables a new kind of positive and reflective dialogue between children's parents and the school on wellbeing and health-related topics.

KNK consists of a technological toolkit and a methodological implementation package. Both are based on experience and collaborative development. The technological toolkit's primary function is activity measurement, massive and diverse data collection and big data analysis combined with machine learning (Moilanen et al., 2018) within a research-grounded theoretical framework of holistic wellbeing (see Figure 8.7).

Activity is measured by an accelerometer that registers even small movements of the user. The movements are time stamped and stored in the sensor's memory. The device collects data about the level of movement and exercise performance, passivity, regularity, the duration of actions, bedtime, length of sleep and several further details. The data collected with the sensor are synchronised via a Bluetooth connection to a terminal, which can be a phone or a tablet. The system uses a proprietary fitness tracker and synchronised software. The sensor's memory is

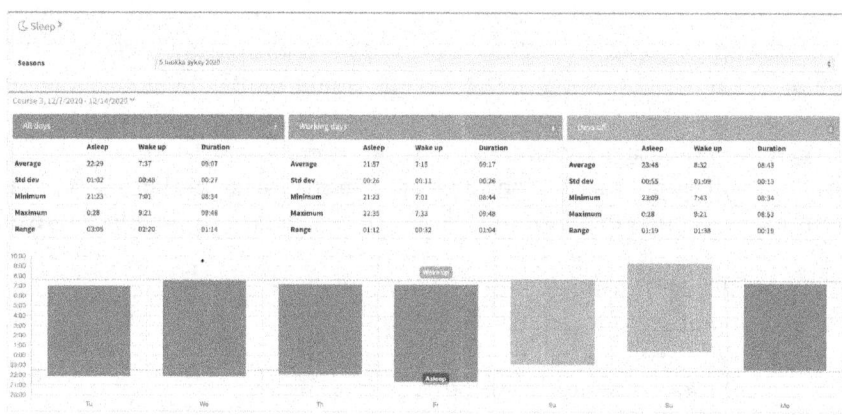

Figure 8.7 Analytic data screen in the KnowNow-Key mobile app

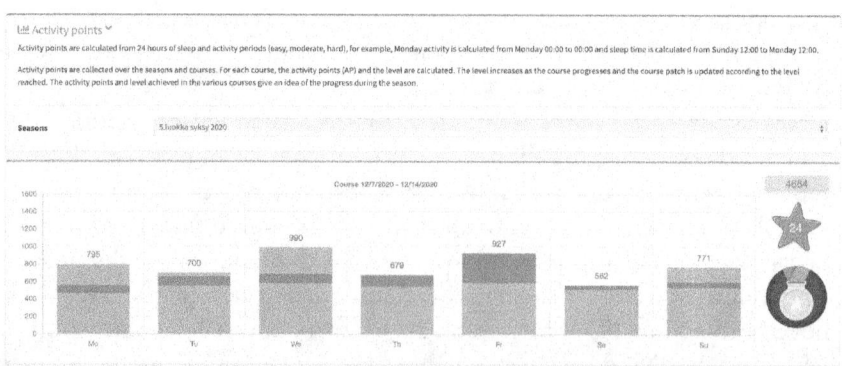

Figure 8.8 Activity points collected in gamification mode in the KnowNow-Key mobile app to increase progress level

sufficient to record events for up to several weeks, depending on the number of measuring points.

The sensor is attached to the wrist like a wristwatch. If desired, it can also be worn on the ankle. The measurement data collected by the sensor is stored on the user's phone or tablet. After synchronisation, the data is visible on the user interface, accessible through any internet browser (see Figure 8.7). Data are processed and evaluated using data encryption, advanced data transmission, machine learning technologies and gamification solutions. All data is protected against unethical access and use. The students' use of the device depends on their own willingness and their parents' consent, which is made in accordance with GDPR regulations. The ethical use of information and the protocol for ethical conduct during the holistic wellbeing pedagogical sessions is adhered to by taking into account the personal risks and procedures of wearable technologies (see e.g. Goodyear, 2017). The training includes comprehensive information on ethical conduct, which forms part of the training programme, which is obligatory for all users. Students' privacy is protected through anonymising the student's identity, thus preventing the knowledge of it being transmitted to the measurement group. The results and measurements can only be seen by the students, their guardians and their teachers without express permission being granted. Students may participate in the holistic wellbeing programme even if they decide not to wear the device.

The sensor collects objective information and transmits it directly from the device to a smartphone or computer. Additionally, collecting subjective information based on users' self-observation is an integral part of the method. Users' mobile or tablet devices collect subjective data in response to daily questions focusing on the following aspects of wellbeing:

- General feeling: in the morning, after school, before bedtime
- Nutrition: breakfast, lunch, snacks, dinner, evening snack
- Amount and type of liquids drunk

Users are also asked their opinion of the measured activities done during the day, spending time with friends, family, screen time, and dividing time between school and home each day.

The data are combined and analysed within the proprietary software programme, which can be described from a research perspective as a mixed-methods process, in which qualitative and quantitative analysis is combined in a pragmatic way. The implementation of the programme doubles as a training event in holistic wellbeing pedagogy, but it is already available as a tool which could potentially become part of everyday practice as well. Meetings with teachers discuss the technical training and provide a comprehensive picture of the entire process, including the aspects of ethical data handling.

After the introductory sessions, devices are launched, and all those willing to participate are asked to proceed doing everything just as usual for a week-long period. During the first week, the device and researchers receive data on the current lifestyles of the participants. The expert team creates a preliminary analysis of the collected data and also collects information on what the members of the school community would like to change in their lifestyle in order to have a more complete experience of wellbeing. Each participant can set personal goals and class- or small-group-based goals are made available.

The second week is called the intervention week. Participants see results in all areas, and they can monitor and follow-up the data collection in real time. During this period participants get a clear impression of how their modified actions influence the objective and subjective data under collection. During the third week it is time to make the changes the participants decided to introduce. After 3 weeks, participants together with the KNK team draw conclusions, and create reports and follow-up strategies, which will contribute to maintaining self-reflection after the training period. The core idea is that participants will be able to introduce new, healthier habits and monitor and influence themselves even without devices. This 3-week, 21-day experience is usually enough to begin a transformation and to share that experience with other members of the learning community.

The programme has been widely implemented in Finland in 2019. From the initial feedback, evidence suggests that schools are eager to have this innovation and the support from the team in their implementation of a pedagogy focused on holistic wellbeing. Cited next are several reasons provided during the feedback sessions:

- The programme and device have been recognised as a means to develop children's and teachers' self-reflection and understanding of health and lifestyle related matters.
- Through raising personal and community health awareness, this focus helps students to author improvement of their wellbeing and learning.
- The students can systematically frame what they can learn about and how they can control their personal development.
- Teachers, parents and students are prompted to reflect on their stress levels and 'readiness' to learn.
- The nurturing of more creative links to subject-based or multidisciplinary and real-life-based approaches to health in learning.
- A contribution to deepening the understanding between the child and his or her caregivers.
- Enhanced communications between home and school.
- Active support to school staff to cope with health-related organisational challenges in their work.
- Associations that indicate a contribution to realising wellbeing-related leadership goals and can unlock new potentials in special education, can be seen.
- Precise and real-time information to support school management.

The responses have been promising, including teachers' and students' opinions on innovative technology and their views on this approach. For example, teachers are mostly very positive about implementing the KNK programme because they are not required to do much extra work. Students are enthusiastic that, as part of the process offered and context generated within the programme, they can track and respond to their health habits in an organised way.

Students usually prove to be committed to making changes to improve their quality of life with the support of the programme. It is also important because teachers are generally asking for 'ready-made' lesson materials to implement the pedagogy for holistic wellbeing in their content teaching. It seems they require more advice, guidance, concrete ideas and hints for discussing various wellbeing-related topics with their students. Additionally, teachers are looking for sources to increase their enthusiasm to start preparing lessons during the training process. This might be because the usefulness of the knowledge-based materials for developing holistic wellbeing-related competencies usually depend on what kind of interest/knowledge/competencies a teacher already has. At the same time, several users have provided evidence that the programme serves as a discussion starter for teacher-student conversations. After the primary activity was finished, the discussion about wellbeing and opportunities for improving a healthy lifestyle continued. Students' request to have more salads and fresh, healthy food available as part of the school meal was one positive response.

To respond to much of this initial feedback, a KNK workbook was also created in the format of a personal development journal and activity log currently in production. It serves as a collection of activities and advice to maintain active discussion and a transformational attitude in connection with holistic aspects of wellbeing throughout the year.

STEAM projects that incorporate embodied cognition and activate creativities

Sinnemäki's commitment to research and continuous analysis, and his willingness to experiment with and mould his pedagogical methods to increase his students' motivation and their overall health, has transformed his learning design. The uncommon, some might say radical, nature of this pedagogy has given him opportunities not only to activate his own creativities but to connect with other creative efforts around the nation of Finland, the European Union and indeed around the world. Among these are his efforts to incorporate embodied cognition activities and to encourage his students to engage in trans/cross/multi-disciplinary creativities.

The Finnish Experience Workshop STEAM Network's (www.experience workshop.org) Erasmus+ project entitled Mathematics in Motion, which aimed to explore ways of learning mathematics through body movement (Fenyvesi et al., 2019), has many connections with Sinnemäki's body-movement-centred learning agenda. This project was partly inspired by Sinnemäki's holistic pedagogical views and conceived in his school. The Erasmus+ project called Poly-Universe in School Education offered opportunities to incorporate and reflect on the concept of embodied cognition in practice with Sinnemäki's students. The goal of this project, just like several other Experience Workshop activities with Sinnemäki's students (see Figure 8.9), was the development of logical reasoning, computational thinking and mathematical problem solving. The University of Jyväskylä's Modelling at School and Kids Inspiring Kids for STEAM Erasmus+ projects opened up ways to implement coding with BBC micro: bits, introducing physical computation, computational modelling, and diagrams for learning and studying various subjects and phenomena beyond the subject limits in multi- and transdisciplinary contexts.

These projects contributed to shifting the focus of Sinnemäki's holistic pedagogy to key competence development (European Commission, 2019) through STEAM. They supported Sinnemäki's and his students' intention to explore various modern technologies as learning tools. Sinnemäki's class, in collaboration with Experience Workshop and the 3D-printer producer start-up called Craftbot, received cutting-edge educational digital fabrication technology. Sinnemäki's students have already opened their own learning paths to introduce European Key Competency areas through digital fabrication, and digital and physical modelling, both in subject-based and multidisciplinary contexts.

Sinnemäki's class's first steps with the 3D printer have already shown its potential to encourage networking, co-creation, and context-based, inquiry-based, ICT-enriched learning (see Figure 8.10). Digital fabrication and modelling contribute to implementing real-world scenarios. Following a cyclical process of design, creation, reflection and adaptation in a digital learning environment seems to be very

Figure 8.9 Experience Workshop's embodied cognition STEAM activity with Jukka Sinnemäki's students to discover the geometry of tessellation through playing with laser-cut Gondos-Tiles. The activity is combined with KnowNow Key data collection. Photo: Kristóf Fenyvesi

Activating creativities

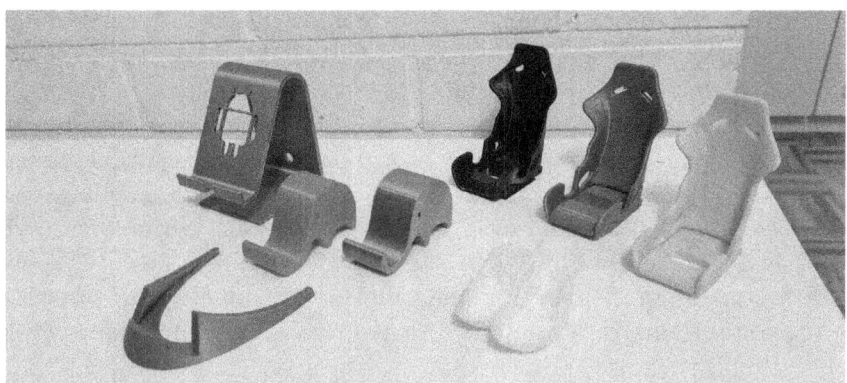

Figure 8.10 3D-printed objects to learn the basics of 3D-printing and study geometrical shapes in industrial design in Experience Workshop's Craftbot project in Jyväskylä Christian School. Photo: Jukka Sinnemäki

useful for promoting inquiry- and project-based learning in a cross-disciplinary manner. Learning, thinking, reflecting and problem solving in action is at the core of the digital fabrication and modelling-related STEAM activities in Sinnemäki's classroom. The 3D-printing projects initiated by the students encouraged peer coaching, supported a wide range of extracurricular activities and career guidance, and strengthened personal skills and competences.

Unlocking research in practice: provocations for group discussion

Jukka Sinnemäki's holistic approach to learning, including the acknowledgement of students' need for physical activity, has helped him become an innovative and risk-taking teacher. His efforts to establish his practice-oriented holistic pedagogy for health and wellbeing has led to several innovations and is having an impact in wider and wider circles. Sinnemäki's students are unlocking multiple creativities, which can contribute to enhancing their positive attitudes towards maintaining healthy and sustainable ways of life and greater achievements in learning.

1. We have described a vision for the classroom that sets as a priority the ability of the students to focus on their own wellbeing as a means to flourish. According to Sinnemäki, 'Students are not empty bottles to be filled, but candles to be lit'. What are the overarching goals for education in the environment/system you work in and what are the main values in your practice? How have you involved the students in the learning process?
2. If you have not already done so, watch the video of Sinnemäki's classroom (KnowNow, 2019). What are your first thoughts? What benefits or possible drawbacks do you perceive in this environment? If you could, what steps in

this direction could you take tomorrow to achieve this sort of environment for learning? Name a few mid-range goals you can make now to achieve such an open atmosphere for learning.
3. We have attempted to make the case that the goals of human wellbeing and flourishing are central to the national curriculum of Finland, citing references to them within the FNCC. Where do you find such statements regarding the central reason for education within your nation/state/community? Are there such statements within your country/locale? These goals represent a 'shared vision' for education throughout Finland (that of elevating human flourishing and wellbeing). What is the shared vision in your country/state/district/school?
4. Sinnemäki's classroom and school environment is largely based on his students' wishes and has a large array of equipment available as alternatives to desk seating that the students are free to choose. Would you encourage such freedom and autonomy to students in your setting? How would it look from students' and teachers' perspective in your school? What are the first steps you could take? Should students share that much power in their learning, or should adults exclusively govern the learning environment?
5. How do you define success in your teaching practice, in students' learning and in your school environment?

Note

1. 'Edupreneur/edupreneurship' are neologisms formed by the concatenation of the terms educator and entrepreneur(ship). Their meanings are derived from that blend, conjuring an environment where the creative efforts and risks taken by educators are both encouraged and rewarded. It is important to note that this environment is fostered by the National Core Curriculum and government policy in Finland. It is critical, therefore, that readers determine whether their schooling environment possesses such a high tolerance of risk in balance with its commitment to the educational process's focus on human flourishing and wellbeing as described in this chapter.

References

Burnard, P., Dragovic, T., Jasilek, S., Biddulph, J., Rolls, L., Durning, A., & Fenyvesi, K. (2017). The art of co-creating arts-based possibility spaces for fostering STE(A)M practices in primary education. In T. Chemi & X. Du (Eds.), *Arts-based methods in education around the world* (pp. 247–281). Gistrup, Denmark: River Publishers.

Cambridge Dictionary. (2020). *Holistic*. Retrieved December 1, 2020, from http://dictionary.cambridge.org/dictionary/english/holistic

European Commission Directorate-General for Education, Youth, Sport and Culture. (2019). *Key competences for lifelong learning*. Publications Office of the European Union. Retrieved January 30, 2020, from https://op.europa.eu/en/publication-detail/-/publication/297a33c8-a1f3-11e9-9d01-01aa75ed71a1/language-en.

Fenyvesi, K., Lehto, S., Brownell, C., Nasiakou, L., Lavicza, Z., & Kosola, R. (2019). Learning mathematical concepts as a whole-body experience: Connecting multiple intelligences, creativities and embodiments within the STEAM framework. In P. Burnard & L. Colucci-Gray (Eds.), *Why science and art creativities matter* (pp. 300–336). the Netherlands: Brill-i-Sense.

Finnish National Agency for Education (FNAE). (2016). *National core curriculum for basic education 2014*. Finland: FNAE.

Goodyear, V. A. (2017). Social media, apps and wearable technologies: Navigating ethical dilemmas and procedures. *Qualitative Research in Sport, Exercise and Health, 9*(3), 285–302. https://doi.org/10.1080/2159676X.2017.1303790

Harris, A. (2016). *Creative ecologies: Fostering creativity in secondary schools*. Creativeresearchhub.com.

Horton, M., & Freire, P. (1990). *We make the road by walking: Conversations on education and social change* (B. Bell, J. Gaventa, & J. M. Peters, Eds.). Philadelphi, PA: Temple University Press.

KnowNow. (2019, September 2). Jukka Sinnemäki teaching philosophy. *YouTube*. Retrieved December 28, 2020, from https://www.youtube.com/watch?v=R97wBeuQdpg&feature=youtu.be.

Linna, P., & Laaksonen, S. (2018). *Finnish edutech sector*. Finnpartnership. Retrieved December 8, 2020, https://finnpartnership.fi/wp-content/uploads/2018/12/Edutech_final-version-002.pdf.

Lovat, T. (2020). Holistic learning versus instrumentalism in teacher education: Lessons from values pedagogy and related research. *Education Sciences, 10*(11), 341. https://doi.org/10.3390/educsci10110341

Lovat, T., Dally, K., Clement, N., & Toomey, R. (2011). *Values pedagogy and student achievement*. Springer Netherlands. https://doi.org/10.1007/978-94-007-1563-9

Lovat, T., Toomey, R., & Clement, N. (Eds.). (2010). *International research handbook on values education and student wellbeing*. Dordrecht, the Netherlands: Springer. https://doi.org/10.1007/978-90-481-8675-4

Moilanen, H., Äyrämö, S., & Kankaanranta, M. (2018). Learning physics outside the classroom by combinating use of tablets and bodily activity. In *Proceedings of World conference on educational media and technology*. EdMedia.

Niemi, H., Multisilta, J., Lipponen, L., & Vivitsou, M. (Eds.). (2014). *Finnish innovations and technologies in schools. A guide towards new ecosystems of learning*. Sense. New York City, USA: SpringerLink.

Szabó, T. P., Fenyvesi, K., Soundararaj, G., & Kangasvieri, T. (Eds.). (2019). *Everyday creativity: Boosting creative resources with Finnish models of education. Teachers' handbook*. Jyväskylä: University of Jyväskylä.

World Health Organization (WHO). (2020). *Health promoting schools*. Retrieved December 17, 2020, from https://www.who.int/health-topics/health-promoting-schools#tab=tab_1.

Yada, T. (2020). *Exploring prosociality and collective competence in exercising shared educational leadership in Finland and Japan*. Jyväskylä: University of Jyväskylä.

Yada, T., & Jäppinen, A.-K. (2019). A systematic narrative review of prosociality in educational leadership. *Educational Management Administration & Leadership, 47*(6), 980–1000.

CHAPTER 9

Cultivating primary creativities in STEAM gardens

Donald Gray and Laura Colucci-Gray with Louise Robertson

STEAM as a hybrid construct of disciplines and ways of knowing the world

The acronym STEAM refers to the interplay and synergies that can be created from the dialogue and interpenetration amongst previously distinct subjects. The acronym emerged from the more commonly known acronym STEM, which stands for the disciplines of science, technology, engineering and mathematics, with the *addition* of the arts:

> Linguistically STEAM can be seen as an expansion of STEM, which is commonly referred to as the assemblage of scientific and technological disciplines driving the promise of economic growth and prosperity. The arts may lack a specific collocation and/or definition, ranging from specific forms of visual art (painting, drawing, photography, sculpture, media arts and design), to a variety of arts including visual, performing (dance, music and theatre), digital media, aesthetics and crafts, and widening even further to include the liberal arts and humanities disciplines.
>
> (Burnard & Colucci-Gray, 2020, p. 1)

The acronym STEAM is contested. The debate characteristically pertains to the position of the arts in relation to STEM subjects in the school curriculum. Specifically, STEM subjects in school belong to that category of curriculum associated with 'vertical' discourses of education. The superiority of vertical discourse epitomised by the sciences, in comparison to horizontal discourses, associated with experience and craft, is based on claims about its truth or power. In this view, the hybridity of STEAM is often seen as a re-assertion of the economic discourse in education, with the arts playing a subsidiary role to STEM, to enhance the appeal of scientific subjects and to develop creativity and innovation as a core twenty-first-century skill. Conversely, Young and Muller (2013) propose a different conception of 'powerful' knowledge, which they refer to as a form of *specialised* knowledge, requiring specialised institutions for its development and delivery. Powerful knowledge is thus 'knowledge that they [students] would not have access to at home or at work and knowledge that takes them beyond their experience' (p. 231). By extension, schools can be empowering to the extent to which children are able to access this form of knowledge and its specialised delivery. In this view, the hybridity of STEAM could be a vehicle for securing a social position, for example by enhancing the prospects of future employment in the manual or craft industries.

Such debates are particularly pertinent to this chapter, which focuses on the educational opportunity of children's learning in the garden, which is in itself a hybrid, theory–practice and multi-disciplinary construct.

Following Biesta (2015), the debate surrounding STEAM calls for an examination of the purposes of education. For example, the pressure to deliver knowledge for qualifications, or to socialise children into conforming behaviours and expectations, may overtake a third purpose, that of 'subjectification': 'which has to do with the way in which children and young people come to exist as subjects of initiative and responsibility, rather than as objects of the actions of others' (Biesta, 2015, p. 77).[1] In this view, we are interested in STEAM gardens as a new concept for the cultivation of new educational sensitivities as they are emerging from the fields of sociology, anthropology, the arts and childhood studies, and calling for new understandings of children as subjects unfolding in a world in-the-making (Lenz Taguchi, 2011). Of particular relevance to this argument are also renovated understandings of creativity. We take the lead from Ingold (2014), who argues for a creativity that moves away from the consumerist focus on novelty and final products, as well as intellectualist notions of creativity as lying in the head, to one in which 'the wellsprings of creativity lie [. . .] in their attending upon a world in formation' (p. 124).

This chapter will thus explore STEAM gardens as a form of education in which attention shifts away from subject disciplines to performative knowledge, one that is powerful not in the sense of asserting power hierarchies over other kinds of knowledge, but in its being linked to action, with the potential to support and foster children's creativities as being and becoming. This is the knowledge that is created by and through social and community exchanges, whereby the arts and sciences are integrated in practical problem solving and design activities, spanning several disciplines and seeking to stimulate children's imagination, storytelling and critical thinking as a set of diverse and multiple creativities. The arts are viewed broadly, from visual and performance arts to craft skills, such as cooking or sowing, seeking to value cultural heritage and to develop school-community collaborations (Burnard & Colucci-Gray, 2020, p. 3).

From these perspectives we will, in this chapter, endeavour to explore STEAM approaches in the garden as a way to develop new ways of thinking in education, rooted in the hybrid space between specialised curriculum knowledge and children's everyday experiences, and resulting from the intra-action of these ways of knowing. As such, we will use the letters of the STEAM acronym to illustrate this shift from *knowing about* to *living in* the world, which arises from a repositioning of children vis-à-vis knowledge and experience. This also means shifting the priorities from a short-term economic agenda to longer-term future-oriented priorities for a safe and sustainable future, with a view to address the growing urgency to change our ways of thinking about our place on the planet in these uncertain and precarious times.

Drawing on research from science studies, neurocognitive science, education and the arts, we will illustrate how new ideas can be built on already recognised practices of school gardens, to reinvigorate teaching with a vitality that can enable young people to renew their relationship with the Earth and the natural world, providing a more optimistic outlook for their unknown futures.

The educational discourse of school gardens

There is a resurgence in interest in school gardens worldwide, which has arisen in response to a range of drivers, from improving the health and wellbeing of children and communities to providing a context for meaningful learning, often with a focus on science learning (e.g. Gray, Colucci-Gray, Donald, Kyriacou, & Wodah, 2019). Internationally, school gardens are viewed as the locus for a broad range of educational purposes and curriculum outcomes, offering the opportunity to connect schools and community, and to adapt curricular planning to include holistic and experiential activities. Indeed gardens have long been recognised as hybrid spaces, incorporating both the artistic and scientific perspective, while at the same time instilling a love for nature, and a deep understanding of the interdependent relationships of all living beings, including humans.

There is a long tradition of eminent philosophers and educationalists – such as Comenius, Froebel, Pestalozzi, Rousseau as well as Dewey – recognising the potential of gardens for the development of the affective and aesthetic dimensions of the self. Essential aspects often referred to are the importance of the senses and the particular, subjective experiences offered by garden-based learning. For example, Dewey (1928) acknowledged the potential of gardens for learning but also the distinction between what we would now call powerful and living knowledge. Comparing learning in gardens with the study of botany, he suggested that there is nothing in botany that could not be 'introduced in a vital way with caring and growth of seeds'. Furthermore, such learning does not belong to a particular study called 'botany' but 'belongs to life' and has a natural correlation with the 'facts of soil, animal life, and human relations'.

In the first instance, gardens offer children the opportunity to come into close proximity with 'nature', although we make the distinction here between 'wild' nature and 'cultivated' nature. Gardens include both, in the sense that human interventions cultivate the garden, but the very cultivation of the garden depends on the activities of the pre-existing 'wild' nature, which is not controlled by the human cultivator. It is through an exploration of the act of cultivation – and the dependency on the 'wild' – that children learn about their creativities. Not as powers to impose a pre-defined schema, but as the expression of 'skilled practice that brings forth the work, and of which it is an outcome, rather than in any set of designs or representations that precede it' (Ingold, 2014, p. 134). It is indeed in the exercise of skilled practice, situated within the opportunities and constraints of time and space, that children can learn about themselves as humans within the natural world and the multitude of interdependencies that exist in the soil, in the plants, in the air. How earthworms aerate the soil, how microorganisms decompose matter and recycle nutrients, how butterflies and bees transfer pollen and assist in the reproduction of plants. We do not view gardens as a miniature of large-scale farming (such as a lab experiment seeking to model a large-scale phenomenon for closer analysis), but rather, as an evolving relationship with our own human nature. As stated by Miller (1993), 'The garden matters to people because it "mediates" between various "oppositions that define human experience", such as "man and nature" or "action and contemplation"'. In that sense, gardens are not simply an education about specific plant species and the rate at which they may be grown, but are also an education of ourselves, how we grow and the qualities we can develop. As mentioned earlier, this understanding of human nature in relation to and not separate from the nature of the garden also resonates with new understandings of creativity. Following Ingold (2014) the creativity of the garden does not begin or end with an idea in mind; and it is different from the creativity of a designer seeking to impose form onto an inert matter, but rather, it is the creativity of the designer and maker, one that 'carries on through, without beginning or end' (p. 126). It is in this sense that this chapter will refer to knowing and learning in the garden as living knowledge, as it grows with the actions of the children.

From school gardens to STEAM gardens

As mentioned already, gardens offer great potential for learning of different subjects, with these subjects usually located within the STEM disciplines (understanding life processes, measuring, construction, etc.), but also offering opportunities for the arts, such as drawing, painting and design, as well as providing inspiration for literacy and other forms of expressive arts using sound and movement. What we argue here is that, while each disciplinary area in itself can benefit from a garden-oriented approach, it is the synergy between the STEM and arts disciplines, which has the greatest potential for children's engagement, through the integration of cognitive, physical and psychosocial development.

In this chapter, we draw upon our experiences as two academics (Gray and Colucci-Gray), who have particular interests in science and sustainability issues, and a former headteacher and artist (Robertson), to integrate the theoretical and practical dimensions of STEM and the arts, which underpin the rationale for STEAM gardens, using pedagogical exemplars. Gray and Colucci-Gray have been working for the past 3 years in partnership with a social enterprise organisation, One Seed Forward, in establishing and developing gardens in regeneration areas in the city of Aberdeen, along with the development of educational materials (Gray et al., 2019). Robertson has considerable experience as a practising artist and former headteacher in primary schools incorporating arts activities into the development of the gardens within those schools. Here we draw upon our respective experiences to look at the potential for science and arts activities in school gardens; specifically we consider how the synergy amongst these activities might be progressed to move from a focus on individual 'curriculum subjects' or skills, to the emergence of a practical knowledge for living in the world.

S: from soil science to the sensing soil

In a landmark article published in the journal *Ecology & Society*, Rockstrom et al. (2009) identified nine 'planetary boundaries' within which human society must operate: the safe operating space for humanity. Of these nine, three levels have been trespassed: biodiversity loss and the biogeochemical flows of phosphorous and nitrogen. Many of these changes derive from large-scale industrial agriculture, with overuse of chemical fertilisers, herbicides and pesticides as well as other large-scale industrial processes linked to increasing human consumption. Yet, such problems are not solely scientific but require a cultural shift in practices as well as perspectives and institutions. The question is, what is the nature of such a shift and how do we go about engendering it for current and future generations?

While scientific practice often tries to separate human experience from the phenomenon being investigated, this practice is also at the roots of a dualistic attitude in western culture, which separates intelligence and bodily experience, with science belonging to the realm of the intellect and the arts belonging to the realm of creativity and the senses (Burnard & Colucci-Gray, 2020). In the same vein, learning as part of school science occurs through the regimentation and limitation of the senses, as children are taught not to tamper or interfere with the outcomes of an experiment. For example, observation in the lab is reduced to simple visual observation of data as recorded by an instrument of some sort, perhaps a thermometer, a light meter or a balance for measuring weights. Occasionally, there may be more subjective, qualitative assessments, for example has it changed colour, does it feel smooth or rough? Such practices are set out to address the specific of 'what is to be learnt' (allegedly responding well to the educational purpose of achieving a qualification), but fail to develop a full sensory awareness of both the environment and the matter that is being observed. As such, the result is a limited, restricted understanding of the world in which children live and grow. It is important for children to bring their own experiences of the world around them to the science class. Only through attentive awareness of their surroundings will they be able to draw out more meaning from the science and elaborate their experiences to a greater understanding, and application of, the other elements of STEM subjects.

While gardens have historically been introduced in schools as a means to develop the teaching of science, and have been linked with the growing of food to encourage healthy eating and greater sensitivity to environmental matters, gardens are also recognised as arenas for artistic, aesthetic and sensorial practice. From this viewpoint, artistic practices can extend sensorial engagement. Their purpose is to develop young people's perceptions in such a way that they notice things, literally developing their sensitivity to observe and take cognisance of those aspects of experience which are more qualitative, subjective and serendipitously beautiful (e.g. the fleeting image of a melting snowflake on the ground or the water droplets on a spider web). Arguably, the integration of artistic sensitivity with a scientific purpose develops a more resilient and more attentive inquiring capability. Engaging the arts and science with the full engagement of the senses was pioneered by J. W. von Goethe in the eighteenth century in his phenomenological scientific method. He stated: 'Insofar as he makes use of his healthy senses, the human being is the greatest and most precise scientific instrument that exists' (Goethe, as quoted in Amrine, 1998, p. 37). And: 'Every act of looking turns into observation, every act of observation into reflection, every act of reflection into associations; thus it is evident that we theorise every time we look carefully at the world' (p. 33). An important point is that much of Goethe's method and his inspiration came from the work he conducted in his garden in Weimar, Germany. In this view, observing the soil does not equate to viewing something from the privileged and yet distant height of the human eye, but it legitimatises the primacy of the body in directing human attention. Such is the education of perception, by which we become practised in both paying attention and responding skilfully to salient aspects of our environment (Gibson 1979, p. 254, as cited in Ingold 2014, p. 135).

Box 1: Soil art

Compare two methods of examining soil. The first is the often-practised 'soil in the jar' investigation, where children will put a soil sample in a jar and shake it up, leaving the soil to settle over time. After several hours, or even days, the soil will have settled clearly into distinct zones: clay, silt and sand layers with organic matter, perhaps, floating on the surface. Here the children are observers but are kept separate from the investigation itself. If we compare this with using the hands to feel the soil, the nose to smell the soil and even the ears to listen to the soil as it is rubbed through the fingers or dropped onto a surface, children will have a very different experience, a sensorial experience that stimulates their imagination: What does it smell like? What does it feel like? Why does it smell like this? Why

> does it feel like this? Why is it this colour? This texture? Starting from their sensory experience, children can investigate the different properties of soil through artistic experiments. The different pigmentation in a range of soils can be used to create paintings, which not only illustrate the specific characteristics of different soils but will also capture what was unique and serendipitously beautiful about that particular artefact and/or sample of soil. For example, understanding that clay is a type of soil leads on to the use of different soil types for modelling and construction, recognising how the creativity of human intellect developed and continues to develop in correspondence with the environment around us.

T: from technology to time

In a world where everything is fast – instant communication, emails, fast food, fast transport, fast fashion – and schooling is determined by dates in the calendar, school term times and exam dates, all of which are mediated through a technology designed to 'speed things up', gardens and gardening remind us of the existence and the importance of different types of time. Miller (2010) uses the ancient Greek terms *chronos* and *kairos* to distinguish between two types of time. *Chronos* is the most familiar to us. It is measurable and sequential, divided into seconds, minutes, hours and days, the times of the day and the year. It is scientific time. *Kairos*, however, is the recognition of the appropriateness of time. It is the right or opportune moment for an event or an act. Children are invariably confronted with the first of these two forms of time: dates are set, times are given and we are programmed to do certain things at certain times, often without giving much thought to the appropriateness of the time. Central to the management of time is technology – in the form of transport or built into computer calendars. Technological artefacts unify the experience of time as a linear arrow proceeding from point A to point B. However, in the garden, *kairos* is paramount. Children soon become aware of the appropriateness of certain acts at certain times (for example picking a berry before time is directly experienced as sourness). Patience becomes a virtue for observing, noticing and, by extension, learning. The pace of learning in a garden invariably becomes slower but slowness does not imply laziness, or tardiness. Slowness can be considered as appropriateness, as in tune with nature's time, the 'right' time being that which aligns with the natural cycles and biorhythms of the planet. This has been recognised by the slow movement, which began with Slow Food in Italy as a counter to the MacDonald's fast-food chains springing up around historical and cultural sites in Rome. Slow Food was the catalyst for a range of slow movements, which now encompasses areas such as slow travel, slow cities and slow education. In the garden, children begin to recognise that speed is not always necessary, or important. The appropriateness of acts and events at particular times is important.

Compost takes time to develop; seeds must be planted at appropriate times, when the weather is appropriate (after frosts have passed) and not by the calendar or clock; germination cannot be rushed but can be nurtured by appropriate care and the right conditions. From this perspective, time is perceived as a multiplicity of different times, in the form of weather patterns, seasonal cycles, intensity and rhythms (e.g., the 'tempo' of the rainfall or of the sunlight in the course of a day or year). Observing the weather and the cycle of the days and seasons is thus a significant experience for children to both learn about and make sense of the experience of 'time'.

Box 2: Weather watchers

In one of the schools we draw upon, children were involved in a weather watchers project, which developed over a whole school year. Here the children used rain gauges to measure the rainfall in the garden, thermometers to measure temperature and wind chimes to capture the wind. The scientific way of gathering information, the technical skills to set up the rain gauges and the use of mathematical skills to plot rainfall and temperature progressed hand in hand with the artistic skills of creating a weather map using a range of materials to make weather symbols. The children could draw upon their sensory experiences linked to features of the weather and the measurements they obtained over time to embrace a holistic understanding of weather. Taken a stage further, they could map close observations of the development of the garden, plant growth and so on with the dominant weather features at particular points over the school year. Patience became a virtue and led to an understanding that *kairos* is as important, if not more so, than *chronos*.

E: from engineering to enactivism

If we are charged with changing ways of thinking, as Rockstrom et al. (2009) intimated, it is important first to consider what form of thinking may have contributed to our ecological dangers. In the sciences, perhaps the most pervasive idea for over three centuries, since the publication of Newton's *Mathematical principles of natural philosophy* in 1687, is that nature operates on a mechanical model. According to this view, everything can be reduced to an understanding of its parts, which operate in a mechanical fashion, thus making prediction possible by analysing simple cause-and-effect relationships. While this mechanical and reductionist model of science has been extremely successful, today we recognise the limitations of such a paradigm, particularly when dealing with complex biological systems. In the twentieth century, new insights have become apparent which show that, while a mechanical model is possible in a closed simple system, it has fundamental flaws in an open dynamic system, which is the foundation on which nature and the Earth's planetary systems operate.

It could be said that modern education operates on the same principle as reductive science. It fragments learning into subjects, with each subject similarly disaggregated into small parts learned discretely and then tested in some form, whether by formative or summative tests or high-stakes examinations. That is not to suggest that there is no place for such learning; the idea of 'bite-size chunks' and similar strategies is firmly embedded in educational practice. In science teaching, however, this often consists of learning the 'facts' or a piecemeal approach to performing experiments, starting with a distinct hypothesis that is often detached and analysed separately from the context and wider relationships within which it is embedded. Education arguably developed into this form of practice as a result of policy directives, which reduced the purpose of education to providing a productive workforce, with little regard for children's wellbeing, nor for the impact that this may have on the life support systems of the planet (Gray et al., 2019).

A key element to be considered when seeking to overturn this model of education and to cultivate children's experiences in the garden is the very concept of learning, which is much more than the accumulation of abstract notions in the head. Recent research and thinking indicates that body-mind-environment interactions play a fundamental role in cognition (Gallagher & Lindgren, 2015), and movement and sensory engagement are important in this process. This was recognised over 100 years ago by John Dewey who would use the hyphenated body-mind to indicate the essential and integrated nature of the two:

> The forces are still powerful that make for centrifugal and divisive education. And the chief of these is, let it be repeated, the separation of mind and body . . . Thus the question of the integration of mind-body in action is the most practical of all questions we can ask of our civilization.
>
> (Dewey, 1928, p. 19)

Here we should also point out that Dewey (1928) recognised the garden as a means to connect intellectual and practical elements within their curricula. However, it is important to note here that Dewey's term 'practical' was not to be understood as the simple mapping of abstract ideas into the practical realm (or the verification of knowledge through an experiment for which the answer was already known). Quite the opposite, in fact: practical engagement would expose children to the questions posed by the garden itself, arising from the myriad of interactions between the weather, the wild and the ability of the child to wonder.

As Gallagher and Lindgren (2015) point out, learning is not a process of reproduction of external phenomena by symbolic representation in the head, but it is about the combination of sensorial and motile engagement of the body with the affective, emotional aspects in continuous interplay with the environment. In other words, what 'enters' our field of perception literally depends on 'what we can do' in that field of action-perception, in terms of its pragmatic meaning. This pragmatic dimension can thus lead to some important reflections about opportunities and constraints within any system, recognising one's limits and reviewing personal choices and actions by acquiring metacognition. We are reminded of John Dewey (1928) in relation to creativity and resistance, as he refers to an ongoing dialectics 'between concrete practices and thinking', and the formation of sustaining habits of both problem solving and problem finding.

> **Box 3: Shoebox gardens**
>
> As part of a competition organised by One Seed Forward, children were invited to construct 'shoebox gardens', the only condition being that such gardens should include some edible plants. The task was not simply a cerebral process of figuring out what the final product would look like in terms of its size and dimensions, but it required manipulation of materials, both living and non-living, understanding of the relationships amongst the different elements, as well as knowledge of what the plants would require for growing. The shoebox gardens could be seen both as artistic creations, responding to aesthetic criteria of form and colour, as well as scientific models, displaying selected variables in interaction. From a pedagogical perspective, we recognise here the features of 'design thinking' – a central process of STEAM education – with its five key principles: defining/observing, empathising, visualising, creating prototypes, and testing/refining (Quigley & Herro, 2019). In two winning examples it is perhaps the empathetic element that is most striking. They connect the 'small story' of the life cycle of the parsley plants and the flowers with a number of other, potentially 'bigger stories'. For example, in a shoebox creation with model dinosaurs and parsley against a painted backdrop of blue sky and erupting volcanoes, there is the story of how the expansion of plants and the extinction of dinosaurs in the Carboniferous era led to the accumulation of biomass, which we now access in the form of fossil fuels. Alternatively, in a miniature 'fairy garden' with its mix of herbs and flowers, there is the story of what creatures may find their source of food from a plant of sorrel, beyond the scale of what humans are able to see, reach or experience. Through the process of making, these children acquired the ability to understand the life of materials, and their instrumental as well as their intrinsic value, as they made decisions about the entire life cycle of the shoebox garden, from its creation to its disposal.
>
> Enactivist theories have been recently discussed in the field of engineering education, as reported by Roth (2017), pointing out how 'the work-related (hand, body) movements that build and manipulate artefacts, or sensing (hand) movements deployed during an investigation, later function

as symbolic movements' (p. 257). And in a similar vein, the field of mathematics education has taken an embodied cognition stance towards learning by recognising the link between abstract thinking and physical gestures (Roth, 2017). These ideas are converging with contributions from the field of childhood studies, pointing to the strong linkages between bodily actions, language and the imagination (Lenz Taguchi, 2011).

Box 4: Garden logos

In another school supported by One Seed Forward, the children were asked to create logos for their new garden space. As artistic endeavours, the logos communicated content knowledge, showing that children are very aware of the need for sunshine and water, but they also recognise the value of butterflies and bees and a variety of plant species. These were only the beginnings of potential explorations as the pupils began their journey into the world of the soil, the plants and animals, and the intricate interactions between them. Yet, it was also the beginning of an embodied literacy, which incorporates nature experiences in the visual and expressive language of the children, thus pointing to the ideational function of artistic literacy. A range of activities can be devised that integrate STEM understanding and expressive arts, combining models, logos and enactive metaphors (Gallagher & Lindgren, 2015) to reclaim the value of scientific literacy in schools not simply as the listing of facts, but as the ability to give shape and form to the imagination.

A: aesthetic awareness in the Anthropocene

As we enter further into the period of the Anthropocene, the human impact on the planet is becoming clearer and more devastating. We are not suggesting that an arts/science partnership will be a panacea for planetary ills, but it should result in individuals who have a more holistic outlook. As Wahl (2005) states:

> The artist's gaze continuously shifts attention between the details of the phenomena and their impression as a whole. Artists intend to intuitively understand the intimate relationship between the part and the whole; to feel the interconnection that unites all detailed diversity into a dynamically transforming whole.
>
> (p. 61)

As mentioned earlier, the artistic quality of perception was recognised by a number of eighteenth-century scientists, such as Alexander von Humboldt, J. W.

von Goethe and Ernst Haeckel, who actively sought to integrate the arts with their scientific endeavours. With the term 'aesthetic awareness' we refer to the capability of 'paying attention', being the physical act of sensorial engagement with things entering the realm of our care and concern. In this way, we follow Biesta's (2015) idea, mentioned earlier, of education as attending to the purpose of 'subjectification', not in the sense of delivering individualised and personal learning packages, but rather in the sense of enabling the formation of the sense of oneself in ongoing communication with the world. In this view, becoming conscious of environmental issues is not so much a process of learning about environmental problems, or following behavioural guidelines for their solution, but it is about awareness of the role that the body plays in the development of the relation, that is, how bodies – humans and non-humans – relate together through the activity of learning.

Box 5: Bug hotels and mini-beast games

A classic example of environmental education activities aimed at learning about and preserving biodiversity is the construction of bug hotels, which were incorporated into the activities undertaken by children. In one of the schools supported by One Seed Forward the children were shown how to construct and assemble the materials for small bug hotels. In this process we note the incorporation of technological craft skills, such as sourcing, cutting and assembling of wooden logs, alongside an understanding of purpose, which incorporated creative design ideas from children themselves. In line with the principles of design-based thinking described earlier (see Box 3), this activity developed both specialised knowledge and skills in STEM while including the ideational, empathetic and communicative power of *craft*, telling a story about the children as scientists-designers-makers, and their close relationships with each other and with the subjects for whom the bug hotel was designed.

Another example of aesthetic engagement in the garden led to the development of hand-crafted games, which led to the discussion of the role that ladybirds and bees play in a garden, and the intricate networks that exist among all the mini-beasts to be found there.

In these examples of craft-based learning we are not simply seeing the application of knowledge, but we are seeing the enactment of relational attention. As children design and empathise, they build stories for their characters and, in so doing, they make them part of their own lives. Such affective and aesthetic elements are powerfully formative moments in young children's lives, and can be built on with ever more creative, expressive and experimentative artistic approaches as they become older and transition into secondary school.

M: from mathematics to mattering

There is growing interest in the idea of a relational materialist approach to education, in which a recognition of the role of the body and our interactions with the material environment around us is fundamentally important in understanding how we come to know and to be (Lenz Taguchi, 2011). Lenz Taguchi (2011) explains that the relational materialist approach draws on the work of Karen Barad and through a relational materialist approach 'we read the world around us from our embodiedness, and being a part of the world, and being in an equal state among other organisms and matter' (p. 40). Because of this, it is impossible to isolate knowing from being as they are mutually implicated.

In essence, a relational materialist approach recognises the importance of the intra-action amongst different entities, each entity acting on another entity in a reciprocal way. The observer, the subject, is no longer deemed to be separate from what is being observed, the object, but intra-acts with the material being observed in a way which affects the observer and the observed. There is no ontological separation between subject and object, mind and body, knower and known: there is a constant coming into being through the intra-action, the ongoing relationship that affects both.

From this perspective gardens have become an important context in which to explore the material encounters that children have and how this influences their learning and being. For example, by adopting 'a relational materialist approach', the focus shifts to the agential capacity of non-human forces as the primal force propelling children's knowing through garden experiences (Lenz Taguchi, 2011; Gray et al., 2019).

This mutual relationship between the child and the material of the garden can, we suggest, generate profound results. Miller (1993) talks about the virtues of gardening in which the activity of gardening improves both people and the land. The living and non-living material of the garden *acts on* the gardener just as the gardener *acts on* the garden, and both are improved. Moreover, as mentioned earlier, some consider the act of gardening to be artistic in itself, enabling children to 'see' with new eyes and to find a new way of thinking about how they relate to the garden, to the natural world.

Box 6: Garden matters in the school

In the school led by Robertson, the garden had grown to incorporate the vegetable growing space as well as the storytelling corner and the play area, with tables located in the garden for more specific activities of construction and observation. We note that the decorative potential of hand-crafted planters was linked to discussions around position (for sunlight) and the requirements for water and nutrients, followed by careful observation of growth and flower and seed production. Nevertheless, there was also the pleasure of harvesting a crop and collecting fresh flowers to take indoors. In such an integrated process of knowing the detail as well as being a part of the whole lies the power of STEAM gardens: they bring the child's experiences to matter in the school by the act of redesigning the space in a way that responds to the child's aesthetic engagement and movement. The garden physically matters as it is physically related to the body-mind.

So, while there is much to do in the way of mathematics in the garden, such as measuring space, calculating areas, graphing growth patterns, weighing produce and so on, we see that matter comes to matter both through the reciprocal actions that each entity acts on the other, and through the development of shared experiences amongst participants, both human and non-human. Just as the fungal hyphae beneath our feet spread out for kilometres; just as the pollen is distributed by butterflies and bees beyond the garden gate, the seeds are spread by human hand, animal fur and faeces, and blown on the wind, the knowledge gained by children is enhanced through their imagination and creativity to encompass the worldwide web of planetary processes. Children are not shaped by the narrow confines of a single discipline, but the disciplines are porous and permeable, inviting ideas, creativity and imagination cultivated through deeper observation and aesthetic appreciation of the life forms around them.

Conclusion: from the parts to the whole and back: cultivating diverse creativities of children and gardens

We have in this chapter argued for the integration of STEM and arts disciplines in the context of the school gardens as a means to engender a radical shift from knowing as the acquisition of specialised knowledge to knowing as being.

Specifically, we have drawn on the particular nature of the garden as both art and science, thus affording the opportunity for a plurality of educational experiences supporting an array of diverse creativities. A garden can be known scientifically, through the classification of plant and animal species and their particular properties and behaviours. However, the garden can also be known qualitatively for its artistic aspects, recognising that colour, pattern and design are integral dimensions of the garden's own creative way of responding to the environment in which it takes its own form. A garden is never fixed, but it actively changes its configuration in correspondence with the temperature, the weather, light and the seasons. Similarly, children attending to the garden also respond to the Earth's changing patterns with their own undergoing of creativity (Ingold,

2014), in a continuously emerging process of becoming, responding to and with the ever-changing becomingness of the garden. As Burnard and Colucci-Gray (2020) state: 'Future-making education needs to unravel, unsettle and rupture, to get underneath the skin of diverse and multiple creativities, in the uncertain terrain of unfamiliarity' (p. 426). Such diverse creativities, however, are not neutral capacities, but they develop within and in between the constraints and the opportunities of a shared Earth. In the face of the current changing climate, we need to consider how our human-constructed distinctive capacities, as well as delineated, disciplinary areas can be literally 'put to work' in a holistic and synergistic way. We need to be able to see the relationships and interdependencies amongst disciplines in the same way that we need to understand and *feel* the relationships and interdependencies within the natural world and our part in that complex web of life. Specifically, the STEAM garden is not a set of activities or simply a place for the application of curricular knowledge, but it is the expression of skilled practice, as Ingold (2014) defined it: 'the capacity of living, growing things continually to surpass themselves' (p. 128).

We conclude with an invitation. It is our responsibility as educators, as parents, as guardians, as human beings, as residents of planet Earth, to strive towards a relational pedagogy that helps us and children to recognise how important our thinking and our behaviours are to the health of the only planet we have, and ultimately to our own health and wellbeing.

Acknowledgements

The authors thank One Seed Forward for hosting the shoebox gardens competition, and the schools, the children and their parents for giving permission to use their examples for the purpose of this publication.

Unlocking research in practice: provocations for group discussion

1. In what way could we come together as a group of colleagues to co-plan for integrated learning opportunities in the school grounds/garden?
2. In what way can we involve our pupils to co-design a school garden and co-plan for shared and meaningful learning outcomes?
3. How can we use arts and craft to involve pupils in sensorial observation of their school environment?
4. How can we create meaningful partnerships with community members to learn together and support the ongoing creativity of the school garden?
5. How can we use arts and sciences in the garden to stimulate children's awareness of time and their place in the natural systems?

Note

1 As detailed by Biesta (2015), subjectification is distinguished from questions of identity, which pertain to the domain of socialisation and culture. Instead, subjectification addresses the qualities of being a human subject such as autonomy, independence, responsibility and the capacity for judgement.

References

Amrine, F. (1998). The metamorphosis of the scientist. In D. Seamon & A. Zajonc (Eds.), *Goethe's way of science* (pp. 33–54). Albany, NY: State University of New York Press.

Biesta, G. (2015). What is education for? On good education, teacher judgement, and educational professionalism. *European Journal of Education, 50*(1), 75–87.

Burnard, P., & Colucci-Gray, L. (2020). *Why science and arts creativities matter. (Re-) Configuring STEAM for future making education*. Rotterdam, the Netherlands: Brill-i-Sense Publisher.

Dewey, J. (1928). Body and mind. *Bulletin of the New York Academy of Medicine, 4*(1), 3–19.

Gallagher, S., & Lindgren, R. (2015). Enactive metaphors: Learning through full-body engagement. *Educational Psychology Review, 27*, 391–404. https://doi.org/10.1007/s10648-015-9327-1

Gibson, J. J. (1979/2015). *The ecological approach to visual perception*. New York: Psychology Press.

Gray, D., Colucci-Gray, L., Donald, R., Kyriacou, A., & Wodah, D. (2019). From oil to soil. Learning for sustainability and transitions within the school garden: A project of cultural and social re-learning. *Scottish Educational Review, 51*(1), 57–70.

Ingold, T. (2014). The creativity of undergoing. *Pragmatics & Cognition, 22*(1), 124–139. https://doi.org/10.1075/pc.22.1.07ing

Lenz Taguchi, H. (2011). Investigating learning, participation and becoming in early childhood practices with a relational materialist approach. *Global Studies of Childhood, 1*(1), 36–50. https://doi.org/10.2304/gsch.2011.1.1.36

Miller, M. (1993). *The garden as art*. Albany, NY: SUNY Press.

Miller, M. (2010). Time and temporality in the garden. In D. O'Brien (Ed.), *Gardening – Philosophy for everyone: Cultivating wisdom* (pp. 178–191). Hoboken, NJ: Wiley-Blackwell.

Quigley, C. F., & Herro, D. (2019). *An educator's guide to STEAM. Engaging students using real-world problems*. New York: Teachers' College Press.

Rockstrom, J., Steffen, W., Noone, K., Persson, Å, Chapin, F. S., Lambin, E., . . . Foley, J. (2009). Planetary boundaries: Exploring the safe operating space for humanity. *Ecology and Society, 14*(2), 32. https://doi.org/10.5751/ES-03180-140232

Roth, W. M. (2017). The thinking body in/of multimodal engineering literacy. *Theory into Practice, 56*(4), 255–262. https://doi.org/10.1080/00405841.2017.1389218

Wahl, D. C. (2005). 'Zarte empirie': Goethean science as a way of knowing. *Janus Head, 8*(1), 58–76.

Young, M., & Muller, J. (2013). On the powers of powerful knowledge. *Review of Education, 1*(3), 229–250. https://doi.org/10.1002/rev3.3017

PART 3

Sculpting 'change' differently in primary education

These chapters stimulate dialogue and awareness of the different ways in which we can extend the repertoire of human faculties for thinking and experiencing change through diverse creativities. This collection of chapters aims to dwell further into the new creativities that are sculpting change in primary education.

CHAPTER 10

Unlocking creative leadership in the primary school

Megan Crawford, Deborah Outhwaite and Matthew Crawford

Introduction

The aim of this chapter, like the others in Part 3 of this book, is to stimulate dialogue and awareness of the different ways in which leadership can be acted out and sustained through diverse creativities. We introduce lenses from our own practice which allow the reader to reflect further on how creative leadership, in and outside multi-academy trusts (MATs), can enhance and support change in primary education for the benefit of all students. Leaders pursuing innovation and creativity is not a new quest, as this quotation from Sir Alec Clegg reminds us:[1]

> They were innovators. They modified their views continuously as they learned from their experiences in their own schools and from the ideas that they picked up outside and wished to try out. *Their professional life was a creative quest.*
>
> (Clegg, 1972, emphasis added)

In 2003, one of the authors of this chapter wrote about invention and wisdom in leadership and management. She drew on business and management theories that stressed the importance of creativity when there is challenge, ambiguity and paradox in the system (Crawford, 2003), and applied it to leadership and management in education. In particular, she focused on Bolman and Deal's (1997) suggestion that it is *personal artistry* that enables managers and leaders in organisations to seek out new patterns and possibilities in any given situation. This is especially pertinent when there are a variety of contexts that leaders work in, and their policy environment is in a state of constant change. Bolman and Deal (1997, p. 420) argue that leaders 'need the capacity to act inconsistently when consistency fails, diplomatically when emotions are raw, non-rationally when reason makes no sense, politically when confronted by parochial self-interest, and playfully when fixation on task and purpose seems counterproductive'.² Thinking creatively about how to make things happen enables leaders to respond to research and policy agendas with what we will call *creative capacity*.

The three authors position themselves at the interface between practice and theory, and in this chapter we will use our own unique perspectives on primary education to identify key aspects of leadership creativities that can both invigorate staff and enhance learning for all the primary school community. This chapter will consider creativities and leadership in the context of the English policy landscape since 2010, especially, but not exclusively, MATs. Although we draw specifically on the English context, we will draw out synergies that will be relevant to other leadership contexts, where individuals and groups are concerned with a creative endeavour, and wish to enhance their *creative capacity*. In England, the familiar tenets of a high-stakes accountability landscape (OFSTED, testing), and what that means to leaders, will be discussed, acknowledging differing viewpoints ranging from what Gunter and Courtney (2020, p. 2) have called 'subjugation to a narrative disconnected from the realities of those required to comply' to that of personal freedom in a fluid system.³ We agree with Coldron, Crawford, Jones, and Simkins (2014) that one's view of this narrative is heavily influenced by one's position in the policy field.⁴ We will explore this dichotomy in more depth, and reflect on the interplay between policy, leadership theory and leadership practice, and the ways in which creative research initiatives can invigorate practice and add to our knowledge of the leadership both of research and of primary schools.

We begin by looking at the idea of *personal artistry* and its relationship to creative leadership, then consider the English policy landscape and how it can help or hinder leadership's relationship with creativity. Following an examination of two case studies, we conclude by looking at ways to unlock creativities in research in practice, and set the reader prompts for thinking further about their own creative approach to educational leadership in the primary school.

What kind of leadership?

There are as many articles on leadership in education as there are leaders in education, but thinking about creative educative leadership (rather than the person who inhabits that position) enables us to take a broader picture of how leadership can flow through an organisation in many different ways or, as Ogawa and Bossert (1997) put it, of leadership as an organisational quality.⁵

Leadership is rooted in the culture of organisations, and we take the view that cultures are socially constructed realities. In any primary school, staff may share assumptions and beliefs that operate unconsciously and, as Meyerson and Martin (1987) suggest, people's definition of what culture is depends on leadership enacting cultural ideas and norms. Stable and shared norms, values and meanings are not always explicit, especially if the policy framework within which schooling sits is either constantly changing, or has norms, values and meanings at odds with those at the local level. Leadership has to bring together these conflicting values and priorities in order to find new patterns and possibilities within a school workplace setting to work for the benefit of students. In this chapter we do not seek to look in detail at political or policy explanations, although these are important, but instead on how culture and meaning can be brought together to harness creativity in individuals and groups.

We argue that creative leadership can be found wherever leaders are willing to reflect on their personal capacities, and engage in building a culture where individuals and teams can flourish, while at the same time dealing with conflicting priorities systemically. One way to facilitate this is to creatively involve parents, teachers and students in what Sergiovanni (2000) calls the 'lifeworld of leadership', which is concerned with values and beliefs.[6] Drawing on Habermas (1987), he adopted two terms – *lifeworld* and *systemsworld* – to describe two separate but interdependent domains. The systemsworld concerns management systems that help life run smoothly, and the lifeworld is more about culture and meaning. Sergiovanni acknowledges the value of both to the school and says that, with proper balancing, they enhance each other. He argues that it is the lifeworld of leadership that should generate and drive the systems in schools. If we are to argue that creative leadership can be found in many places within the current systems in England and elsewhere, we can also argue that it is the deeper understanding of the lifeworld of leadership that shapes the creative.

Of policy landscapes

We noted earlier that the policy framework within which primary schools sit in England is heavily dominated by the view that individual schools have freedom to innovate, whilst at the same time placing a heavy accountability framework on schools to guide them. A school's relative position in the system in England is defined by various parameters, of which it could be argued that OFSTED is the most important in terms of reputation, power and individual school finances. In other systems in the UK, other factors in the devolved administrations come into play; and in other jurisdictions the power of the individual school to be creative is constrained by other local policy issues, national culture and the power of individuals to challenge creatively. Although this chapter focuses on England, we would like to think that some of the questions we raise, and the case studies that we discuss, can allow readers to look at their local lifeworld in a different way. In particular, Habermas (1987) noted that there is a crossover and that actions can be simultaneously in both worlds, and that strategic policy drivers in the systemsworld should be influenced by the lifeworld and not vice versa.[7] Sergiovanni saw, even 20 years ago, that the way structures were beginning to invade the cultures of schools was problematic – the systemsworld was winning over the lifeworld. By separating the two, educators have allowed the systemsworld to dominate. How, then, do we bring in creativity and allow some rebalancing of the lifeworld of leadership where there is local generation of goals influenced by local values? This is what we wish to explore in the next sections as we turn to our own reflections on creative lifeworld leadership in a country where it could easily be argued that colonisation of the systemsworld is now fully grown. We argue that leadership, therefore, has to be creative and purposeful, emergent and adaptive.

The authors of this chapter all work within the systemsworld as chair of a MAT, director of a teaching school alliance, and CEO of a MAT. Two of the authors also work within higher education in various roles, and our intention is to bring together both our experience in primary schools and our knowledge of the lifeworld of leadership from an academic perspective. Next, we turn to the role of MATs, which could be viewed as inherently part of the systemsworld, given that they are centrally policy driven.

The role of MATs

A brief overview of MATs may be useful to those reading this chapter outside England. Academy schools were created in the early 2000s under a Labour government; they were a new kind of English state school because they were funded directly by central government. Initially, the policy focused just on schools in the most challenging circumstances. This remit was then extended in 2010, by the Coalition government, to any school which met certain broad conditions. Although many secondary schools (nearly three quarters by 2018) converted quickly, primary schools moved much slower, with only a quarter converting in this same time period, many staying with the Local Authority (LA) the middle tier between government and schools in the pre-2010 system. Crawford, Maxwell, Coldron, and Simkins (2020) note 'new definitions of the middle-tier as schools and other stakeholders are redefining relationships, locally and nationally'.[8]

Although the systemsworld continues to drive primary schools to become academies, the 2019–2021 COVID-19 pandemic showed the need for local authorities to be able to distribute key system resources (laptops and internet access via dongles in emergency situations such as the first lockdown, for example). The expanding collection of MATs across the country may well be able to enact such policy in the future, but as local authorities still run the majority of primary schools, what we currently have in play is two systems, each with vested interests. MATs have been driven by neo-conservative policy, through governments that are likely to be in power until at least 2029 (because of the way in which the UK electoral system works, and the 2011 Fixed Term Parliament Act). Those inhabiting the lifeworld need to discover how to best use these new systems, not just for the children that we engage with daily, but for the staff teams that we run and are responsible for.

MATs are by no means a one-stop shop; they come in a vast range of sizes and varieties. They have been viewed as a political strategy to erode the power of one side of the spectrum. Trust boards are undoubtedly encouraged to recruit from the business world, but that is because they 'scale up' and create large organisations (entirely funded from the state purse), and on a practical level require the skill set of those who have run large organisations. Current policies may govern the rest of the working lives of senior leaders who are currently in the system. Those from an education background who work with MATs are interested in the ways in which leaders can be supported to get the most out of this policy direction, and its significant and long-lasting policy reach, whilst it is enacted locally.

The MATs under discussion here are examples of structures that have attempted to harness local creativity and purpose. For example, they are led by people who have masters and doctoral qualifications in education leadership, and who wish to gain a wide perspective on appropriate ways forward for trusts that will outlast the current views from the systemsworld in order to progress the needs of the communities that we work for. The fact that these organisations are publicly funded

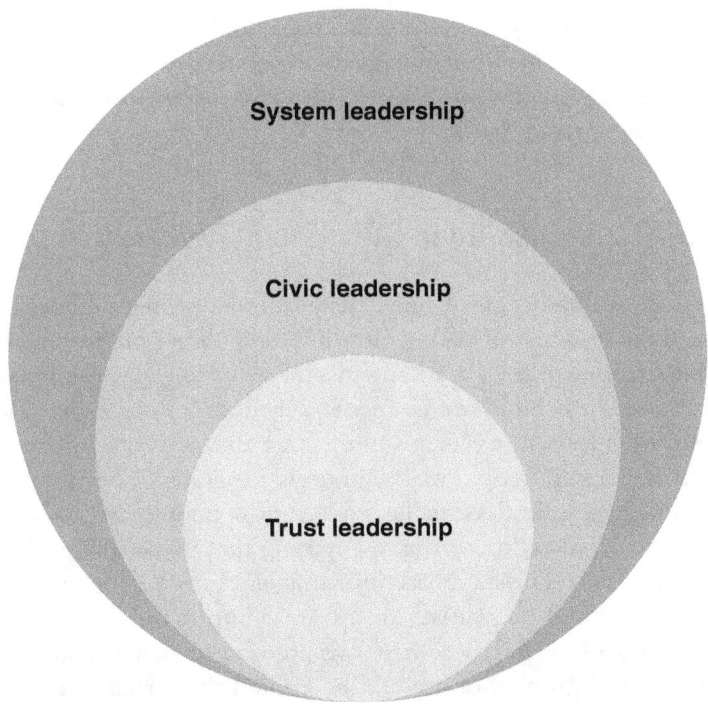

Figure 10.1 Cruddas's three nested leadership narratives (source: Cruddas, 2020)

is important here. Cruddas (2020) has written about the need to recognise three 'nested' leadership narratives, as seen in Figure 10.1.[9]

1. The first is about trust leadership: how we talk about ourselves, what we do and why we do it. School trusts create the conditions for deep collaborations among teachers and leaders to improve the quality of education.
2. The second is about civic leadership: how we work with others to advance education as a wider common good. Civic trusts create the conditions for purposeful collaboration between and among trusts and other civic organisations.
3. The third is about system leadership: not in the old definition of 'working beyond the school gates', but rather how we need to act on, rather than just acting in, the system. System building goes beyond collaboration and engages deliberate system design and system building.

We are all leaders who use the creative capacities generated in our MATs by discussion, experimentation and teamwork in order to develop our trusts to the best of our abilities; to develop our teams' civic duties; and to enable our education system to develop a stronger, wider sense of system design and to build leadership that lasts. Although there are aspects of government policy that we might not personally agree with, our focus is on creating a lifeworld of learning for both staff and students. This is a key leadership dilemma, and each reader needs to take a view on the juxtaposition of policy and their personal values, which can be explored further both in Sergiovanni's work, and also writers such as Greenfield (for an overview, see Rizvi (1994)).

Primary MATs: unlocking creativities in research in practice

So, what does creativity look like in leadership in primary schools? We have already discussed the systemsworld's imprint on policy direction, so here we would like to examine the lifeworld view and discuss how *meaningful* we can make the work that we do, in order to build *creative capacity*. If those in leadership roles wish to move a team forward, there are many things that they can try, but the most important concern is helping people make progress in *meaningful* work. This progress can be shown if we, as leaders, make explicit how people's work is contributing, and importantly avoid saying or doing anything that makes people believe their work is of little value. This emphasis on *meaning* links to the three dimensions that Sergiovanni (2000) emphasises are of great importance to the lifeworld: culture, community and person. The first two are tied to beliefs and our connections to a specific social group. So, it could be argued that, even in a larger policy environment that emphasises one particular way of conceptualising schooling, local school culture and its community is still of great importance to the lifeworld of the school, and perhaps also the wider MAT. This will be illustrated in Case Study One which follows. In Sergiovanni's definition of the lifeworld, the aptitudes and experiences that we develop as individuals help us to understand how our own meanings are shaped within a culture. His argument is that, when colonisation occurs, *meaning* is lost in all three of these areas. Eventually, he suggests, all those involved from parents to teachers and students become disinclined to commit to new ideas, and to re-think practices. We argue that creative approaches can halt this erosion, and renew the parts of the lifeworld of leadership that really matter to move learning forward.

Tang (2020) argues that creativity in leadership is often witnessed by colleagues but perhaps not acknowledged by wider educational structures.[10] Arguing about creative leadership in Singaporean contexts, Tang wrote that creative leadership should be actively encouraged and the level of '*creative capacity* is delineated by the frequency of idea generation, quality of originality and sophistication as well as impact on the breadth of the community' (2020, p. 8). This suggests that leaders of schools need to create personal and professional spaces in their lives in order to refresh their creative capacity.

Case studies

As we saw earlier in this chapter, Clegg (1972) noted that leaders are innovative. Creative practices can be seen in the following cases, drawn from Embark Federation (an education charitable trust serving 3,000 children and families across nine schools in Derbyshire). Each case study aims to explain how the creative leadership displayed has enacted the lifeworld, and to provide examples of personal artistry that have prevented colonisation and the ensuing loss of meaning. Helping to keep students, parents and teachers engaged in their practice and inclined to challenge and change is a key part of creative practice in leadership. As you read the case studies, be prepared both to challenge your ideas and also to bring your own artistry to the case. What would you do in a similar situation?

Case Study One: the Embark Award and involvement in performing arts

Matthew Crawford's first headship taught him the importance of performing arts in children's learning. He recounted:

> My then deputy Kathryn Mason drove it: the children-led assemblies and other performances, and you could see the confidence and self-esteem it gave them, and the knock-on effect on their learning. The results were benefiting from that work and we were in the top 10 per cent of schools for attainment and progress.

As Trust Leader of Derbyshire's new and rapidly growing Embark Federation, Matthew has extended his belief in the value of performance to programmes that are soon to be run in 12 primary schools. This has allowed him to scale up the schools' ambitions to create some extraordinary opportunities for their pupils, many from areas of deprivation:

> If a child is struggling in maths, rather than give them double maths in the afternoon I learned to give them something they were good at and really enjoyed. They then applied themselves better the next day in English and maths. A lot of this was around confidence, self-esteem and the real-life skills that arts give to children, and seeing it in action encouraged me to do even more of it across all our schools when we became a multi-academy trust. We want the very best for all of our children and want them to be able to access a wide variety of opportunities.

The trust's vision is to create schools that 'stand out' at the heart of their communities.

So, with the economy of scale that is possible for a trust, Embark hired a part-time fundraising and events manager, Rosie Mclaughlin, who organised inspirational events for the children and the funding. Her background was in the arts after studying at the prestigious Mountview Academy of Theatre Arts in London. Matt's vision was inherently creative, but he used creative leadership practices to drive it forward and embed these creativities. Inspired by Bourdieu's concept of 'cultural capital' (Bourdieu & Passeron, 1990)[11] (before OFSTED embraced it), the idea was to actively broaden the experiences the children have in their school, and to do this well they needed additional funding to support the Embark Award, 100 events that they wanted all of their children to have completed before they moved on to their secondary schools.

At the start, Embark brought two talented West End performers, Victoria Farley and Sophie Isaacs, to work with 70 children in workshops where they recorded the Federation Song. 'The behaviour of our children and the work they managed to get out of them in just one day was out of this world. That was the start of it, encouraging us to do more', says Matthew. The children – a mix of those who were passionate about the arts and classmates who otherwise would never get such opportunities – were chosen by each school. Later, another 42 children went to London's West End for workshops at Pineapple Dance Studios, lunch, the Lion King matinee and to meet the cast. None had visited London before. Matthew said:

> It was a trip of a lifetime! It is aspirational and inspirational for them to meet these top performers as well as helping with people skills like self-esteem and holding a conversation – all these things are important as you hopefully go on to "stand out" in the job market. One pupil said it was the best day of her life.

Matthew – who took up his first executive headship just 2 years before the MAT launched in January 2019 – is proud of all his schools and says his role is to model the leadership he is looking for. He is proud that each school has 'autonomy in the right places' and cites an inspirational piece of advice from former National Schools Commissioner Sir David Carter: 'What's the MAT dividend, what is it doing for the children? If you are the parent, what's the benefit of your child's school being in the trust? That's always resonated with me'. He added:

> Individual schools haven't got the time or the finances to put on these kinds of events. It's just adding that little extra 1 per cent to the schools. They're already fabulous places to be. This is just adding a little extra bit of inspiration.

The outcome of this work is that the trust has brought in £50,000 over 12 months, which has all been spent to achieve a range of events including a trip for disadvantaged pupils to the West End; successful artists and illustrators working with the children; a jazz day with Hot House for all the children that play instruments; West End stars visiting all of the schools during World Book Week to bring the stories to life; and a concert with four West End stars for the staff, governors and trustees. This last event was a 'thank you' on behalf of the trust leadership for all the work that everyone had put in, as Matthew said: 'A way of acknowledging that we had all gone above and beyond, but these events that grow our collective cultural capital are really worth getting the buy-in with from across our staff teams'.

Matthew Crawford believes that increasing the children's aspirations, self-esteem and confidence has had a huge impact on their work:

> We always say that children are unable to write if they haven't got experiences to draw upon, and as a trust we are trying to create these for our children. Our Embark Award mentioned earlier has played a key role in this too. The aim is for all our children to have achieved the 100 activities of the award before they leave school at 11, which include things like visiting the theatre, attending a sporting event and raising money for a local charity.

Points to mull over:

- What are the values that drive this approach?
- Can this work be related to the idea of the lifeworld of leadership, and if so, can you relate it to the idea of personal artistry that Bolman and Deal (1997) suggest is vital?
- What particular leadership skills do you think Matthew drew upon to develop leadership creativities in action?
- Is modelling leadership always the best way to progress ideas?
- Making meaning is a large part of this case study. What do you do as a leader to enhance meaning?

Case Study Two: devising an effective COVID-19 response strategy

During the international coronavirus pandemic, Embark Federation focused on creating a resource for all stakeholders to help overcome the challenges that arose with the outbreak of COVID-19. The trust led a Reconnection to Recovery and Resilience Programme focusing on the social, emotional and mental health needs of all. The programme was shared widely across the trust landscape, through the Confederation of School Trusts and local authorities, as well as in the media in June 2020, so the strategy has now had the opportunity to have a positive impact on around four million children.

Embark schools share a collective goal, working as a team to create stand-out schools at the heart of their communities. Four core beliefs – family, integrity, teamwork and success – underpin the Reconnection to Recovery and Resilience Programme, designed to put the social, emotional and mental health/wellbeing needs of all at the centre of the experience. COVID-19 was the biggest leadership challenge the trust has faced so far, and trust leaders focused on guiding families, and their Embark community, through an ongoing crisis, where they said that they want schools to continue to be vibrant places where children love learning.

The Embark team were determined to enable all stakeholders to thrive, bearing in mind the huge range of experiences individuals were likely to have:

- increased stress and anxiety levels (from the threat of COVID-19, or as a result of the loss of their normal routine)
- mixed experiences of home schooling and economic problems (including parental job losses)
- poverty, bereavement
- witnessing or experiencing domestic abuse (instances of which have sadly risen by around 30 per cent in recent months).

The trust drew upon the help of Sharon Gray OBE, specialist leaders of education and national leaders of education, as well as the leaders and staff from across the Embark Federation, and also leaders from local secondary schools/special schools. The aim was to support all involved – plus those further afield – allowing time/space to reflect on experiences of lockdown. It created opportunities for people to express thoughts, emotions and, ultimately, increase resilience, helping everyone to move forward with positivity – enabling them to flourish and thrive.

Nine teams were established from across the schools, and then the trust headteachers identified staff to work in each group based on their strengths. Each team was responsible for one of nine stages forming the basis of the Reconnection to Recovery and Resilience Programme (see Figure 10.2).

Team 1 looked at how to best stay connected with families: children were encouraged to keep scrapbooks recording simple events, whether that was making a cup of tea with Dad, or joining Joe Wicks, an internet trainer, for

Unlocking creative leadership

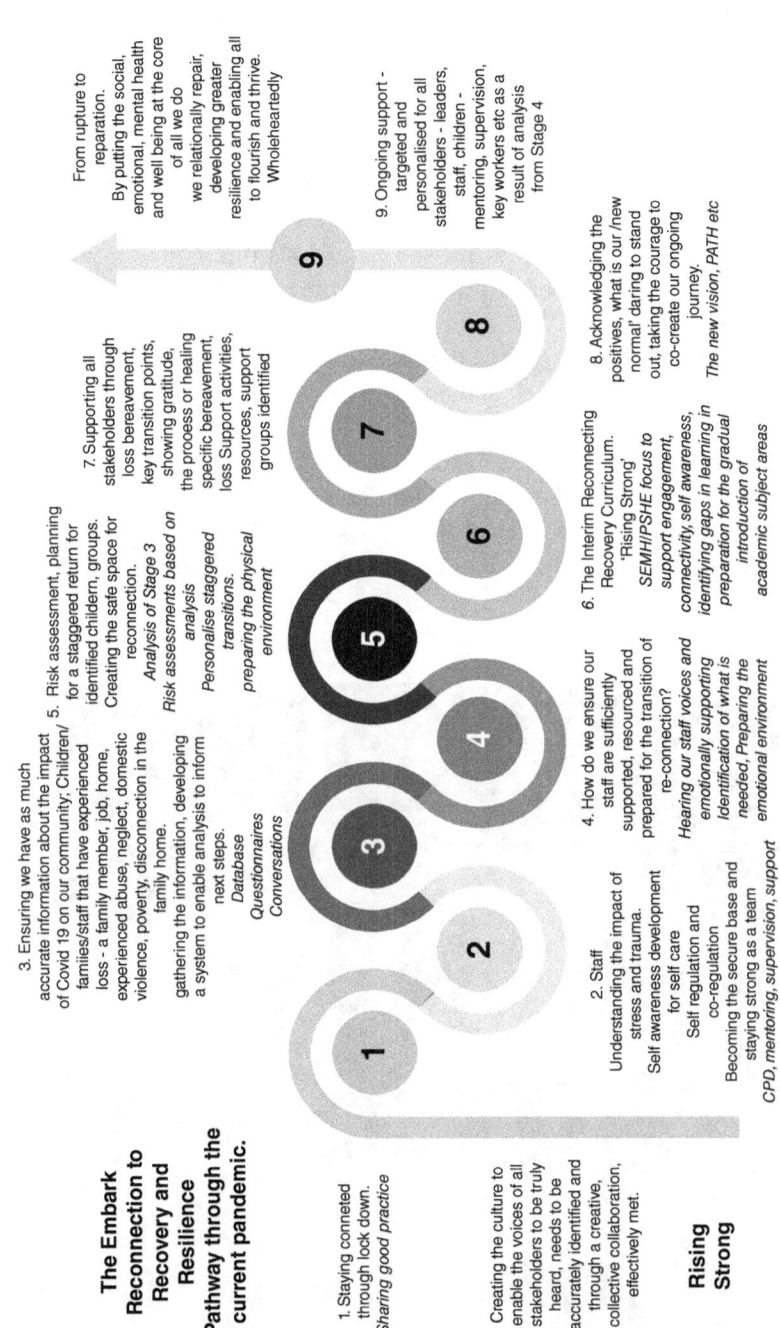

Figure 10.2 The Embark Reconnection to Recovery and Resilience Pathway through the pandemic

their morning exercise. Team 2 looked at how best to deal with the return to school, and with the interruption of learning. In part they used time capsules, including future artefacts such as the letter all households received from the UK Government urging people to stay at home. Team 3 devised methods of identifying the right support for our families, for example, through questionnaires, phone calls and doorstop visits. Schools used their family support teams for this. Team 4 utilised senior leaders to work together to plan how to re-connect with staff who had been shielding during the lockdown. How were the workforce going to re-connect effectively? While Team 5 reached out to staff with special educational needs expertise and devised plans for vulnerable children to return to school, Team 6 reached out to specialist staff in early years and across all years groups that would enable all children to re-connect when returning to school in September and rise strong from the pandemic. For example, the staff of classes aged 7-11 (the Key Stage 2 team) made a book of hope and a rising strong mural (see Figure 10.3).

Team 7 looked at what they needed to do as a trust moving forward, whilst Team 8 focused on the sustained and ongoing support that was required and how to best put it in place; and Team 9 looked at the professional development needs of the wider staff group in order to meet their shifting landscape. All the

Figure 10.3 Photograph of the rising strong mural with children and staff in one of the Embark Federation schools

schools remained connected during lockdown and worked together, sharing their expertise to ensure they were ready to welcome children back. The trust leadership felt that the existence of the nine teams allowed them to plan their journey to recovery together.

The trust leadership, including the trustees – who were actively involved throughout – felt that the schools could not return with a 'one-size-fits-all' approach. Hence the recovery programme, in line with government guidance, carried out bespoke risk assessments for each of the nine schools, which have varying catchments. The schools have used the tools and resources in the Re-connection & Rising Strong Toolkit to prioritise the emotional wellbeing of their children and their families. Positive relationships and quality resources from the toolkit have led to a successful reconnection, despite the continuation of the pandemic. Since the return to school in September, attendance was high, prior to the third lockdown and further school closure, with the majority of trust schools regularly recording more than 97 per cent attendance:

> The first day the girls were back I was wondering how they were. I knew the school had done everything possible to welcome the children back in a happy, positive way but I worried whether [they would enjoy] themselves. When they came home they were so happy to have had that day at school – eager to return.
>
> (Parent/Keyworker, interview, June 2020)

> We know that we've created something with this programme that will be massively beneficial. Our role as leaders is to continue putting emotional needs at the heart of everything we do, because then children are able to learn and benefit – and move through this crisis.
>
> (Sarah Armitage, Chair of Trustees, interview, June 2020)

Professor Barry Carpenter led a webinar, which has been shared across the UK, on what the trust has done and how it has worked; the trust received positive feedback from settings that are using the programme nationwide – from Durham to Devon. The Welsh government have also sent the programme to all their schools, as have the Youth Justice Board to their stakeholders. The trust has made a positive impact on children in so many different areas, but critically has united as a trust community like never before, living out its values and core beliefs. The programme has also attracted attention internationally, including as far as Australia and New Zealand.

Matthew Crawford feels that the trust's future vision is that 'through our recovery approach we bring our trust community to an increasingly positive place from which to move forward, rupture to repair, from adversity enabling our schools to unite, and through this relational approach gaining greater resilience'. When leaders are considering how to sculpt change differently, resilience is important, as is developing a repertoire of ways of thinking about and experiencing change through diverse creativities. Personal artistry and creative capacity for all are key. Points to mull over:

- Many different kinds of personal artistry in leadership are embedded in this case study, some individual, some organisational. Which ones would you draw upon if you were implementing a similar initiative?
- What do you understand by using strengths to develop creative capacity mentioned earlier? Think about what is meant by 'headteachers from across the schools in the Trust identified staff to work in each group based on their *strengths*'.
- Write down three strengths that you could bring to a similar initiative that inform your personal creative capacity.
- You may want to explore some of the ideas introduced in this chapter about leadership and teamwork further. This chapter's references offer a starting point for delving further into these ideas.

Conclusion and prompts for further development

The authors of this chapter come from different backgrounds, values and viewpoints, but we are all passionate about learning. Our focus is on the part everyone can play in enhancing experiences for children and, as Sir Alec noted at the start of this chapter, our professional life is a creative quest. We also believe that remembering the importance of the *lifeworld of leadership* will enhance each individual's *personal artistry*, and the team's *creative capacity*. This chapter has also hinted at the fact that, as with much in education, there are contested ideas around leaders, leadership and policy. However, our focus in this final section is to make you, the reader, think a little more about the *person* in the lifeworld, having read the case studies and gained a little of the background of the three authors. Sergiovanni (2000) tells us that *person* refers to our own individual competencies that help us understand our own lifeworlds, and aid us as we seek to find meaning and significance in what we are doing, especially in the challenging times in which we write. You will have seen that we suggest that culture, community and person are intertwined, and this can be seen in our second case study. Repairing and reconnecting through creative leadership of communities takes a great deal of energy not only from those involved in leadership, but also in managing the anxiety that may come from international events. At the same time, that reconnection enables leaders to continue to offer strategies and support to those who have key roles to play in primary schools, and to develop a resilient culture for personal development. Bolman and Deal (1997) do this in their book on re-framing as they set out to find different ways of looking at the same situation, or to build personal capacity to understand the ebb and flow of organisations. Reading Bolman and Deal is one useful way of understanding how professional communities work together. As they put it, 'No single story is comprehensive enough to make an organisation truly understandable or manageable' (p. 13). Making creative connections between what *needs* to be done and what *can* be done in the complex world of education involves using creative insight to illuminate some of the more cerebral processes. If you are able to unpack some of the ideas we have suggested, it will be because you have insight from your personal creative practices! To finish, we would like to offer you some prompts for personal development, based on some of the ideas we have suggested in this article. Please use as you will to inform your own thinking and creativity, or re-write them (creatively) to suit your own context and theme.

Unlocking research in practice: provocations for group discussion

1. What is your 'rule of thumb' when dealing with a situation that requires creative thinking? Can you write down three strategies that you always use, and then add a new one?
2. Leaders are often told they need to communicate a vision. Is this a creative leadership practice, and if not, why not?
3. Now that you have read this chapter, write down the key takeaway for you that you can apply to where you are working now. What can you do to make whatever it is even better for your students?
4. Can you be creative in leadership practices even if you are not officially designated a 'leader'?
5. What is your next leadership task? How can it be done differently to the last time you carried it out?
6. What aspects of personal artistry have you developed over the last 3 years? Write down what helped you develop these, so that you can develop others.

Notes

1. http://www.educationengland.org.uk/documents/speeches/1972clegg.html
2. Bolman and Deal (1997) is recommended reading for their examples that frame different aspects of leadership. They help leaders see different viewpoints and solutions to problems.
3. Gunter and Courtney (2020) challenge many of the taken-for-granted assumptions about policy and ask readers to think clearly about their value base.
4. Coldron, Crawford, Jones, and Simkins (2014) is a very useful article for readers outside the English system, explaining how power is manifested there. It contains excellent examples of how leaders reflect on their practice.
5. Ogawa and Bossert (1997) is a great place to begin if you want to understand the difference between *leaders* and *leadership*. The book as a whole provides a very useful start to thinking about leadership.

6 Sergiovanni (2000) is recommended reading to take you further on the journey into the lifeworld and systemsworld as they pertain to schools.
7 Habermas (1987) is useful reading for further exploration of some of the theoretical insights behind the idea of the lifeworld and systemsworld.
8 Crawford, Armitage, and Upton (2020) use research to look at how local authorities and MATs have synergies in the system. They ask the reader to reflect on what matters about leadership in practice.
9 Cruddas's (2020) report is very useful for readers in the English system, encouraging us to think about how we move forward with the policy of trusts. She asks teachers and leaders: what system do we want to work in?
10 Read Tang's (2020) thesis if you want to explore personal creative capacity in more depth.
11 Read Bourdieu and Passeron (1990) to understand more about the concept of cultural capital. How does this concept apply to your setting?

References

Bolman, L. G., & Deal, T. E. (1997). *Reframing organizations: Artistry, choice, and leadership.* San Francisco, CA: Jossey-Bass.

Bourdieu, P., & Passeron, J. C. (1990). *Reproduction in education, society and culture* (2nd ed.). London: Sage.

Clegg, A. (1972, August 3). *Making the whole world wonder* [Speech]. Bingley College of Education, Bingley, UK.

Coldron, J., Crawford, M., Jones, S., & Simkins, T. (2014). The restructuring of schooling in England: The responses of well-positioned head teachers. *Educational Management, Administration and Leadership, 42*(3), 387–403.

Crawford, M. (2003). Inventive management and wise leadership. In N. Bennett, M. Crawford, & M. Cartwright (Eds.), *Effective educational leadership* (pp. 62–74). London: Sage.

Crawford, M., Maxwell, B., Coldron, J., & Simkins, T. (2020). Local authorities as actors in the emerging 'school-led' system in England. *Educational Review.* Advance online publication. https://doi.org/10.1080/00131911.2020.1739625

Cruddas, L. (2020). *Systems of meaning: Three nested leadership narratives for school trusts.* Confederation of School Trusts. Retrieved from https://cstuk.org.uk/assets/CST-Publications/10027_CST_Three_Nested_Leadership%20_White_Paper%20(002).pdf

Gunter, H. M., & Courtney, S. J. (2020). A new public educative leadership? *Management in Education.* Advance online publication. https://doi.org/10.1177/0892020620942506

Habermas, J. (1987). *The theory of communicative action, Vol 2, Lifeworld and system: A critique of functional reason.* Boston, MA: Beacon Press.

Meyerson, D., & Martin, J. (1987). Cultural change: An integration of three different views. *Journal of Management Studies, 24*(6), 623–646.

Ogawa, R. T., & Bossert, S. T. (1997). Leadership as an organisational quality. In M. Crawford, L. Kydd, & C. Riches (Eds.), *Leadership and teams in educational management* (pp. 9–23). Buckingham, England and Philadelphia, PA: Open University Press.

Rizvi, F. (1994). Tom Greenfield and educational administration. *Curriculum Studies, 2*(1), 119–127. https://doi.org/10.1080/0965975940020106

Sergiovanni, T. J. (2000). *The lifeworld of leadership: Creating culture, community and personal meaning in our schools*. San Francisco, CA: Jossey-Bass.

Tang, S. (2020). *Programmes, policies and practices which hinder/augment Singapore-based teachers' intentions to further increase their pedagogical creative capacity: A sequential exploratory approach* (PhD thesis). University of Liverpool.

Further reading to frame the second case study

Crawford, M. (2020a, July). 'Rising strong' – A pathway to recovery and reconnection. *Trust*. Retrieved from https://trust-journal.org.uk/2020/07/10/rising-strong-a-pathway-to-recovery-and-reconnection/

Crawford, M. (2020b, July 5). There are no shortcuts on the road to recovery. *Schools Week*. Retrieved from https://schoolsweek.co.uk/there-are-no-shortcuts-on-the-road-to-recovery/

Crawford, M., Armitage, S., & Upton, A. (2020, June 22). How a tailored programme can help schools reopen. *Department for Education Teaching blog*. Retrieved from https://teaching.blog.gov.uk/2020/06/22/how-a-tailored-programme-can-help-schools-reopen/

How parent-teacher collaboration is helping pupils back to school safely. (2020, June 12). *Independent*. Retrieved from https://www.independent.co.uk/news/uk/how-parentteacher-collaboration-is-helping-pupils-back-to-school-safely-a9537026.html

How schools in England are helping pupils return to the classroom. (2020, June 29). *Independent*. Retrieved from https://www.independent.co.uk/news/uk/schools-england-return-coronavirus-classrooms-rules-guidelines-summer-a9575491.html

Pupils return to primary schools after coronavirus lockdown. (2020, June 2). *Bishop's Stortford Independent*. Retrieved from https://www.bishopsstortfordindependent.co.uk/news/school-reunion-it-s-back-to-class-for-pupils-in-england-9111742/

School's back! How England's primaries have prepared to welcome more children after months of lockdown because of coronavirus. (2020, June 2). *Daily Mail*. Retrieved from https://www.dailymail.co.uk/femail/article-8376095/Schools-Englands-primaries-ready-welcome-children-coronavirus-lockdown.html

CHAPTER

11

Learning at a snail's pace: *what if* and *what else* is happening in a South African primary classroom?

Karin Murris, Joanne Peers and Nadia Woodward

From '*What if* and *what else* are the children doing'? . . .

We re-turn[1] to data created as part of an international project on Children, Technology and Play (CTAP), a collaborative mixed-methods project between the University of Sheffield (UK) and the University of Cape Town (SA), funded by the LEGO Foundation (see Marsh et al., 2020).[2] Karin was the Principal Investigator of the South African part of the study involving seven pre-primary and primary schools in South Africa and 1,286 parents. Joanne was one of the researchers on the project, working closely with two schools, four children and three teachers, including Nadia, a Grade 1[3] teacher. Two of the children in her class were involved in the ethnographic, qualitative component of the project as case study participants. Nadia did her 1-year teacher qualification (PGCE[4]) with both Karin and Joanne at the University of Cape Town.

Lecturers' routine use of pedagogies such as philosophy with children (P4C) and Reggio Emilia is at the heart of the PGCE Foundation phase. Both teaching philosophies are characterised by using questions and transmodal methods that involve the creative arts, are divergent and generate further questioning (cf. Murris, 2016). Unlike using questions that 'Google can answer', P4C and Reggio Emilia celebrate questions that focus on concepts that children have raised themselves and with meanings that are puzzling at any age. These philosophical questions provoke further enquiries that spiral into unknown territories of knowledge creation for both teacher and child. Rooted in academic research, in this chapter we present seven vignettes that reveal how change can be unlocked and sculpted differently by asking new questions, stimulating thinking and experiencing change in primary education through diverse creativities and dialogue about learning and teaching in schools. For example, in the vignettes we focus on in this chapter, the concepts (e.g. symmetry) are doing this transformative situated work in between human and non-human bodies by re-shaping concepts and examining how they work to help us think differently about teaching practice (Murris & Haynes, 2020).

Enquirers of any age do not follow a linear trajectory, nor do they go 'round and round in circles'. Instead, like fractals,[5] they 'spiral together' inwards and outwards, and with and through other material bodies. In principle, enquiring processes can go on forever (Murris & Haynes, 2002, p. 45). Defying quick settlement through fact-based answers, philosophical questions open up enquiries and generate thinking classrooms that resist knowledge transmission and 'banking' approaches to education. Brazilian educator and critical pedagogue Paulo Freire (1970/2014, pp. 124–125) famously introduced this notion of 'banking':

> A careful analysis of the teacher-student relationship at any level, inside or outside the school, reveals its fundamentally *narrative* character. This relationship involves a narrating Subject (the teacher) and patient, listening objects (the students). The contents, whether values or empirical dimensions of reality, tend in the process of being narrated to become lifeless and petrified. Education is suffering from narration sickness.
>
> The teacher talks about reality as if it were motionless, static, compartmentalized, and predictable. Or else he expounds on a topic completely alien to the existential experience of the students. His task is to 'fill' the students with the contents of his narration – contents which are detached from reality, disconnected from the totality that engendered them and could give them significance. Words are emptied of their concreteness and become a hollow, alienated, and alienating verbosity.

'Banking' is still a powerful descriptor of how teachers tend to teach in South Africa, even in the early years, leaving little space for learning through play, let alone through play with technology – the topic of the CTAP research project. In that sense alone, Nadia's classroom is an exception. For her, the aliveness of reality is a given, as opposed to reality being 'motionless' and 'static', as in the banking model. Nadia adopts P4C and Reggio Emilia inspired practices as a powerful way of teaching the South African national curriculum in a government school in the Western Cape. This kind of teaching can be theorised as 'posthumanist', because critical posthumanism takes the relationality between human and non-human bodies as the starting point rather than individual existence, and does not assume that only humans are intelligent. We have written about and extensively theorised these posthuman pedagogies in practice elsewhere (Murris, Reynolds, & Peers, 2018). So, what difference does it make for teaching practice and why does it matter?

One way of showing the difference it makes is by starting with a question that makes perfect sense when writing about teacher research: '*What if* and *what else* are the children doing'? In fact, by asking this question, data could be created that is unexpected, rather than searched for by ready-made codes that are already implied in the research questions and predetermined by the research design. For example, what was really noticeable in the CTAP project (and an unexpected finding) was the open-ended dialogues taking place between some of the teachers, children and researchers (see Marsh et al., 2020). Also, the different roles usually taken up by children, teachers, parents and researchers as distinct and separate started to shift and to become far less demarcated and bounded. This is clearly evident in the vignettes that follow. But theorising our practices through critical posthumanist theories invites a rephrasing of our original question that matters ethically and politically. It takes the reader on a sticky journey that leaves slimy traces that cannot be erased. Inspired by a snail's way of life (its body and movements), we pay attention to the dynamics of the relationships between the researchers (Karin, Joanne), the teacher (Nadia), the children and the more-than-human (e.g. the technology), thereby moving away from human exceptionalism and a human-centred orientation. With Nadia as co-researcher of her own teaching, our analysis troubles the adult-child binary and invites a rephrasing of our original question to a less human-centred orientation to teaching and educational research: '*What if* and *what else* is happening in a South African early years classroom'? We finish by offering some philosophical and pedagogical ideas about how photography can be used for documenting learning, thereby inspiring a kind of teacher research that includes the more-than-human – in particular the school's geopolitical setting.

. . . To '*What if* and *what else* is happening in a South African early years classroom'?

To include the geopolitical setting of the school in our analysis and to examine how the more-than-human[6] participates in knowledge generation, we re-turn to the data generated by the CTAP project. Re-turning is a posthumanist pedagogy, as well as a research methodology. Critical posthumanist and quantum physicist Karen Barad (2014) explains the difference between 'returning' and 're-turning' through the familiar visual metaphors of reflection and diffraction. Returning is associated with reflection (how light returns from where it came once it hits the mirror), while *re*-turning is about diffracting (Barad, 2014, pp. 184–185). Thus, if returning implies a going back in time to what once was in linear time, re-turning in teacher research involves always already being entangled with/in a world that is not at a distance.

Knowing is a material and discursive practice that changes the world in its materiality – a worlding practice. Each and every knower, independent of age, cannot step 'out of the world' and reflect on it (gaze at it), because relations are always already there and bring individual bodies into existence. Re-turning and diffracting as methodologies disrupt the idea that with our mind's eye (and leaving our situated bodies behind) we can go back in time, detaching ourselves from the now, and then going back to earlier events without affecting the past. For example, when *reflecting* on a lesson we taught last week, we assume that the lesson is an objective fact, frozen in time and space and untouched by someone remembering the event. For critical posthumanism, events do not exist in an absolute sense, but rather emerge from and through their intra-action and are distinct only in relation to their mutual entanglement (Barad, 2007). In other words, the question '*What if* and *what else* is happening in a South African early years classroom'? cannot be answered by isolating the events that happened as individual elements. Barad's relational ontology[7] implies a radical reworking of the traditional notion of individual subjects (children) in the world and seeing the relations between (human and more-than-human). We trace (not map from a distance) some of the trails and lines that matter in the learning that was produced diffractively.

We explore some examples from Nadia's teaching and Joanne's research in Nadia's class to bring this writing alive by moving multidirectionally in re-turning to the research data created by Dictaphones, wearable cameras and mobile phones. Of course, research does not happen in isolation. Before the research started in the school, that is, before Nadia signed consent forms, invited two families to take part in the ethnographic part of the project and selected her two research participants, Joanne walked in (research can be a bit like 'parachuting in'). A quick reminder, Joanne is one of Nadia's teacher educators; she visits the school to observe the case study children in class, conduct focus groups with small groups of children, and interview Nadia and the two children and their families at home. When exactly does the school or the classroom become a research site? Is it possible (or even desirable) to draw clear boundaries? We start with an *intra*-view[8] between Joanne and Nadia. Joanne started with the pre-set questions all researchers in the CTAP project were using, in England as well as South Africa.

Through their specificity and by paying care-ful attention to detail, vignettes can be helpful to change practice. They highlight the complex issues involved in pedagogical decisions and the implications of changes to theoretical frameworks underpinning practice. Our first vignette introduces Nadia's approach to teaching with technology when exploring insects. Six other vignettes will take the ideas further by paying attention to snails and their movements as part of the world.

Vignette 1: when digital devices are limited

>**Joanne**: So, let's go with how you are using technology this week, in terms of the bee, oh the insects. Ja. So are you using it, how is it being used to facilitate learning?
>**Nadia**: Well, my choice in terms of how I . . . what I use for digital technology is obviously based on my limitations of what I have accessible to me, but based on what I have accessible, I am.
>**Joanne**: Okay, so we are interested in understanding how this sort of play with technology or media might develop the following skills, holistic skills, and

would be interested in your perspective and observations on each. So, some of the examples now of them building, that roadmap or when they are transferring some of the experiences from having done things of technology. So you were in the hall and looked at insects and then they came and did something. So in the area of physical, social, cognitive and creative and emotional skills. How would you say that technology is helping in the area of physical skills?

Nadia: Well, I mean I think yesterday's example of looking at real insects and then transferring that into an art project, we . . . they started off with facts about insects. Okay, how many body parts, how many legs. You know, and then it went into a creative arts project and then some kids got really creative. They went beyond that and some of the insects, and then some were, stuck really true to what they had seen, they made sure they were three body parts, they made sure there were six legs and so on.

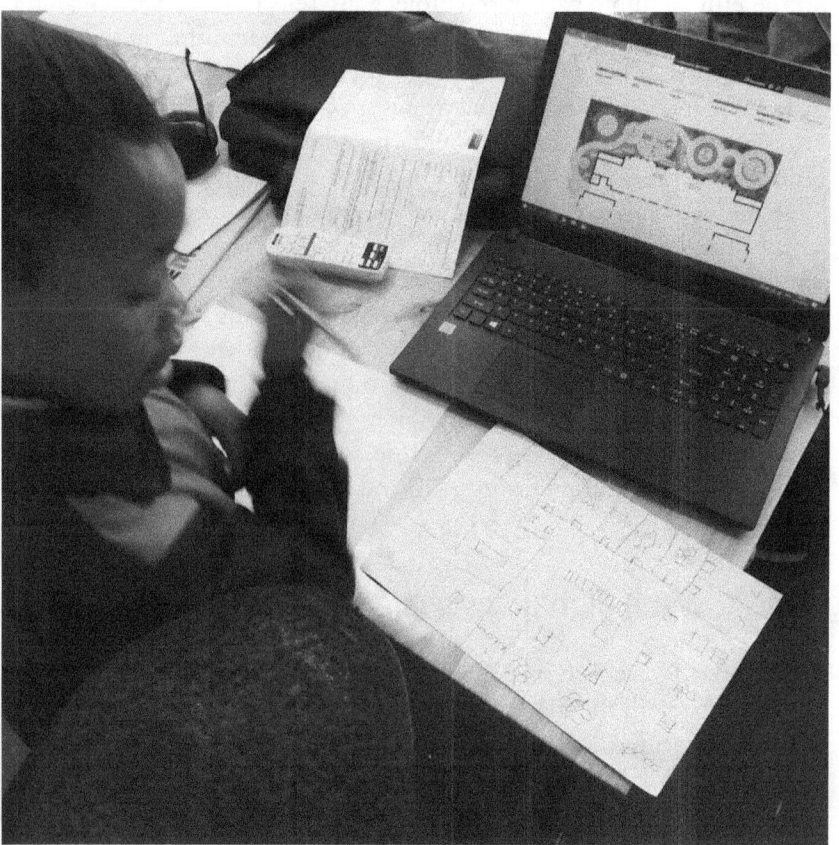

Figure 11.1 Creative entanglements with/in devices

Learning at a snail's pace

> Signpost: What are the possibilities for learning even when digital devices are limited?

Joanne's first question does not come from nowhere. She has situated the more general question about Nadia's use of technology by looking around and *noticing* what is hanging on the wall, so-called prior to when the research started. Working with the constraints of the questions laid out in the research instrument, Joanne and Nadia weave in and out of the questions by including the artefacts of learning that are present in the classroom, for example, art and documentation on the walls, activities and constructions left on Nadia's desk. The vibrancy of the materials in the room creates an atmosphere for Nadia and Joanne to move around the classroom during the intra-view. The intra-view becomes more complex as it opens up the questions to include the children's work and Nadia's practice, which is evident in the loose ends and spirals of learning and enquiries that is very present in the

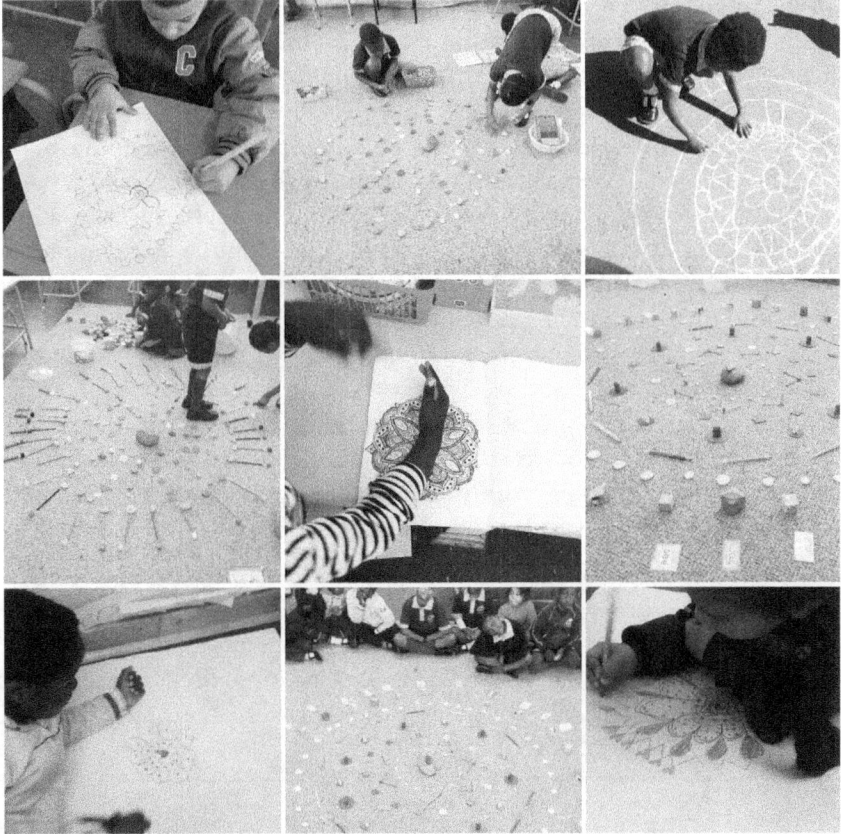

Figure 11.2 Multimodal work with mandalas

classroom. In particular, the materiality and discursive reconfiguration of one particular wall shows the pedagogical documentation of the learning in progress – all of which is entangled with (and has performative agency as part of) the research data. Giving an exact time of when research starts in a classroom is suddenly more complex than originally assumed.

> Signpost: Nadia creates photograph collages so that parents are included in the learning process.

So, what is Nadia's documentation about and why is it important? Inspired by the Reggio Emilia approach to early childhood education, the photos are an expression of children's active engagement with concepts using their '100 languages' that go beyond the spoken and written word (Regio Emilia Approach, 2020). Through various encounters of thinking with the materials, learners are given opportunities to diffract through their own and each other's learning by re-turning to the photos again and again. The documentation is there to document/record/hold up to the light the learning for later re-discovery, re-investigation and re-imagining. The technology is entangled and part of distributed agency (not just child or teacher agency) in learning, and its pace creates possibilities for a rare kind of hospitality, collaboration and sense of belonging in a school, also for the non-human.

The children in Nadia's class are actively involved in creating this documentation with the materials. They are given the freedom to display on the walls/cupboards/windows/desks any creations or materials created in the learning process (the evidence of their learning). Children also engage in the process of documenting their learning, or that of their peers, by asking Nadia if they can use her phone, then walking around and photographing what they regard as the learning taking place. The documentation board is alive and ever-changing with no intention of being a display board, but a means to share and document learning to be re-visited, re-imagined and re-constructed. The documentation also plays a role in the way Nadia plans and engages with the curriculum while still working with the curiosity generated by particular concepts and ideas.

> Signpost: Documentation is a collaborative process. In Nadia's classroom, collaboration includes participation from parents, children and teachers, but also the non-human such as furniture, atmosphere and technical devices.

Nadia's teaching with insects, but also with flags, map making, moon and mandala, were pushed forward and pulled up by the children in different ways over the

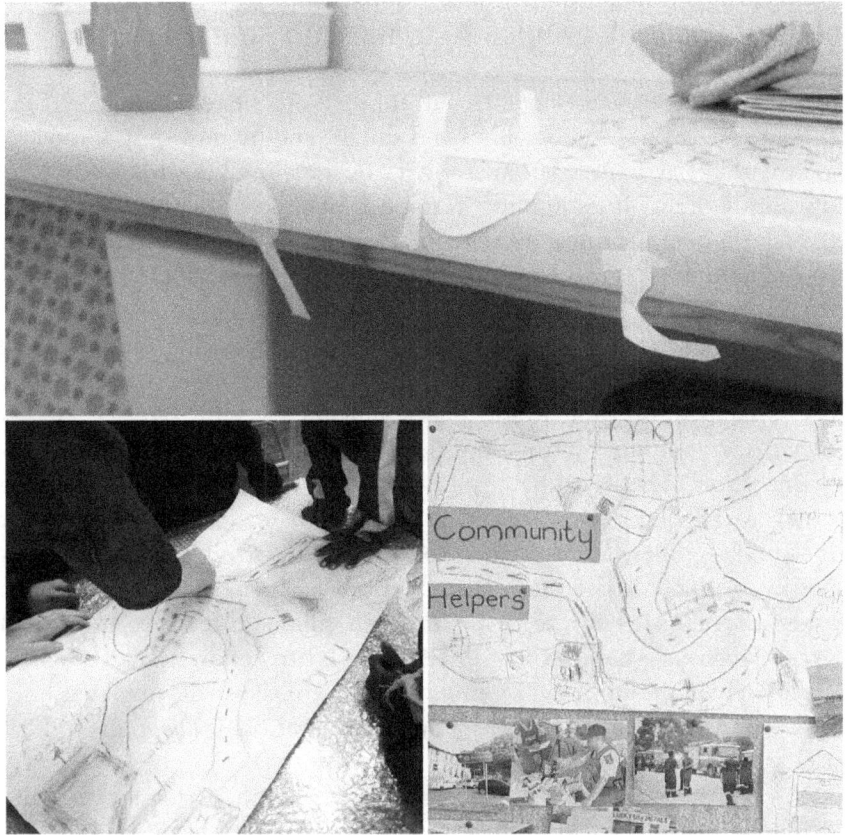

Figure 11.3 Documenting thinking and ideas

course of a few months. They reveal the ongoing movement of learning and they left lively trails on the data of the CTAP research project.

We diffract through Nadia's teaching and Joanne's intra-actions with the human and more-than-human, for example, the video camera and mobile phones that made it possible to do this writing (Murris & Menning, 2019). Nadia read the transcripts of the intra-views with Joanne. In the re-turning, it dawned on her that learning is not unilinear and does not spiral upwards or downwards in one direction. Curriculum is one of many moving lines. We find inspiration in Ingold's philosophy of lines to try to articulate some of these interesting findings and how they affect us as practitioners. Nadia does not resist the curriculum, but relates to it within the multiplicity of lines: sticky lines, slimy traces, whirlwinds, spiralling with multiple lines. Nadia allows herself and the children to be taken by these lines.

For the analysis of the vignettes, we will engage with a *philosophy of lines* as part of our methodology of *re-turning*.

Ingold's philosophy of lines to think with snails

We analyse the earlier vignette and more short vignettes next by thinking with Ingold's (2015) ideas about lines and spirals, and by regarding knowledge making as a worlding practice. The materiality of spiralling lines opens up possibilities to disrupt the linear lines implied in notions of child development and progress, and to reconfigure learning as more complex in terms of deciding what *is* – what is *real*. Included in what is real is also the more-than-human as part of a notion of agency that is distributed and does not reside *in* the individual human. Indeed, the notion of distributed agency helps us not only to rephrase the child-centred question 'What if and what else are the children doing'? to the question 'What if and what else is happening?', but it also puts out a line by which we can start describing 'what *is* happening' by troubling linear causality (when I do x, y happens). And the question 'what *is* happening'? is answered *at the same time* (disrupting unilinear time) as the questions *what if?* and *what else?* are happening in the classroom. Re-thinking lines, or re-turning to how lines work in teacher research, makes it possible to include the more-than-human (e.g. materials, place) in what happens when learning. It helps to de-centre both child and teacher, and troubles human exceptionalism – the idea that intelligence is situated in human consciousness and exclusively *in* the human. We link the figure of the snail, spiralling lines, teaching and learning to show *what is happening* and *what else is happening* in Nadia's Grade 1 classroom.

A common creature in school gardens in South Africa is the snail. The snail deposits its anterior and it pulls up at the rear in a continuous motion, repeating this pattern in slow and thoughtful movements. Ingold describes how the snail 'alternately pushes forth and pulls up, leaving its slime trails on the ground' (2015, p. 7). He suggests that this 'rhythmic, push-pull cycle' seems fundamental to the life of most if not all animate creatures including humans. Ingold draws attention to the whorl on the snail's back as he builds his argument for the ongoingness and intertwined movements in the world and, in the case of our chapter, education. We follow our curiosity about the theory of lines which puts forward lines as relational and entangled be(com)ings within education. According to Ingold (2015), lineology is the oldest of subjects.

Lineology can be found in any early years education classroom in South Africa. A common example is noticing how a line is drawn between mathematics, art and language as separate subjects in a school curriculum (dividing lines often mirrored in teacher education). Ingold suggests that the subject of lines is in fact a part of everyday life. Even though it is old, it is at the same time the newest of subjects as its scope is wonderfully broad, for it 'includes walking, weaving, observing, singing, storytelling, drawing and writing' (Ingold, 2015, p. 54). How then can we think in education about lines and their movement? Perhaps by resisting thinking about learning lines as linear, fixed and bounded by subjects (as also the case in Freire's 'banking' notion of education) but spiralling instead, as in P4C and Reggio Emilia, as we have seen in this chapter? Teaching and learning involve multidirectional and ongoing lines *ad infinitum*. Ingold himself underscores this in his book *The Life of Lines* (2015), noting the centrality of the entwining of lines – the way in which lines of place are entangled with education. For example, in Nadia's school, the way in which the children travel to and from home, back to school, inside and outside the classroom, expresses their entanglement with place – as always already entangled with the children's learning. It is unusual to think of place as part of agency in teaching and learning, but if we move away from individual human bodies and take as our starting point complex phenomena consisting of entangled, spiralling lines, it becomes clear(er) why place matters.

Snails and their relationship with lines: a homology, not an analogy

The snail as a non-human body does not work in an analogous way to describe Nadia's teaching as *like* that of a snail. A snail leaves traces and slimy trails along the ground, on the leaves, sand and playground. As we re-turn to the data, we notice that the spiralling moves of Nadia's teaching also leave traces and slimy trails in the way in which the children participate in the classroom and her teaching – the relation is the *same*. It is a homologous, not an analogous, comparison. This matters, because the snail's body and its function are not simply used to *represent* human teaching and learning. Teaching, learning and re-searching are part of a worlding process. We as humans are not simply reflecting upon the world with words and describing it as if we are not always already entangled and part of it. What strikes us is how Nadia follows, re-turns, connects up and links in with the children's traces of learning and interest. In the vignettes that follow, we disentangle several spiralling lines and slimy traces to show the 'how' of Nadia's emergent curriculum. We also argue why it matters and for whom, and hope to offer an imagination of how teaching can be done that is not 'banking', that is, 'motionless, static, compartmentalised', or 'predictable' beforehand, which takes all life out of teaching – not only for children but also for their teachers. Neither is her teaching 'alien to the existential experience of' her children, nor is 'content disconnected', nor does she see it as her task to 'fill' the students, nor are her words 'emptied of their concreteness'. At the same time, she is teaching the South African curriculum that is not explicitly posthumanist, nor enquiry based and content driven. So how does she do it?

Let us first have a look in more detail at what a snail is and what it does. The title of the chapter could easily be misconstrued. We are not arguing for a slowing down (at a snail's pace) of teaching, because, for example, children might not be able to keep up with the pace of the curriculum. We are not arguing (as some might) that the children Nadia teaches live in poverty, hence they cannot keep up with a universalised curriculum that does not take into account children's socio-economic and political contexts and their home languages. Instead, the snail as a figuration is about the slowness of *movement*, not slowness in (objective) time.

Table 11.1 Vignettes for learning at a snail's pace

Vignette	Snails	Questions about learning	Questions for teaching practice
2	movements are slow	How can we reconfigure the pace of learning?	How would teaching change if it were in slow motion?
3	lines are tangled with other lines	What if learning about concepts was an entanglement of lines?	How could teachers pay attention to entangled lines in the classroom?
4	leave traces behind	What traces are left behind as part of the learning process?	What traces do teachers need to pay attention to?
5	engages with different materials as it moves along	How is learning entangled with different materials?	How can the teacher offer multimodal learning opportunities?
6	shells are spirals and coils	What if learning is multidirectional like spirals?	How can we teach a curriculum that moves from question to question, opening up more questions?
7	move across surfaces and in between places	How can learning emerge if it moved through spaces?	In what ways could teachers open up unusual outdoor and indoor spaces at school for learning?

To adopt animals as narrative characters in posthumanist writing is common and deliberate. It is a way in which we can pay tribute to their complex ways of be(com)ing in the world and their intelligences.[9] A snail's complex way of be(com)ing with/in the world is summed up in Table 11.1.

Vignette 2: snails' movements are slow

The curriculum can assume movement at a particular pace that expects learning to move along a straight line and in a forward motion. Through her process of learning and engaging with children, Nadia begins to notice how concepts and ideas tend to linger longer than anticipated. A concept or particular interest among the children explored in the first part of the school year may re-turn at multiple moments during the rest of the year. For example, the mandala becomes one of the slow spirals that keeps re-turning in many different forms in Nadia's classroom (see Figure 11.2 and Figure 11.4). We see the slow spirals as re-turning and

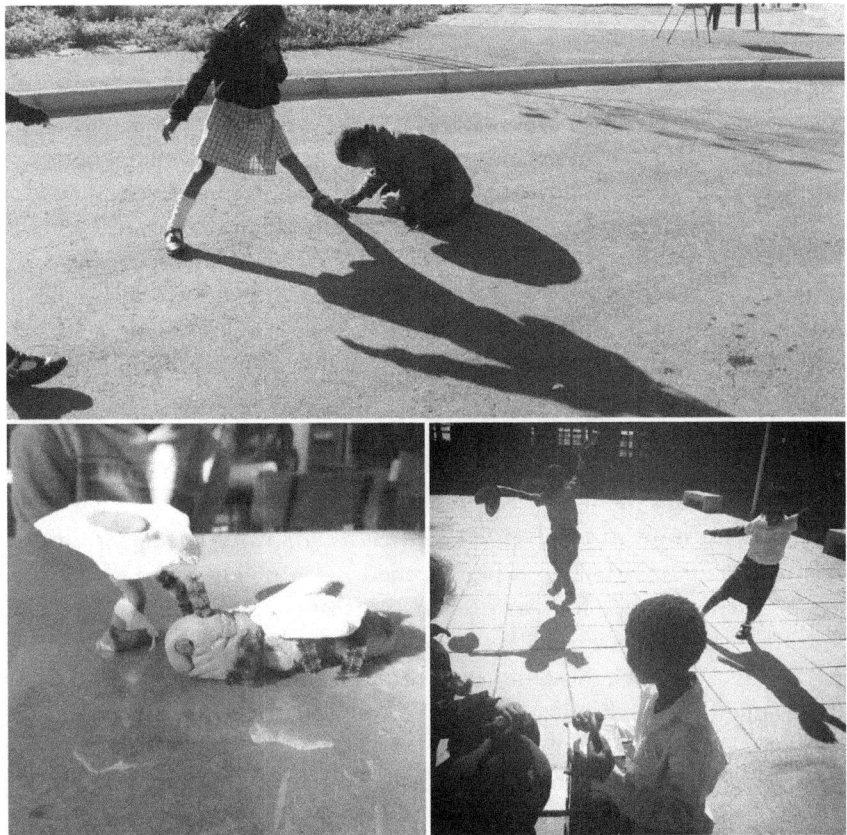

Figure 11.4 Slow paces

reappearances of concepts in Nadia's classroom. For example, the thinking with mandalas is made visible through her use of documentation and captures the slimy trails of thinking and learning (see Figure 11.4). Threaded lines of symmetry, investigated through patterns, shapes and mandala making, bring slow movements into the learning as children play and create new thoughts. This is in contrast with the usual conception of pace as speeding teaching up to reach developmental milestones or curriculum outcomes, Nadia's pace takes unilinear time into account, but *also* offers a different pace of learning and knowledge making. It is not a matter of either/or, but and . . . and . . .

Vignette 3: snails' lines are tangled with other lines

The curriculum is one of many tangled lines of learning in any classroom. At the time of this research, in Nadia's class, the curriculum learning outcome for mathematics is 'symmetry'. As a teacher, she has to regularly weave and thread different lines together creatively by responding to what is happening around her, sensing what might be expressed, though not yet articulated. As it happens, the introduction of the mandala by a child in the classroom works as a provocation for changing the teaching methods. In listening carefully to the children, by following on from their work with the mandala, Nadia is able to move between mathematics, literacy and the life skills curriculum requirements. The key here is to pay close attention to what affects the children and to notice their diffractive play with shape, form and design. When the children create mandalas using materials found in and around the class, they begin to pull laminated sight words off the wall to incorporate into the large mandala. Letters, pencils, mathematics counters, dice, blocks and laminated words are used in an entangled and elaborate creation of a class mandala. The children move their way around the mandala reading the words. The mandala is left out on the carpet for the full day, while the children make sure they carefully stepped over it as they move across the classroom. This process is gently guided by Nadia.

The classroom is set up in a way that children have the freedom to use many of the resources available when needed. The children therefore do not always look to the teacher for permission to create, but rather, when inspired by an idea they know, they are allowed to act on it. This is unlike many other schools in South Africa where authoritarian adult-child relations are more common. In P4C and Reggio Emilia, authority is negotiated with the children (Murris & Haynes, 2020). Classroom agreements are set up so that children understand that being given the freedom to use materials also means they have a responsibility to look after the resources and return them when they do not need them any longer. Counters, blocks, Lego, paper, stationery and wooden letters are all available and stored on the counter for children to pull out, use and then return. Nadia observes the way in which the children are working, noticing what discoveries are being made and how familiar ideas have re-turned for reinvestigation. She draws attention to details that may inspire other children to follow similar lines of learning or to find their own lines. The lines of learning are tangled as the children move between new curiosities and previous learning and ideas. For example, the children connect the concept 'symmetry', first discovered in their body maps, and then explore the shadows of their bodies with the symmetry they explore in the image of the mandala. Nadia is keenly aware of what is happening, observing the children as they work, not as a means to correct and steer them (though an element of this remains), but by noticing what they are exploring in the moment and being open to what else is going on, which is more than she ever imagined would happen when she planned the lesson. By re-turning, the past learning is enriched, deepened and reconfigured. Some children re-turn to the tracing of bodies after making their mandala (see Figure 11.5). They pull various strands of their learning into the mandala. Having a sound knowledge of the South African curriculum, Nadia is also able to see when what the children are engaging in can tie into those curriculum needs. In the mandala work, Nadia is able to draw links to various mathematics curriculum outcomes such as symmetry, shape, space,

Learning at a snail's pace

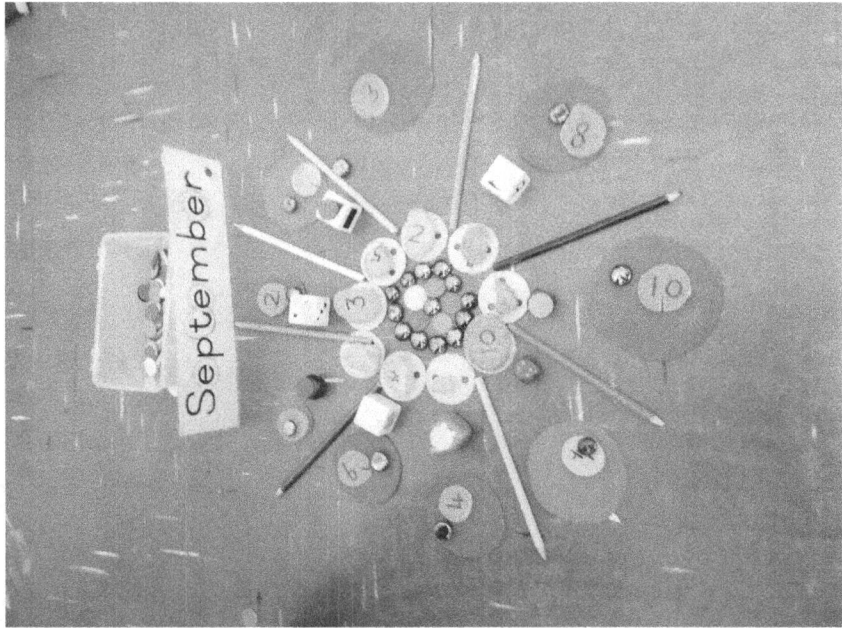

Figure 11.5 Curriculum one line among many lines

pattern, measurement, counting out objects, sorting and more. The children effortlessly pull literacy resources into their mandalas, which allow opportunities for reading and working on letter recognition.

> Signpost: Have you returned to Table 11.1 yet? Have these vignettes made you ask different questions to the questions in the table?

> Signpost: Teachers can use one activity to draw multiple lines of learning. Nadia regularly crosses literacy, mathematics and science in her teaching.

Vignette 4: snails leave traces behind

Documentation is seen within Nadia's classroom as a living document on every surface imaginable. The children pin up images of mandalas, insects, maps, flags and letters as they create them, sometimes pull down old ones to recreate them or to edit, adjust or turn them into something else. Nadia understands the many ways in which documentation can work in a classroom space to serve the needs of the children and to leave traces behind for the teacher and curriculum advisors.

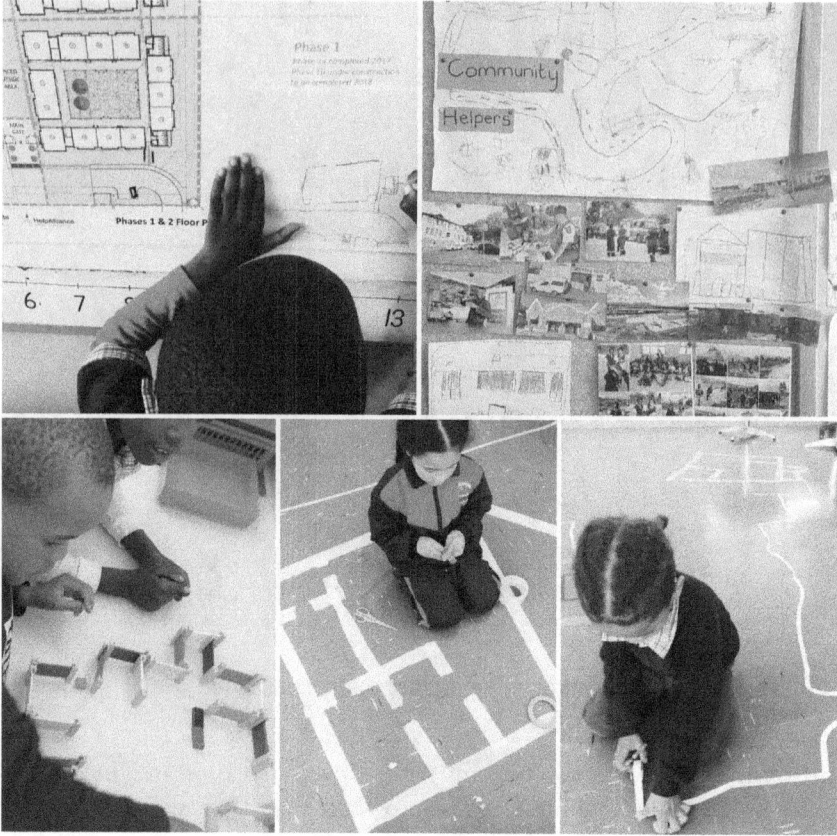

Figure 11.6 Documentation on different surfaces

The documentation allows Nadia to have materials for diffraction that will in turn inform the way she plans her lessons for the days and weeks to come. When she sees what the children have decided to place up for documentation purposes, she is able to see which parts of their learning they value and believe to be important or of interest.

Vignette 5: the snail engages with different materials as it moves along

Nadia responds to the children's curiosity about insects (see Vignette 1) by preparing an enquiry which invites ideas and opportunities for finding out more about insects. This starts with a dialogue in the classroom, followed by some online researching and then moving into the art room. During the morning, the children are given a range of different materials to learn more about insects. Joanne's research with the children takes place while Nadia spent time in the art room with

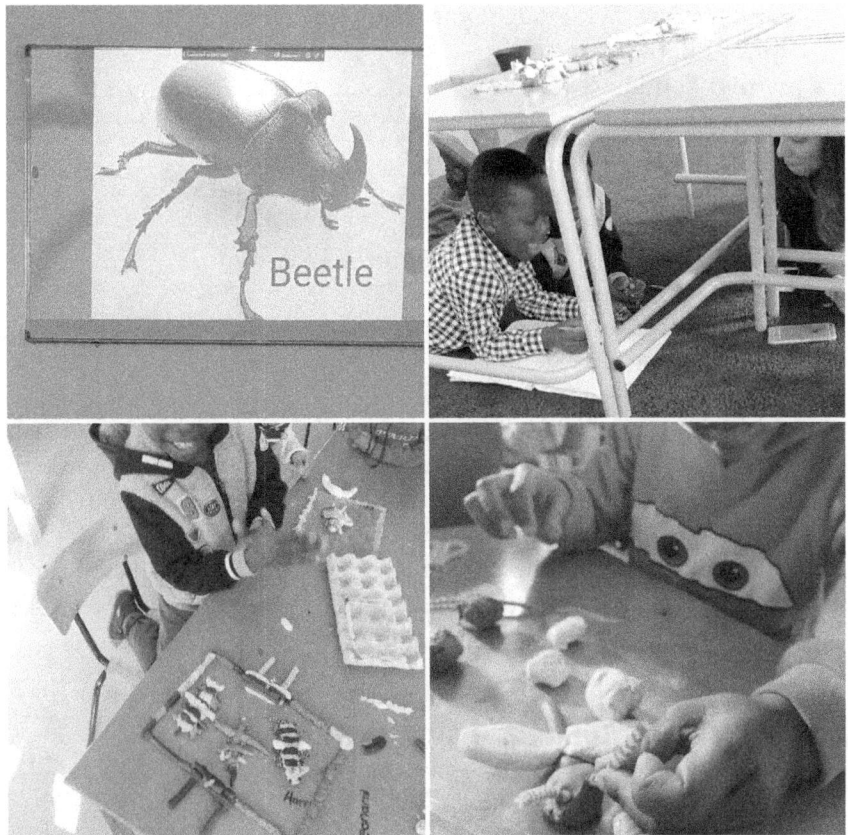

Figure 11.7 Insects on the move

the children. The focus group children autonomously make the decision to bring some of the playdough insects with them to the focus group session with Joanne. Learning about insects is not limited to a particular lesson or teacher, but rather is an ongoing worlding process. The insects become part of the research data as they become entangled with technology, play and learning.

> **Joanne**: So at the moment, I feel like there's lots of insects flying around here.
> **Child** 1: There's one insect.
> **Joanne**: And there's lots of insects on the table and we've also got some of our thoughts from last week.

The children playfully continue with their ideas about insects through song as one child teaches Joanne and the focus group about his knowledge about insects.

> **Sipho**: Insects, insects coming all the way
> From different gardens, playing on the way.

Joanne: Wow! Who taught you that beautiful song?
Sipho: I know it.
Joanne: You know it? Okay, let's all sing it!
[Everyone singing together:]
Insects, insects coming all the way
Playing in the garden on their way.
Joanne: Okay, let's start it again.
Group singing: Insects, insects coming all the way
Playing in the garden
[a bit of confusion as to what lyric comes next, Sabelo helps by singing the final line:] on their way.

Combining Ingold's (2015) proposed inter-running spirals and Barad's (2007) concept of intra-action, the song 'Insects, insects coming all the way. From different gardens, playing on the way' (sung by Sipho) is one of many intra-spiralling lines with/in this collaborative enquiry with child, insects, Nadia, school, Joanne, learning, bodies and play. The coiling of planned activities based on the research instruments, the flying insects, carpet, movement and hand gestures is entangled in the performance of corresponding lines.

Vignette 6: snails' shells are spirals and coils

As overlapping loops, the spiral also 'comes back in on itself' when the children create mandalas in their school's carpark using white chalk. Nadia notices how the children cross over and in between different themes and concepts while exploring. The very space they used a few weeks prior for creating body maps and, in weeks prior to that, tracing out their shadows, now became a space for mandalas, patterns, numbers and bodies. The lines of learning are made visible in this space as the spiralling of different drawings is chalked onto the tarmac.

Figure 11.8 Playing on their way

Vignette 7: snails move across surfaces and in-between places

The children move seamlessly through the physical spaces of the school classrooms. On many occasions, the corresponding lines with learning about homes, maps and mandalas are in multiple places. The children are seen walking home and returning later to play and add more detail to the drawings they made earlier. This example shows the relationship between learning in schools, home and the children's environment as they travel with their learning through and in between different locations. In Figure 11.9, a home is being made with petals and flowers for bees. A correspondence of lines of thought about homes and insects is being produced on the pavement.

Drawing a line under it

This chapter offers opportunities to re-configure early years and primary practice through a notion of collaborative learning that includes the more-than-human

Figure 11.9 Homes in different places

(snail) and, as a result, renders children living in poverty capable, rich and resourceful. Nadia's twofold use of photography ('what if') in her teaching in the Global South offers a re-imagination of what *is* happening and what else could be happening in classrooms, also in the Global North.

Through the character of a snail with its home on its back and sticky trails, we follow the traces and read the classroom in the geopolitical context of a South African informal settlement. Celebrating slowness, snails have their own pace and also bring their own home with them. Snails have/are homes. Re-turning to what has already been 'covered' in teaching helps to make the learning stick when reading a classroom that is entangled with 'pace', 'place', 'slowness', 'homes' and other concepts that reconfigure 'collaborative learning'.

As Barad (2014, p. 182) argues, returning does not imply a 'going back'. 'The world "holds" the memory of all traces; or rather, the world is its memory (enfolded materialisation)' (Barad, 2014, p. 182). Re-turning to Nadia's teaching, we extend a line and tangle with Ingold's proposition:

> To make a straight line, it is necessary to connect two points, for example by means of a ruler, prior to advancing from one to the other, using the edge as a jig to guide one's movements. But a living line, which must perforce find its way as it goes along, has

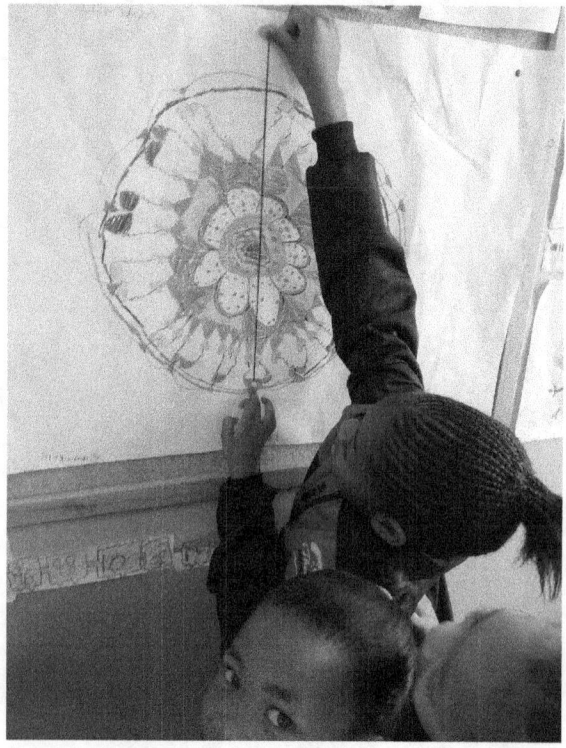

Figure 11.10 A meshwork of lines

continually to attend to its path, adjusting or 'fine-tuning' the direction of its advancing tip as the journey unfolds.

(2015, p. 58)

Unlocking research in practice: provocations for group discussion

Table 11.1 is a collaboration of vignettes and questions created through our chapter writing as co-authors with/in our computers and smartphones. As we return to them, we believe they are one of the lines that keep the spiralling of this chapter moving. It reminds us that learning does not start with questions or end with them. So instead of finishing with another set of questions, we invite readers of this chapter to re-turn to the 12 questions in Table 11.1 as they are enmeshed. We do this as part of the never-ending work of tracing, leaving slimy traces and thereby opening up new traces with questions yet to come.

Notes

1. For the significance of writing 're-turn' instead of 'return', see the next section.
2. Permission for the use of the data and images was granted by the School of Education, University of Cape Town. For details see Marsh et al. (2020).
3. Grade 1 in South Africa is attended by 6 and/or 7-year-olds.
4. PGCE stands for the Postgraduate Certificate in Education. This 1-year teacher education qualification in South Africa will no longer exist after 2020 for the Foundation phase (5-8-year-olds) and the Intermediate phase (9-12-year-olds) and will be replaced by a 2-year degree.
5. A fractal is the visual representation of a mathematical formula (by giving colours to numbers). Flower is one of a class of formulae that create simple three-dimensional shapes which grow more complex as the shape is repeated in miniature around the edges of the first shape. Its infinite, spiralling complexity renders it a useful metaphor for the community of enquiry pedagogy of philosophy for children.
6. The more-than-human refers to non-human bodies, e.g. snail, phone, floor, slime, wooden blocks, pencil, atmosphere.
7. *Onto* means being. So ontology is the science of what is, or exists.
8. The use of 'intra' instead of 'inter' in this chapter indicates an ontological move from individual existence to a relational one. Introduced by Karen Barad (2007), *intra-action* is at the heart of her agential realism and based on a diffractive reading of the findings of quantum theory that assumes that entangled phenomena, not individual bodies, are ontologically prior in metaphysics.
9. See, for example, the spider and brittle star in Karen Barad's work (2007).

References

Barad, K. (2007). *Meeting the universe halfway: Quantum physics and the entanglement of matter and meaning*. Durham, NC: Duke University Press.

Barad, K. (2014). Diffracting diffraction: Cutting together-apart. *Parallax*, *20*(3), 168–187. https://doi.org/10.1080/13534645.2014.927623.

Freire, P. (1970/2014). *The pedagogy of the oppressed* (30th anniversary ed.). New York: Bloomsbury.

Ingold, T. (2015). *The life of lines*. Abingdon, UK: Routledge.

Marsh, J., Murris, K., Ng'ambi, D., Parry, R., Scott, F., Thomsen, B. S. . . . Woodgate, A. (2020). *Children, technology and play*. LEGO Foundation. Retrieved December 21, 2020, from https://www.legofoundation.com/media/2965/children-tech-and-play_full-report.pdf

Murris, K. (2016). *The posthuman child: Educational transformation through philosophy with picturebooks*. Abingdon, UK: Routledge.

Murris, K., & Haynes, J. (2002). *Storywise: Thinking through stories; Issue 2*. Newport: DialogueWorks.

Murris, K., & Haynes, J. (2020). Troubling authority and material bodies: Creating *sympoietic* pedagogies for working with children and practitioners. *Global Education Review*, 7(2), 24–42.

Murris, K., & Menning, S. F. (2019). Introduction to the special issue. *Video Journal of Education and Pedagogy*, *4*, 1–8. Retrieved December 21, 2020, from https://brill.com/view/journals/vjep/4/1/vjep.4.issue-1.xml.

Murris, K., Reynolds, R., & Peers, J. (2018). Reggio Emilia inspired philosophical teacher education in the Anthropocene: Posthuman child and the family (tree). *Journal of Childhood Studies*, *43*(1), 15–29.

Reggio Emilia Approach. (2020). *100 languages*. Reggio Children. Retrieved December 21, 2020, from https://www.reggiochildren.it/en/reggio-emilia-approach/100-linguaggi-en/.

CHAPTER

12

'What can be otherwise'[1]: embodying a collective *phronesis* (or practical wisdom) for sculpting new creativities in primary education and beyond

Julia Flutter

Introduction

To my surprise, my life's sixth decade has introduced me to the world of sailing, and I have found myself, literally and figuratively, at sea. From the moment I first set out on this oddly unsettling and challenging quest, it has proved to be, in every conceivable way, a voyage of discovery. Having absolutely no nautical knowledge, my learning curve was necessarily steep to allow me to become part of a small crew, sailing 800 miles from West Scotland to the English Channel. Experiencing this voyage and its moments of near disaster led me to reflect afterwards on the value of the different kinds of teaching and learning responsible for my survival. Rather like teacher education, official sailing courses provide knowledge of theory and regulations as well as hands-on learning under expert supervision, but I quickly discovered that coping with life at sea also demands a different kind of wisdom – a practical, embodied and collective wisdom – that comes from being part of the seafaring community. This community willingly shares its expertise and local knowledge, and always stand ready to respond to a fellow sailor's emergency call. Practical wisdom also builds with the craft knowledge obtained from one's own direct encountering of different winds, waters and ways of doing things. Teaching, like sailing, depends upon developing this kind of practical wisdom, I believe.

To become an accomplished educator (or sailor) who can meet whatever challenges arise in the classroom (or at sea) with confidence, calm and diligent care in order to reach the chosen destination, one needs more than theoretical principles, research, policy and regulations to hand – such professional expertise requires a collective and cumulative practical wisdom derived from becoming part of an expert community and from honing one's judgment through practice and reflection.

In this chapter I want to explore this notion of collective practical wisdom further, as I look at the voyages of primary educators, education researchers and arts practitioners in this book. I will also be introducing and expanding on this idea of practical wisdom, referring to it by its other name, *phronesis*, coined by the Classical Greek philosopher Aristotle, whose work has offered inspiration and direction to educators for over two thousand years. The journey through this chapter charts the spiralling trails of new creativities we have been encountering throughout this book to discover where they lead and to consider what new possibilities could emerge from these innovative starting points. However, we begin this chapter with an activity which helps to set the compass for our journey of exploration, before we move on to look at the examples of collective phronesis unfolding in classrooms, schools and research. In the concluding section, I will be considering some of the wider implications and new horizons for sculpting new creativities through collective phronesis for teacher professionalism.

Opening the box: A creative beginning to our journeying together

Before we venture further into this chapter, I would like to present an activity which takes you on a journey of exploration into your own creativities.

The activity

Begin by imagining that you have set out on a long voyage to explore the New World. During your voyage, you land on an island and there you discover, hidden inside a cave, a beautiful wooden box. Tantalisingly, you cannot yet see what is inside because it is closed and locked. A small brass key lies in your hand. You notice it is engraved with the word 'if'. Place the key in the keyhole and turn the key, slowly and gently. The lock clicks open. Lift the lid and look inside. What do you find in the box?

Now, imagine what you have discovered inside the box. Through drawing, writing, singing, speaking, sewing, carving or by whatever means you wish, convey to someone else (an adult or a child) what you discovered in the box and what its discovery meant to you. Take as long as you wish to complete this activity and, while you set about imagining and creating the box

'What can be otherwise'

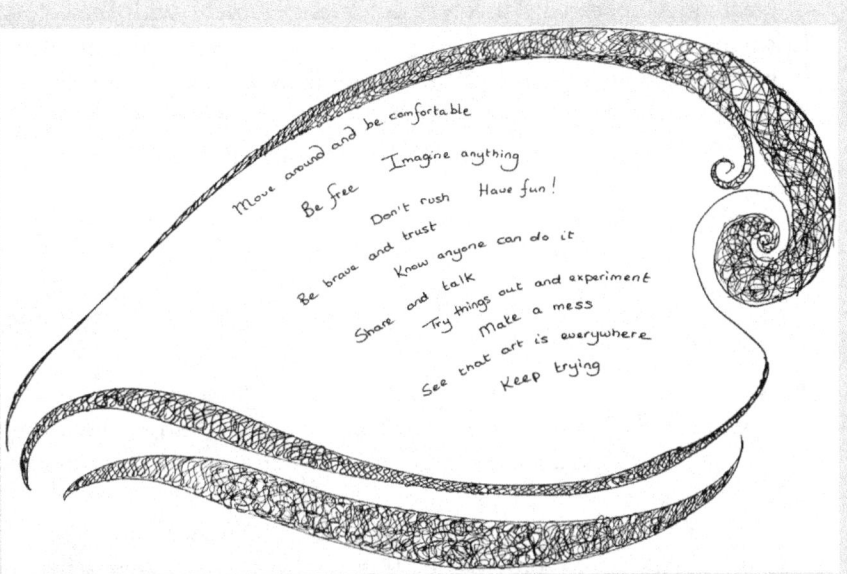

Figure 12.1 Children's wishes (see Lee & Stepney, this volume)

contents, remind yourself of the children's wishes described in Elsa Lee and Sarah Stepney's chapter (this volume), heeding their advice as you explore your own creativities (see Figure 12.1).

Reflecting on the activity

Afterwards, note down your responses to the task and think about the following questions:

- How did you feel as you set about working on this task?
- What inspired your thinking about the contents you chose?
- Was the 'wish list' helpful to your thinking and creating?
- Were there aspects of the task that were particularly challenging? If so, why?

If you would like to share what you have created, please tell me about it by visiting the *Unlocking Research* website (unlockingresearch.org) to upload an image or text.

Enabling new creativities

Hopefully the activity will have helped you to touch base with the experience of being creative and it is also intended as a reminder that the teaching and learning of creativities necessarily involves direct engagement with these forms of knowledge and skill. Of course, we know that learning does not simply happen through a process of exposure and continuous practice. As our guide on this journey, Aristotle argued over 2,000 years ago that it is not only by doing that we acquire knowledge, skills and capacities but through being taught:

> as a result of building houses well, people will be good house builders; but as a result of doing so badly, they will be bad ones. If this were not the case, there would be no need of a teacher.
>
> (Aristotle, 2011, p. 27)

As we have seen throughout this book, the role of educators in nurturing children's creativities is far more subtle and complex than simply providing opportunities to be creative and steering children towards a fixed measurable outcome or performance.

The aim of this book, together with the other books in the *Unlocking Research* series, is to support all those who are engaged with primary education in bridging the gap between research, theory and practice. Although these accounts reflect the practices and outcomes within specific contexts, each affords us richly detailed insights that have resonance for all those engaged in primary education. Each of these vignettes of practice and research add to a growing repository of teacher professional knowledge, derived from lived experiences of teaching and learning within classrooms and schools. Narrative case studies like these are vitally important because, as Bent Flyvbjerg (academic researcher and Chair of Oxford Global Projects) argues, such context-based evidence produces 'the type of context-dependent knowledge which research on learning shows to be necessary to allow people to develop from rule-based beginners to virtuoso experts' (2006, p. 222). Each of the narrative case studies presented in this book therefore offers us opportunities to explore and to learn from new vantage points. We can now begin to draw these insights together, forming a map or assemblage through which it becomes possible to discern more clearly the 'new ways of thinking about expertise, pedagogies and learning contexts' that we have been encountering and to begin to 'reimagine primary education futures that focus on creative environments, ecologies and practices' (Harris, this volume).

Although many who advocate for research-informed practice in education tend to emphasise the importance of large-scale quantitative studies, using methods such as randomised control trials, it can be difficult to translate these theories and evidential findings into recommendations for sustainable practice outside the parameters and funded resources of a research project intervention. Whilst these kinds of evidence raise awareness, suggest new directions for practice, generate theories and highlight trends to inform policy, they also tend to be used to construct off-the-shelf solutions that rarely reflect the variance and specificities across different contexts and circumstances, or the subtle nuances of educational practice. Rather than seeking to proffer 'solutions', the vivid narrative case studies presented by the authors in this book afford us differing perspectives on teaching and new creativities that can be used as springboards for professional discussion, collaboration and an opening out towards new possibilities for developing practice and thinking. As Pamela Burnard and James Biddulph suggest in Chapter 3, this collaborative approach to research and practice enables educators to imagine what might be, to explore options and to ask questions in a spirit of professional collegiality. Joining an innovative, collegial community of enquiry results in a strengthening of educators' confidence for sculpting new creativities. In the next section I look at how educators can navigate through these new waters using a collective phronesis as a compass to guide their directions of travel.

Finding collective phronesis

The first book in the *Unlocking Research* series, *Inspiring primary curriculum design*, invited teachers and researchers to begin unlocking the door between research and practice, opening up new pathways for enhancing practice (Biddulph & Flutter, 2021). We acknowledged that bridging this gap is not unproblematic, however, and we recognised the obstacles, constraints and uncertainties that can impede teachers' efforts to develop research-informed practices. We argued that, while theory, evidence and practice contribute to the development of professional knowledge and expertise, educational practices and decision-making also hinge crucially on ethical considerations. Drawing on Aristotle's philosophical idea of intellectual virtues, we suggested that:

> teachers, individually and collectively as a profession, [should] engage with published research evidence and theory (*episteme*) and consider this knowledge alongside wisdom drawn from their expertise and experience of their own classrooms and contexts (*techne*); in combination, these two strands give rise to a range of differing possibilities for action and it is through the third strand (*phronesis*) – involving reflection and informed, ethical judgement – that action can be decided upon and taken.
>
> (Biddulph & Flutter, 2021, p. 177)

Phronesis is becoming increasingly recognised as an important facet of professionalism and of public decision making more generally. However, there are differences of opinion regarding precisely what phronesis means and entails. Elizabeth Kinsella and Allan Pitman offer this definition which places an emphasis on its key role in shaping professional action: 'Phronesis . . . is an intellectual virtue that implies ethics. It involves deliberation that is based on values, concerned with practical judgement and informed by reflection. It is pragmatic, variable, context-dependent and oriented towards action' (2012a, p. 2). The case studies in this book reveal a common thread that has clear resonance with this definition and help us to expand our conceptualisation of what this concept can offer. We have seen how teachers' values-based deliberation, informed by theory, evidence and practice, can profoundly transform their thinking and practice, and this finding beckons us towards a proposal for a new conceptualisation of phronesis as a cornerstone for the teaching profession.

Throughout this book (the third in the *Unlocking Research* series), we have seen how the phrase 'evidence-informed' forms only part of the complex interplay of professional knowledge development and practice. Phronesis in education involves more than a straightforward, uncritical accumulation of evidence or putting together a pedagogical repertoire; it requires an individual and shared professional disposition that strives to embody ethical objectives and embraces an ongoing commitment to reflective practice and improvement. To help us to explore what this collective phronesis involves it may be helpful to begin by focusing on an example. I have chosen Chapter 10, 'Unlocking creative leadership in the primary school' by Megan Crawford, Deborah Outhwaite and Matthew Crawford because phronesis in action can often be discerned more readily at the level of management decision making and it is possible to identify how phronesis influences and transforms professional life with clarity. Explicitly expressed personal and institutional values are the starting point in phronesis and will be continuously threaded through the decisions and actions which take place as part of a sustained creative quest which aims to seek out new patterns and possibilities (Crawford et al., this volume). The chapter's authors emphasise that values, together with shared norms and meanings, have to be made explicit at the outset, in order to find new patterns and possibilities within a school. The values underpinning the programmes described in the two case studies are immediately identifiable in Megan, Deborah and Matthew's unfolding narrative as they describe the school trusts' objectives: for example, in terms of progressing the needs of their communities and through creating the conditions for collaboration among teachers and leaders. The authors also emphasise the importance of those in leadership roles making explicit how people's work is valued and contributes to the creative capacity of the schools and trusts by supporting opportunities for dialogue and reflection.

Values, therefore, are clearly expressed at the outset and are used to steer the creative questing of collective phronesis. This questing then moves onward, navigating via relevant knowledge drawn from theoretical principles and research (*episteme*) and practical, context-based experience (*techne*) towards its destination. In Chapter 10 we see a theory from business and management studies being applied to leadership and management in education (Crawford, 2003), and providing a structure for thinking about creative leadership which feeds forward into the development of the two case study initiatives. Local knowledge of the schools, trusts and the communities they serve allowed each of the initiatives to be tailored to respond sensitively to the needs of these differing contexts. The chapter authors express their collective phronetic approach as being positioned 'at the interface between practice and theory'.

Of course, many educators, schools and organisations are research informed, so what distinguishes the work described in Chapter 10, and our other chapters, as examples of collective phronesis? To answer that question, I will return briefly to my sailing analogy. If we simply draw on ad-hoc use of theory, research and practice-based experience to guide our direction and leave values aside, we risk leaving ourselves at the mercy of the tides of circumstance (such as policy, social and economic pressures, and so on). In adopting collective phronesis, we initiate a values-driven questing that harnesses knowledge and experience (*episteme* and *techne*) to unleash creative possibilities and, importantly, to test that our actions are directing us the right way – towards the destinations we are aiming for. Whilst the tides of policy and social pressure still operate, collective phronesis urges us to consider responding to these influences in ways that run less risk of throwing us 'off course' and align with our professional values.

Alison Peacock, Chief Executive Officer of the Chartered College of Teaching, points out in the second book in the *Unlocking Research* series, *Reimagining professional development in schools*, that the future of teacher professionalism hinges crucially on 'practice and policy [being] informed by a combination of professional knowledge and wisdom, combined with the theory of research evidence' (Peacock, 2021, p. 21). Based on the testimonies of the chapter contributors in this book series, and on my own experiences across three decades of working with teachers and learners in education research, I would suggest that teacher professionalism is also founded on two other important principles: collegiality and creativity. The notion of collegiality expresses the collaborative sharing of values and knowledge which underpins professionalism. In education, professional collegiality lies at the heart of movements like university – school research partnerships, the Chartered College of Teaching and teacher-led research movements (both online and face to face). An interesting example of collegiality in an educational research initiative was the Consulting Pupils about Teaching and Learning Network[2] coordinated by Jean Rudduck and colleagues in which primary and secondary schools across the country supported each other to set up their own school-based research projects involving innovative pupil voice projects. This ground-breaking network enabled teachers across primary and secondary sectors to work collaboratively and to share their research experiences, findings and outcomes of pupil voice initiatives as part of an ongoing conversation.

Creativity, as one aspect of teacher professionalism, requires a willingness to innovate, to reflect and to be open to challenging taken-for-granted assumptions and habitual ways of doing things. As all the contributors to this book have shown, creativities can act as catalytic forces sparking new ways of thinking, acting and being. However, embarking on these creative journeys requires the momentum of a collective phronesis which harnesses together values and knowledge (*techne* and *episteme*). Figure 12.2 presents an example of one such journey in the form of a visual assemblage depicting Chapter 8 (Fenyvesi, Brownell, Sinnemäki and Lavicza): this assemblage illustrates how collective phronesis originates in values and flows outwards into practice and beyond, contributing to the building of new theory and professional knowledge.

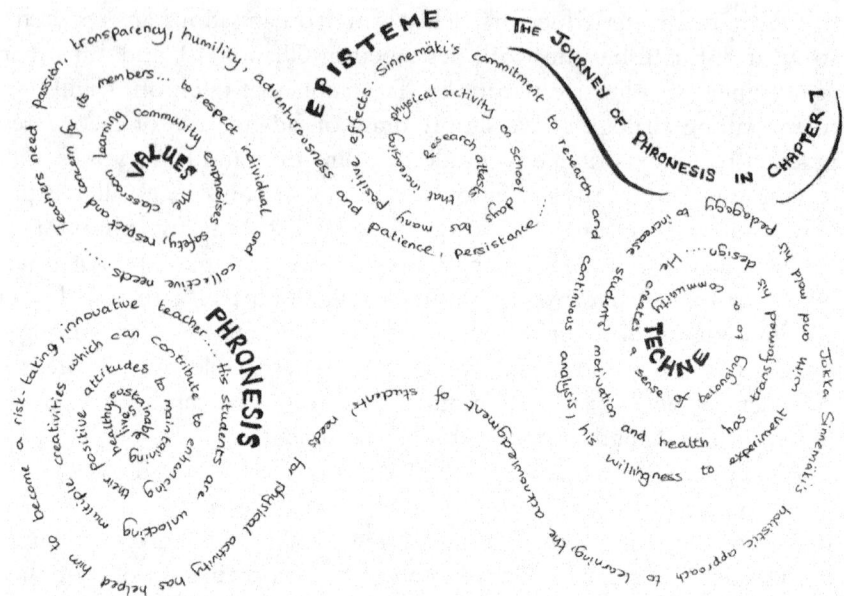

Figure 12.2 The journey of phronesis in Chapter 8 (Fenyvesi, Brownell, Sinnemäki and Lavicza)

Imagining 'what can be otherwise' for primary education

Collective phronesis is not a process, nor can it provide a set of step-by-step tips for busy teachers or inspirational buzzwords for staffroom posters and, yet despite its origins in ancient Greek philosophy, it is far from being a cerebral philosophical idea. Collective phronesis is profoundly pragmatic and reflects 'a practical rationality concerned with the actual doing of things within the embodied nature of lived experience' (Pickup, 2020, p. 11). We can observe this collective phronesis playing out in each of the narrative case studies presented in this book. This collective phronesis is crucial because, as American researcher Austin Pickup argues, it configures teaching as more than an act of 'delivery' or a repertoire of pedagogical strategies:

> The first implication of an embodied phronesis is that it reframes the practice of teaching as an ethically engaged act rather than a technical procedure . . . a theoretical framework of embodied phronesis 'works' to disrupt the dominant frame of the teacher as technician and reorient teachers toward a more ethically and materially engaged conceptualization of the profession.
>
> (Pickup, 2020, p. 16)

Naturally, it is always tempting to look for road maps that seem to promise the quickest route to achieving objectives and resolving dilemmas. However, collective phronesis is not a mapping exercise, it is a disposition – a collective mindset – that envisions and enacts professional decision making and practice as collaborative, ongoing and multifaceted. Rather than a set of instructions, collective phronesis invites us to move onwards deliberatively, allowing time to reflect on the spiralling 'snail trails' of evidence, theory and practice like those described in Chapter 11 by Karin Murris, Joanne Peers and Nadia Woodward. Paying such close attention to evidence from practice and engaging critically with theory and research opens up 'new ways of thinking, being and doing' (Harris, this volume). The implications of building professional expertise in this way through collective phronesis potentially extend beyond the creation of opportunities for professional reflection and critical dialogue (*praxis*). As Canadian researchers Elizabeth Kinsella and Allan Pitman suggest, the ramifications of adopting the disposition of phronesis can potentially be far-reaching:

> Phronesis provides a language and a vision for practice that resists a passive acquiescence to the discourses of professional life that are increasingly instrumentalist, technicist, and managerial. The professional is not simply a technician; rather, the professional is charged with the tasks of making complex interpretive judgements and taking action, as spaces for learning and for professional development . . . Phronesis is a concept of interest, and of hope, for elaborating current conceptions of professional knowledge and for advancing an approach to practice in the professions that seeks to fill the void in current practices – an approach that is felt as a morally informed guiding force oriented toward a wiser path.
>
> (2012b, p. 171)

Taking this idea of collective phronesis a step further, it becomes possible to discern an exciting possibility of change at a society-wide level: for if this practical wisdom is embodied as a constitutional foundation for teacher professionalism, it could lead 'educators to new knowledge and new processes of becoming as they strive toward "what can be otherwise" (Aristotle, 2000, p. 107) in a more socially just world' (Pickup, 2020, p. 18). Figure 12.3 sets out a proposal for this reconceptualised concept of collective phronesis, showing its potential as a driving mechanism in a dynamic interplay between policy, practice, theory and research which could help to replace the fragmentation and tensions that have long plagued education. Each cog's movement in this assemblage sets in motion actions and reactions in the others via the central cog to reflect the way in which the guiding force of collective phronesis can serve to mediate between policy, practice, theory and research. Clearly such a vision would also be pertinent to other professions, including the medical, legal and financial sectors, and it could relate to any scale of system, whether local, national or international.

To illustrate collective phronesis, we can turn to a high-profile example. The Cambridge Primary Review[3] (2004–2010), led by Robin Alexander at the Faculty of Education, University of Cambridge, was the largest independent review of primary education conducted in England. I was a member of the review's core

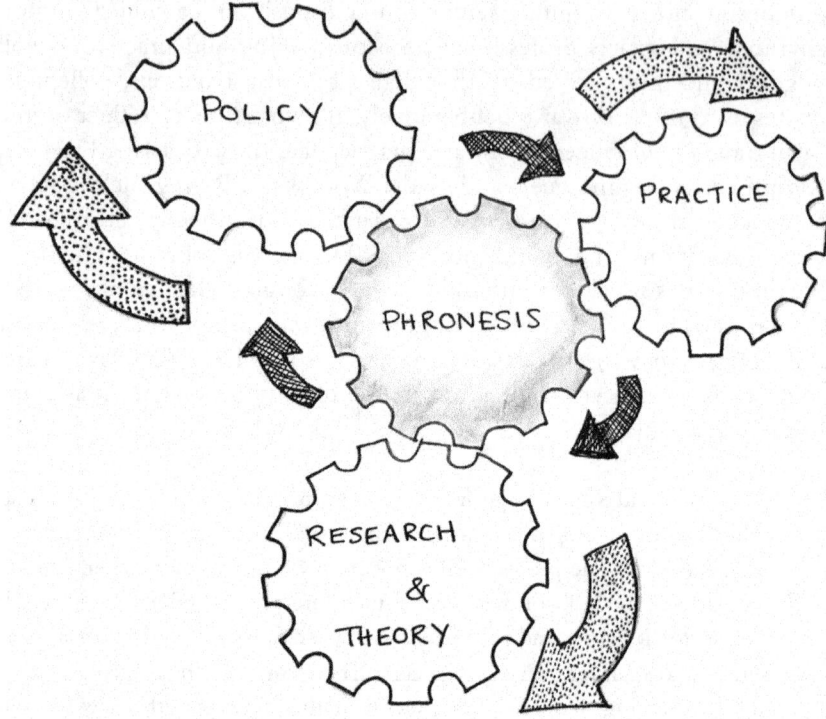

Figure 12.3 Collective phronesis as a pivotal force for policy, practice and research

research team and a co-author of its final report, and later I served as a director for the Cambridge Primary Review Trust, which sought to build on the review's recommendations. From the moment of its inception our team placed a profound emphasis on the importance of aims and values in thinking about primary education, as our remit explains:

> With respect to public provision in England, the Review will seek to identify the purposes which the primary phase of education should serve, the values which it should espouse, the curriculum and learning environment which it should provide, and the conditions which are necessary in order to ensure both that these are of the highest and most consistent quality possible, and that they address the needs of children and society over the coming decades.
>
> (Alexander et al., 2010, p. 15)

The review's evidence gathering included an extensive trawl of rigorous, up-to-date theory and research, and a comprehensive overview of England's policy relating to primary children's lives and learning spanning 40 years. Alongside this formal evidence (*episteme*), we also sought opinion-based data through interviews, focus groups and written submissions to gather people's experiences of, and perspectives on, primary education (*techne*). Contributors included children, parents, educators, policy makers, teacher educators, educational and professional organisations, employers, community and faith representatives, and many others.

After analysing these different strands of evidence, the emergent findings fed into a values-driven quest to put forward a tentative new vision for primary education (*phronesis*) which combined 'evidence, analysis and conclusions together with recommendations for both national policy and the work of schools and other relevant agencies' (Alexander et al., 2010, p. 15). It is important to note, however, that the review was not seeking to put forward solutions: our conclusions and recommendations were set out for discussion, not as prescriptions. We hoped that our efforts would feed into public and professional debate to stimulate changes in policy and practice at all levels. At system level, the review exemplifies how phronesis could operate through bringing policy, practice, research and theory into a closer frame of reciprocal interaction. However, the review's emphasis on community and localism also reflects the ideographic facet of phronesis which acknowledges context as a central consideration in educational practice, policy and thinking. This idea is a key argument that also finds resonance with many of the narrative case studies in this book. The review's final report specifically calls for recognition of local agency and context with respect to all aspects of primary education:

> The conclusion . . . is that within a broad statutory framework of aims and principles such as we have discussed, detailed aims, along with the fleshing out of curricula and decisions about pedagogy, are best determined at the level of the community and school or group of schools. Local initiative implies considerable variation in the culture of individual schools, in accordance with the diverse aspirations and experiences of the many different communities which public education serves. Such variation has its problems in a society in which the movement of families from place to place and region to region is commonplace but in general it is a source of strength within a broad statutory framework. It encourages innovation, strengthens commitment, and empowers the schools themselves. And few things are more important than to restore to schools and their members a sense of empowerment and self-respect.
>
> (Alexander et al., 2010, p. 200)

In this example we can see how phronesis presents a fundamentally different, and potentially transformative, way of thinking, being and acting. Using a framework of collective phronesis set the Cambridge Primary Review onto a certain course which started out from an explicit foundation of values and aims, before moving on to raise questions about how these values can best be enacted. It then gathered evidence and theory to seek answers, charting, evaluating and analysing this material carefully and using it creatively to present new possibilities in furtherance of its values and aims. If we as educators, both individually and collectively as a profession, choose to adopt a similar course we will find it easier to avoid being engulfed by policy directives and external pressures, and led astray by the beguiling chimera of quick-fix solutions. Collective phronesis offers a powerful steer to our decision making and frames the search for evidence and theory to address specific needs and questions in relation to our practice. We can then interpret and apply policy in ways that align more closely with our values, and our decisions can be supported and justified by recourse to research evidence, collective professional expertise and substantive theory which has been tried and tested against the lived realities in primary education settings.

Travelling hopefully

Perhaps the activity at the beginning of this chapter reminded you of another story about the opening of a box: Pandora's box? In this well-known, cautionary tale, Pandora's curiosity releases all the evils of the world and from her fictional misfortune we learn the lesson that some boxes are best left undone. We could speculate that, if Pandora had been wise enough to carry out some research or consulted others, then her story may perhaps have had a more positive outcome. Creativity, imagination and curiosity can be used for good – to delight and inspire, or deepen understanding of ourselves and the universe we are part of – or for ill – to devise new forms of cruelty and combat, of ways to deceive and commit crimes. What determines the choice of path is a largely a matter of ethics and of wisdom. Together with knowledge and skills, creativities are generally regarded as amongst the most important educational objectives in modern societies, and yet our current curricula find little space for developing the capacities for practical wisdom that ultimately determine what an educated person, an educated profession or an educated society do with their funds of knowledge, skills and creativities.

As I write, the world faces an ongoing global pandemic and is waking up to the consequences of climate change: it is becoming sharply apparent that future generations will need to be equipped with collective phronesis to respond to such world-scale dilemmas. As COVID-19 has taught us, when faced with life-or-death decisions, actions cannot be wholly determined by recourse to science and technology. Brooklyn-based American philosopher, Richard Bernstein, provides us with a starting point in our search for answers, writing with disquieting prescience in 1983:

> At a time when the threat of total annihilation no longer seems to be an abstract possibility but the most imminent and real potentiality, it becomes all the more imperative to try again and again to foster and nurture those forms of communal life in which dialogue, conversation, phronesis, practical discourse and judgment are in need for being concretely embodied in our everyday practices.
>
> (Bernstein, 1983, p. 229)

Education undeniably holds the key to humanity's future but if we do not yet have answers, what can be taught? As primary phase educators, this responsibility may feel daunting and, at times (particularly in 2020), overwhelming, but what gives us heart and hope is that there is always one constant point of light to steer by: the children we teach. Children have an incredible affinity with the game of 'if . . .'[4] and, when presented with an activity like the one at the beginning of this chapter, they release their imaginations and creativities in ways that are unfettered by the narrowed confines of adult expectations, as you will discover if you try doing so. Each new generation brings with it a chance of doing things differently and fresh ways to imagine 'what can be otherwise', but navigating future choices and challenges will require opening the box of creative possibilities unlocked with the key of collective phronesis.

Unlocking research in practice: provocations for group discussion

1. Choose a chapter in this book and trace out the spiralling trails of phronesis within it. How are the authors' values expressed? What kinds of knowledge (*techne* and *episteme*) do the authors draw on? How is this knowledge used to open up new creativities and possibilities?
2. Thinking about your own context, what does your school need to know in order to respond effectively to the needs of your local community? What kinds of opportunities are there for creating stronger links between your school and the community?
3. How do you think policy and practice should interrelate? Could it be beneficial for policy makers and practitioners to work together more closely? By what mechanisms could this be achieved?
4. Using both the chapters in this book and other case studies on the *Unlocking Research* website (www.unlockingresearch.org), find and map out new ideas that inform, inspire and guide your own creativities and practices.
5. Read the 'Prelude' by Professor Joy Higgs, Director of the Education for Practice Institute, Charles Sturt University, Bathurst, Australia (in the following section). In what ways do you think the professional practices of the two young teachers, Tironis and Novitius, might differ?

❖ ❖ PRELUDE ❖ ❖[5]

Professor Joy Higgs
Charles Sturt University, Australia

In the autumn of his years,
Veteratoris (the experienced practitioner)

paused at the end of his day
to ask his young novices his usual question,
What have you learned this day?

Tironis (the beginner) replied:
I have decided I want to be a great teacher.
How can I learn to teach like you?
Novitius (the newcomer) asked:
I want to be a good practitioner.
How can I learn to be wise like you?

Veteratoris reflected for a while,
wondering how to answer.
Finally he replied,
let me tell you a story.

When I was a young man,
I went to visit a great and wise man
called Aristotle.
He told me the mystery
of the three intellectual virtues
who spent their time pursuing
teaching, learning, and practice.

Episteme, a youth of some stature
brought the virtue of independent knowledge.
He loved science with a passion
and applauded truths that were universal,
invariable, and independent of context.

Techne was the practical one.
Her desire was to create
and to learn how things worked
and how to make things
that suited the current task and goal.
Her favourite answer was 'it depends.'

Phronesis was the quiet achiever.
She often pondered over whether
her planned actions would be wise and proper
as well as practical.
She was fascinated by two ideas
praxis – a tantalising blend
of reflective, right, and transformative practice

and poiesis — developing technique
through artistry and creativity.

Veteratoris finished his story by saying,
to me, each of these three virtues
demonstrates excellence of mind.
I want you to think about
what you want for your future
and what sort of person,
teacher, or practitioner
you want to be —
Tironis and Novitius —
and come back next week
with your answers.

Barely had he finished speaking
when Tironis exclaimed:
I don't need a week — I know already.
If I am to become a great teacher
then science must be my guide.
I will spend all my time
searching for The Truth
I will teach from strength not 'maybes.'

❖

One week later,
Novitius waited after class
to speak to Veteratoris.
She said:
I want to be a good practitioner
so I need to learn the virtue of Techne.
I want to critique my practice
so I need the virtue of Episteme
to learn new ideas and strategies
that science can offer.
And, more than everything else,
I want someday to be wise like you
to make what I do
make a positive difference to people's lives
so I need to accept the challenge of Phronesis
to bring reflection, ethics, and practicality
to my journey of becoming
a good and wise practitioner.

❖ ❖ ❖

Notes

1. Aristotle (2011). Although Aristotle's works reflect a very different time and context, his thinking on ethics and the nature of knowledge catalyse new lines of reasoning that continue to have resonance with modern-day realities. Over the two millennia since his death, the quest he set in motion to consider 'what can be otherwise' goes on, calling each new generation to reconsider the question of how life can be lived virtuously for the good of all.
2. This network was part of the Economic and Social Research Council's Teaching and Learning Research Programme Phase 1 Network Project 'Consulting Pupils about Teaching and Learning' co-ordinated by Professor Jean Rudduck and based at Homerton College, University of Cambridge (Rudduck & Flutter, 2004).
3. The Cambridge Primary Review was led by Robin Alexander from 2006 to 2012. Its award-winning final report, *Children, their world, their education* (Alexander et al., 2010) has received international recognition for its transformative vision for achieving excellence in the primary phase.
4. As identified by researchers such as Craft, Cremin, Burnard, Dragovic, and Chappell (2012) as 'possibility thinking' at the heart of all forms and types of creativity.
5. Higgs, J. (2012). Realising practical wisdom from the pursuit of wise practice. In E. Kinsella & A. Pitman (Eds.), *Phronesis as professional knowledge: Practice wisdom in the professions* (pp. 73–85). Brill/Sense. Reproduced with kind permission of Professor Higgs and Brill/Sense.

References

Alexander, R. et al. (2010). *Children, their world, their education: Final report and recommendations of the Cambridge Primary Review*. London and New York: Routledge.

Aristotle. (2011). *Aristotle's Nichomachean ethics: A new translation* (R. C. Bartlett & S. D. Collins, Trans.). Chicago, IL: University of Chicago Press.

Bernstein, R. J. (1983). *Pragmatism and hermeneutics beyond objectivism and relativism: Science, hermeneutics and praxis*. Philadelphia, PA: University of Pennsylvania Press.

Biddulph, J., & Flutter, J. (2021). Unlocking research to new possibilities. In J. Biddulph & J. Flutter (Eds.), *Inspiring primary curriculum design* (pp. 174–179). Abingdon, Oxon and New York: Routledge.

Craft, A., Cremin, T., Burnard, P., Dragovic, T., & Chappell, K. (2012). Possibility thinking: Culminative studies of an evidence-based concept driving creativity? *International Journal of Primary, Elementary and Early Years Education*, 41(5), 538–556. https://doi.org/10.1080/03004279.2012.656671

Crawford, M. (2003). Inventive Management and Wise Leadership. In N. Bennett, M. Crawford, & M. Cartwright (Eds.), *Effective educational leadership* (pp. 62–74). London: Sage.

Flyvbjerg, B. (2006). Five misunderstandings about case-study research. *Qualitative Inquiry*, 12(2), 219–245.

Higgs, J. (2012). Realising practical wisdom from the pursuit of wise practice. In E. Kinsella & A. Pitman (Eds.), *Phronesis as professional knowledge: Practice wisdom in the professions* (pp. 73–85). Rotterdam and Boston, MA: Sense.

Kinsella, E., & Pitman, A. (2012a). Engaging phronesis in professional practice and education. In E. Kinsella & A. Pitman (Eds.), *Phronesis as professional knowledge: Practical wisdom in the professions* (pp. 1–12). Rotterdam and Boston, MA: Sense.

Kinsella, E., & Pitman, A. (2012b). Phronesis as professional knowledge: Implications for education and practice. In E. Kinsella & A. Pitman (Eds.), *Phronesis as professional knowledge: Practical wisdom in the professions* (pp. 163–172). Rotterdam and Boston, MA Sense.

Peacock, A. (2021). The importance of the Chartered College of Teaching: A professional body for the future identity and status of our teachers. In E. Hargreaves & L. Rolls (Eds.), *Reimagining professional development in schools* (pp. 9–22). Abingdon, Oxon: Routledge.

Pickup, A. (2020). Embodied phronesis: Conceptualizing materially engaged practical wisdom in teaching, teacher education and research. *Journal of Thought, 54*, 4–22.

Rudduck, J., & Flutter, J. (2004). *How to improve your school: Giving pupils a voice.* London and New York: Continuum.

Afterword: sculpting new creativities in primary education

Alison Peacock

How can we begin to unleash creativity within our schools? We have read here about what individual teachers, settings and groups of schools have achieved, always, it seems, swimming against the tide of national policy. Essentially, we need teachers who have the confidence, the understanding, and the intellectual and moral drive to enact this vision of a bolder future. The conception and creation of the Chartered College of Teaching is a creative act in itself. My self-determined role as Chief Executive at the Chartered College of Teaching is to create the conditions for professional growth; to begin to shift the culture of what it means to be a teacher; and to enable the profession to develop into a much more confident, informed version of itself, thereby enabling teachers to be recognised for their capacity to think, to respond, to truly put learning first – and to be creative and imaginative in so doing.

My vision for the future of the profession is that we should collectively *own* the concept of career-long professional learning. We must accept that the role of a teacher is complex and challenging, and cannot possibly be mastered within early-career education and experience. Is this where creativities arise? Teachers can build on their practical wisdom by moving beyond intuition through learning from others, through collaboration, discussion and study. This is why I moved from headship to establish a new professional body. I could see that, if we wish to liberate education and enable creativities, we need teachers to be intrinsically motivated rather than waiting for external approval and judgement. This intrinsic motivation will build once we are able to provide opportunities for career-long deep learning and reflection and as this book and the whole series of *Unlocking Research* suggests, we need hope, imagination and boundless possibility thinking. We are beginning this process at the Chartered College by offering teachers access to a research database, to articles, to research summaries and to the opportunity to study for chartered status. We have chartered accountants and engineers – why not teachers?

Afterword

Study combined with moral purpose and the capacity to act is empowering and builds self-efficacy. If we can create a proud expectation that to be truly professional is to embrace lifelong learning, we will begin to see transformative impact in our classrooms. As a professional body that is voluntary to join and open to all teachers, the Chartered College of Teaching offers a chance to engage with learning about teaching in a manner that does not depend on the school budget or institutional priorities. This is about building individual teacher expertise that benefits the learning of others whilst also building the confidence that comes from knowing not just what is being taught but crucially *why* and *how*. This is about engaging everyone in our profession to think, be and act in ways that challenge the status quo and through which we take the responsibility of our profession for ourselves.

My own research as a headteacher was centred around 'learning without limits' (Hart, Drummond, Dixon, & McIntyre, 2004; Swann, Peacock, Hart, & Drummond, 2012; Peacock, 2016). The research team uncovered seven key dispositions, defined as characteristics of creative ethical leadership. I discuss these in the following section and offer these dispositions as an insight into the invitational approach I believe we need to build across the profession. The result could be confident, informed professionals able to surpass external accountability demands. The profession needs to collectively show effectiveness borne out of true connection with every child through the core ambition of building deep learning through trust, co-agency and inclusion.

The first of the seven dispositions is *openness*. Contributors to this book show their openness to ideas, to possibilities, to surprise. This is in contrast to the 'safer' pedagogies based on the belief that there is one right way and that outcomes should be knowable and predictable. *Questioning* is a disposition that understands the restlessness that comes from constantly seeking to improve, with the humility to understand that this is challenging and means taking others with you on the journey. To question is to eschew reliance on others' certainties and ready-made solutions. How else are we to find creative ways forward? *Inventiveness* means having the capacity to approach challenges with new ideas rather than age-old approaches. This means resisting compliance with imposed answers. To teach and to lead in this manner requires the disposition of *persistence*. It requires pursuing what feels right with the professional courage to make changes that reject simple solutions in favour of ethical, values-led action.

As our schools begin the journey of recovery caused by the impact of contemporary world crises, we need to ensure that we offer *emotional stability* to our communities. Within an emotionally stable environment it is OK to take risks, to try new ideas, to explore, to play, sometimes to fail. The opposite of this, of course, is for school to be somewhere that makes you feel labelled, guilty, in need of remediation. I think our teachers need to be the holders of that safe space that school represents for many children, our colleagues, our parents and carers as we rebuild our lives for the future. We need a much stronger focus on reducing inequity as opposed to 'catching up'. Our schools should be at the centre of rediscovering joyful community through sport, the arts, dance, drama, an orchestral enactment of all that binds us.

The sixth characteristic that builds learning capacity is *generosity*. Teachers should be encouraged to welcome and celebrate difference as a strength. We need to resist the push towards desire for uniformity and deficit thinking, instead moving towards a joyful clamour for greater diversity. Our profession should demonstrate *empathy* in all that we do. At the Chartered College of Teaching we celebrate collegiality and collaboration. We constantly strive to help our profession through building mutual supportiveness. When we work in this manner, we reduce the tendency towards fear, defensiveness and blame.

Creativity comes in many forms. This book celebrates diverse, ambitious thinking about the role of education, our teachers and schools in the future. Let us work together to help teachers on this journey as we move beyond simply doing what we are told to do, towards doing the things that make our hearts sing. And together our chorus will sing louder.

An example of this principled creative approach is described in the vignette that follows:

> We noticed that one of our Year Six boys, Andrew, was increasingly unhappy and angry. As we began to discover where this anxiety came from, it became clear that he was missing his father who was at home in bed each day with a long-term illness. In talking with the family we decided to offer Dad a paid role as lunchtime playleader, coming in to school each day to eat lunch with his son and to provide companionship throughout the lunch hour. This small action made a huge difference to both Andrew and to his father both in the immediate short term but also in the longer term too.
>
> This response to a challenging situation comes from the capacity to look beyond the immediate deficit issue of poor student behaviour and difficulty of supervision during playtimes, towards a creative approach with positive long-lasting impact.

References

Hart, S., Drummond, M. J., Dixon, A., & McIntyre, D. (2004). *Learning without limits*. Maidenhead: Open University Press.

Peacock, A. (2016). *Assessment for learning without limits*. London: McGraw-Hill International.

Swann, M., Peacock, A., Hart, S., & Drummond, M. J. (2012). *Creating learning without limits*. Maidenhead: McGraw-Hill International.

Index

achievement 5, 11, 33–34, 114, 124–125, 127, 137–135, 143
aesthetics 4, 146
affect: affective 71, 84, 107–111, 114–115, 117–120, 148, 157
Ahmed, S. 40, 68–69
Alexander, R. 43, 91, 97–98, 211–213, 218
Amabile, T. 79
amazement 7
animating/ animacies/ animated 26, 63, 65–73, 190
Aristotle 204–211
artificial intelligence 77
arts 8, 19, 46, 52, 63–64, 73, 96, 146–151, 156–157, 159, 171–172, 182, 204, 223
assessment 10, 84, 127, 134
attainment 30, 171
attitudes 55, 64, 132, 143
autoethnography 110
autonomy: children 12, 99, 137; professional 10, 102–103

Baca, F. vii, viii
Barad, K. 105, 184, 198, 200, 109–110
beauty 151–152, 204
becoming 5, 7, 12, 14, 23, 52, 64–65, 70, 76–77, 80–81, 97, 114, 125, 147, 156–157, 160, 204, 207, 211, 214
Beghetto, R. A. 11
behaviour: behaviour management 172; children in classroom 104
Bellfield, T. 26–44
belonging 116, 125, 150, 188
Biddulph, J. 26, 49–52

Biesta, G. 147, 157, 218
bodily-spatial approach 42; spatial/bodily practice 57–67
Bolman, L. G. 136, 165, 173, 178
Bossert, S. T. 166
Braidotti, R. 79
Brownell, C. S. 8, 123–145
Burnard, P. 160

Cambridge Curiosity and Imagination (CCI) 63, 101–110
Cambridge Primary Review 15, 76
Cameron, J. 49
care: affective 117; caring relationships 53, 117, 129, 153; relationship building 6, 38, 130
change 3–12, 18–20, 22–23, 39–41, 48, 55, 59, 70–71, 79–80, 91–95, 99–105, 109, 112–113, 119, 125, 127, 131, 136, 140, 148, 163, 165, 183, 185, 211, 214
Chappell, K. 37, 78, 85
Chartered College of Teaching 209, 221–223
child-led curriculum 100
children: agency 65, 72, 120; empowerment 213; global citizens 3; imagination 68, 71, 95, 104, 147, 159; independent 70; learning 5, 23, 70, 93, 147, 171, 191; relationships (with teachers) 26, 69; voice 12, 98, 99
Children, Technology and Play (CTAP) 182, 184
circle: circle time 58; practices of care 143; space 58
Cixous, H. 95–96
Clapp, E.P. 32
classroom: environment 40, 117; management 12; outdoor 117; space 134

Index

Clegg, J. 34
co-design 5, 27, 95, 98, 100; approaches 23, 100
cognitive-psychological approach 42
Coldron, J. 166, 168
collaboration/ collaborate/ collaborative 5, 8–9, 12, 16, 18, 20, 26–27, 38, 62, 68–69, 76–78, 80–84, 86, 96–97, 99–100, 102–103, 124, 127, 130, 134–135, 138, 142, 147, 170, 182, 188, 198–201, 207–209, 211, 221, 223
collective 13, 22, 37, 39, 62, 79–81, 118–119, 123, 127, 132, 134–135, 173–174, 203–204, 207–215, 221–222
Colucci-Gray, L. 160
communal 5, 14, 58, 60, 82, 214
concept: curriculum 98; learning 134, 137; local 13–14, 97, 118; stakeholders 19
conservation area 68
context-dependent knowledge 142, 206
Continuing Professional Development (CPD) 175
Cook, P.J. 107–122
Courtney, S. J. 166
COVID-19: laptops and internet access 168; Reconnection to Recovery and Resilience Programme 174
Craft, A. 27, 28, 31
Crawford, Matthew 171, 173, 177
Crawford, Megan 166, 168, 208
creative: agency 46, 65; agent 8; curriculum assessment 19; ecologies 8, 10–13, 19–22, 77–83, 85, 118, 131–132; encounters 81, 204; industries 81; leadership 104, 165–167, 171–172, 178–179, 208; learning 104, 108, 124; mentorship 18; pedagogies 77, 107; practitioners 32, 112, 171; skills 11, 82–84, 113; thinking 11, 71, 77, 85, 179
creativities activate 209–210; aesthetics-imagination 4; child-centred 6; curriculum 6, 93–103; curricula 141–143; distributed 8; diverse 5–13, 19–20, 22–23, 92, 94, 132, 159–160, 163, 165, 178, 183; diversifying 26; ecologies 43; ecologies model 20, 77, 78, 81–83, 131–132; educational contexts 78–83; education approaches 76; embodied 108–110; everyday 6, 8, 12–18, 50–51; gardening 115–117; group 8, 32; imagination and curiosity 214; individual 8; intercultural 6, 8; intercultural creative learning 59; interdisciplinary 6, 92; leadership 6; learning 46–47; linguistic intelligence 5–6; mathematical education 5–6, 113–115;

multiple 4–6, 10, 24, 77, 133–134, 143, 147, 160; musical intelligence 5; participatory 8, 20, 44; pedagogical approaches 118; pluralisation 6; problem solving 104; relational ecologies 83–85; spatial 6, 27, 34–39, 61–70; STEAM garden 30; teacher professionalism 209; transdisciplinary 12, 18, 23, 29
creative partnerships 96, 98
creative pedagogue 107, 111, 120
creative pedagogy 110, 118
creativity 4–8, 10–13, 18–21, 23–24, 27, 38–39, 41–43, 46–47, 76–85, 91–93, 100–102, 108, 110, 112, 128, 131–132, 147, 149, 150, 155, 159, 166–170, 179, 209, 221, 223
Cremin, T. 37
Cruddas, L. 170
cultural: cultural capitalism 172; diversity 47, 57; participation 131; value 57
cultural capital 97, 105, 172–173
culture: classroom 110; organisational 93, 101, 103; school 131, 170
curriculum: assessment 10, 19; children's needs 8; change 136–146; community 98; creative 19, 27–28, 93–103; curriculum-led internal decoration, corridors 54–60; design 93–94; English National 65; Finnish National 124, 126, 129–133; hidden 18, 52, 64; interdisciplinary 120; local 130; mathematics 194–195; national 77, 82; opportunities 9; pedagogical programme 127; primary design 207; primary education 45, 82, 92, 107, 115; Relationships and Sex Education and Health Education 67; South African National 183, 191; subjects 150

dance 146, 223
data-logging 125
Deal, T. E. 165, 173, 178
Deleuze, G. 117, 119
design and technology 152
desk-based activities 72
Dewey, J. 109, 117, 148, 154, 155, 220
Dezutter, S. 8
dialogue 20, 48, 51, 107, 114–115, 131, 137, 146, 165, 183–184, 196, 208, 211, 214
digital: devices 185–189; diffracting 184; fabrication technology 142–143; fitness tracking devices 125; tablet device 139
discourse 4, 7, 20, 48, 57, 77, 91, 146, 148, 211, 214

225

Index

diversifying 4, 7; animation 65–66, 73; camera 185; photographs 43, 53, 68
drama 223
drawing 53, 146, 149, 190, 204
Dyer, E. 37

early years 98, 176, 183–185, 190, 199
earth 45, 115, 148, 154, 159–160
ecology/ ecologies: creative ecology 8, 10–12, 13, 19–22, 77–83, 85, 118, 131; ecosystem 78, 85; of practice 10, 77, 83
education 3–13, 18–24, 26–27, 36–37, 41, 45–48, 50–51, 59, 64, 73, 76–85, 91–92, 94–95, 97–98, 100, 102–103, 108–109, 113, 115, 124–125, 129–133, 143–144, 146–149, 151, 154, 156–158, 165–166, 170–171, 174, 183, 188, 190, 204, 206, 208–209, 211–215, 221, 223
edupreneur/edupreneurship 2014 113, 134–135, 144
Eldem, F. 14
elementary education *see* primary education
Embark community 174
Embark Federation 171, 174, 176
embodied cognition 209
embodied dialogue 48
embodied/ embodiment 10, 23, 48, 65–66, 68–69, 71–72, 76, 82, 84, 105, 107–110, 117, 119, 120, 137, 141, 142, 156, 158, 203, 210, 211, 214
embodied literacy 156
emotional: enjoyment 33, 77; development 126; disposition 222; engagement 154; social 174, 175; wellbeing 131
empowerment 47, 213
engagement 5, 11, 28, 42, 52, 65–69, 71, 73, 83, 93, 99–100, 103, 129, 149, 151, 154, 157, 159, 188, 206
engineering 153–156
enjoyment 33, 77
enquiry 13, 80, 85, 191, 196, 198, 201, 207
environment/ environmental 6, 10, 12–14, 18–21, 27, 29, 34, 40, 42–43, 71, 76–77, 79, 81, 83–85, 92–93, 102–103, 108, 112, 117, 123–125, 127, 131, 133–135, 137, 143–144, 150–152, 154, 158–160, 165, 170, 199, 212, 222
environment/ environmental/ environmental education activities 157
Erskine, B. 30
ethics: ethics and wisdom 214; relational 53, 80, 81, 83, 85

European Key Competency 142
evaluation/ evaluative framework 42, 102
evidence based 206
excitement 116, 117
Experience Workshop activities 142
exploration 13, 20, 47, 48, 71, 93, 149, 156, 180, 204

Fenyvesi, K. 8, 22, 102, 132, 141, 209, 210
financial literacy 113
Finland/ Finnish Education 123, 124, 129–131, 133, 135, 140–141, 144
Finnish National Core Curriculum for Basic Education (FNCC) 124, 126, 129–133
fixed mindset 11
flow 150, 178, 209
Flutter, J. 22, 48, 98, 105, 207, 218
freedom: to make mistakes and learn 68; material engagement 69; memory-making ideas 73; of movement 66; personal 166; policy landscapes 167–168
Freire, P. 3, 183
Fuji Kindergarten 37
Fulbridge Academy 27; corridors 27–32; learning streets 35–38; use of decorated corridors 39–41; working with/within existing buildings 38–39; working with/within limitations 34–35
future-makers 143–144; future-making 38–40

Gallagher, S. 154
gardens: creativity 6, 159–160; fairy 155; Indigenous 115–117; large-scale farming 149; learning 148; logos 156; miniature 149; oriented approach 149; play 198; school 148–149, 219–225; secret 68, 71; shoebox 155–156; space-making 216; STEAM 147, 149–150
Gardner, H. 5, 27, 28
GeoGebra community 17
geography 28, 116
Gerver, R. 22, 101, 104
global: citizenship 3; civic interests 91; community 6, 12, 48, 96; crises 3, 6; wellbeing 83, 124, 133
Gray, D. 148–150, 154, 158
Greene, M. 9
growth mindset 11
Gunter, H. M. 166

Habermas, J. 167
habit 50, 107–109, 111, 115, 118–120

hand-crafted games 157
Haraway, D. 105–110
Hargreaves, E. 92
Harris, A. 19–20, 27, 32, 118, 131
Harwood, V. 117
Hermida, Y. 32
Hickey-Moody, A. 102, 107–109, 117–120
holistic 20, 22, 23, 64, 66, 77, 82, 104,
   123–124, 126–130, 132–134, 136–143, 148,
   153, 156, 160
hope 3, 5–6, 8–10, 12, 18, 23, 34, 45, 49, 56,
   58, 80, 85, 99, 176, 191, 211, 215, 221

identity/ies: embodied dialogue 48; relational
   66; subjectivities 161
imagination: children 71, 104, 147, 159;
   creativity-aesthetics 4; educational 130;
   embodied 71
Indigenous gardening 115–117
Indigenous students 117
Ingold, T. 147, 149, 160, 190, 198, 218
innovation 4, 13–14, 24, 77, 79, 84, 91–93, 95,
   98–103, 105, 108, 124–125, 132–134, 136,
   140, 143, 147, 165, 213
inquiry-based learning 142
institutional values 208
intelligences: artificial 77; linguistic 5; logical-
   mathematical 5; musical 5
interaction 36, 46, 55, 95, 115, 131, 154–156,
   158, 213
intra-action 67, 79, 85, 148, 158, 185, 189, 198, 201
intercultural 77; ism 47–49
intercultural creative learning 52–54; matters
   80–82; professional reflections 86
interdisciplinary 5–7, 21–22, 92, 108, 120
Ivinson, G. 147, 157

Jones, S. 166
journaling 49
judgements 98, 101, 161, 207, 211, 221

knowledge/ knowing/ knowledge transfer 114

Lavicza, Z. 102, 123–145, 209, 210
Law, J. 34
leadership: civic 170; creativity 6, 104,
   165–167; educational 130, 132, 137, 166;
   school 10–11, 22, 26, 62, 72, 76, 81, 95;
   system 170; theory and practice 166; training
   and development 101; trust 170, 173, 177
learning: children's 5, 23, 54, 70, 93, 126, 147,
   157, 171, 191, 212; classroom layouts 41;

designed spaces 59–69; enlivening 100–110;
   learning environments 39; play-based 100;
   professional 12–13, 19–20, 46, 51–52, 102,
   118, 221
Lee, E. 22, 62, 65, 72, 205
LEGO robotics 111
lifeworld 167–168, 170–171, 173, 178, 180
Lindgren, R. 154
linguistic intelligences 5
literacies 27, 30
logical-mathematical intelligences 5
Loughrey, M. 3–25, 91–106

Martin, J. 166
material: material-discursive 184, 188;
   materiality 107
mathematics 5–6, 8, 107, 113, 115, 141, 146,
   156, 158, 159, 190, 193–195
matter 3, 5, 8, 23, 26, 40, 45, 46, 47, 50, 52,
   57, 60, 69, 77, 99, 104, 140, 149–151,
   158–159, 171, 180, 183–185, 191, 193, 214
Maxwell, B. 168
Mayfield Primary School 102–112
McLaughlin, T. 32–33, 59–60
mental: health 174; mental transformation 127;
   mental wellbeing 129–133, 135
Merleau-Ponty, M. 57–58
Meyerson, D. 166
Miller, M. 149, 152, 158
moral purpose 95, 222
Moule, L. 49
Mountview Academy of Theatre Arts 172
motivation/al 5, 12, 27, 93, 102, 123, 127, 132,
   135, 137, 141, 221
Muller, M. 147, 152
multi-academy trust (MAT) 100, 165, 172; role
   of 168–170
multiculturalism 47
multidisciplinary approaches 140

National Advisory Committee on Creative and
   Cultural Education (NACCCE) 91, 138–139
National Curriculum 52, 66, 91
National Foundation for Education Research
   (NFER) 92
National Literacy Trust 33–34
Nature, natural resources 5, 11, 19–20, 23,
   32–33, 48, 77, 79–84, 92, 101, 108, 118,
   127, 141, 148, 149, 153–154, 210, 218
new materialism 63, 66, 67
non-human: actors 82; non-human
   collaborators 76, 78, 80

Ogawa, R. T. 166
One Seed Forward 170
oracy 34, 42, 43
Organisation for Economic Co-operation and Development (OECD)
outdoor learning 63
Outhwaite, D. 165–180

participatory action research 84
participatory approach 23
participatory design practices 11
partnerships 4, 19–21, 60, 78, 81, 83–84, 96, 98–99, 102, 116, 131, 150, 156, 209
Peacock, A. 209, 222
pedagogy: approaches 6; creative 22, 107–120; documentation 188; practice, in Finland 123–144; strategies 210; values pedagogy 126, 130
Peers, J. 183
perform: performative 5–7, 24, 147
personal artistry 165, 166, 171, 173, 178, 179
personal values 208
Peters, T. 34
phronesis 6, 21–22, 204, 207–215
physical: activity 127; environments 123–130; physical-mental balance 127; physical wellbeing 131, 135
Pickup, Austin 210
planning 38, 68, 72, 96, 110–112, 117, 148
play-based: playful learning 12; activities 120; play-based curriculum 100
play 20, 36, 57, 83, 131, 198
playful 72, 80
playing 51, 68, 146, 198, 210
Portelli, N. 107, 111
possibility thinking 8, 22, 46, 58, 218, 221
posthuman/ posthumanism/ posthumanist/ posthumanising creativity/ the posthuman turn 6, 73, 84, 183
posthumanism 79; creative ecologies 77–78; lens 102–120; partnerships 81; perspective 109–111; policies 81–82; posthumanising 121–125; posthumanising wheel (Kerry Chappell) 78; posthumanists 113–116; posthumanist theory 122; process 80
practice 4–6, 8, 10, 13–14, 20, 32, 46, 48–49, 55, 58–60, 62, 67, 69–74, 84, 92–96, 100, 107–108, 110, 113, 117, 119, 124–125, 131–132, 136, 149–151, 154, 160, 166, 183–185, 187, 190, 204, 206–214
primary education 33, 35, 42, 45; partnerships 99–109; school corridors 51–61; school design 36–37; schoolscape approach 51
programmatic lessons 38
products and novelty 218
products-processes policies-partnership 124–132
professional development 20, 42, 43, 96, 124, 176, 209, 211
professionalism: personal-professional reflections 52–53; the posthuman child 18; primary educators 3
professional learning 12–13, 19–20, 46, 51–52, 102, 118, 221
professional practice 13, 48
project-based learning 120; project 127
prosociality 197
pupil voice 98–99, 209

quality: children's learning 5, 23; of education 170
questioning 26, 41, 52, 98, 125, 182, 222

real-life-based approaches 140
Reconnection to Recovery and Resilience Programme 174
relationality 110; between children and adults 111; relational materialist approach 158
Relationships and Sex Education and Health Education 64, 67
research 3–5, 7–12, 14, 18–23, 27, 33, 42, 45–46, 48–49, 52–55, 57, 77, 83–84, 92, 99–100, 110, 125, 133, 141, 154, 166, 180, 184–185, 187–189, 204, 206–207, 209, 211–214
researcher: making meaning 65; reimagining 10; researcher's reflexivity 48
researching, unlocking in practice 45–51, 116–120; creative learning 87–90; ethnic minority immigrant children 88–90; interculturality 95; journal practice 83; project-based approaches 120; real-life-based approaches 140; reflexive approaches 82; research commitments 55, 83, 141; researching teacher position 82
resources 23, 35, 37–38, 40, 68, 71, 73, 84–85, 104, 105, 110, 115, 116, 119, 168, 177, 194, 195, 206
response-ability 11, 48
rethinking 3, 7, 41, 49
risks: agency 46; empowerment 47; play 46; possibilities 46, 58, 103; risk immersion 67, 80; risk taking 9–10, 58, 77, 102–104, 124, 143

Index

rivers of experience 49–52
Robertson, L. 146–162
role models 117
Roth, W. M. 155
Roulstone, S. 34
Rudduck, J. 98
Rush, R. 34

Sawyer, K. 2003 8, 77
school: ethos 43; primary 6, 12, 20, 27, 37, 57, 62, 76, 81, 97, 123, 129, 133, 150, 166–168, 170, 172, 178, 182, 208; school-based research projects 209; school change 19, 99; secondary 82–83, 95, 157, 168, 172, 174, 209
schools, gains for 98, 126, 169
science 6, 28, 30, 73, 96, 115, 148, 150–151, 214; engineering, arts and mathematics (STEAM) 6, 13, 24, 77, 124, 132–133, 142–143, 146–150, 155, 159–160
scientific literacy 156
scientist 97, 156–157
Senior Leadership Team (SLT) 27
Sergiovanni, T. J. 167, 170, 178
shared understanding/experiences 69, 108
Silver Dragon World 39
singing 51–52, 84, 190, 198, 204
Simkins, T. 166, 168
Sinnemaki, J. 102, 123–137, 141–144, 209–210
small group projects 36, 116, 185
social skills: social media 7, 135; social networking 110
soil science 150–152
South African National Curriculum 183, 191
space: classroom 128, 134, 195; corridors 30, 33, 35–36, 38; gardens 82; outdoors 73, 135; spaces 30, 34, 36–39, 82, 135
Spirals of Enquiry 70
sports equipment 127
STEAM: activities 143; garden creativity 6; hybrid construct 217–220; projects 141–143
STEM 13, 146, 149–151, 156–157, 159
Stepney, S. 62–74
storytelling 45
students 14–15, 26–28, 32–33, 37–39, 41–43, 73, 76, 80, 82, 84–85, 97, 107–120, 132–137, 139–144, 165, 167, 170, 183, 191
study reform project 38
subject-based approaches 140
sustainability 18, 62, 77, 78, 131, 149

systems: activity 10, 11, 20; evaluative 102; holistic 20, 22, 153; knowledge 102; school 109, 167; system leadership 170
systems world 167
Szabo, T.P. 8, 13, 18, 24, 132
Szynalska McAleavey, K. 26–44

Taguchi, Lenz 158
Tang, S. 171
Taylor, Frederick Winslow 101
teachers 5–6, 8, 10–14, 16, 18, 20, 33–34, 38, 41–42, 45, 48, 51, 56, 58, 59, 62–64, 70, 72–73, 76, 81–82, 84–85, 95, 108–112, 115–116, 119, 120, 126, 130–131, 133–134, 136–137, 139–141, 167, 170, 171, 180, 183, 184, 191, 207–210, 221–223
teaching: teacher pathways 39; values pedagogy 126, 130; *see also* pedagogy
teaching artist 130
team 6, 27, 34, 72, 95–97, 101, 107, 140, 169, 170, 173–174, 176–178, 212, 222
technology 96, 111, 123, 127, 133, 135, 137–140, 152, 183–188, 197, 214; design and 124, 142, 146, 157; digital 142
temporality 112–115; time 112, 113
testing/assessment 24, 84, 85, 155, 166
themes 29, 39, 45, 46, 51, 92, 198
thinking 54, 73, 146–148, 150–153, 155–157, 159; creative 11, 71, 77, 85; critical 77, 82, 84, 147; divergent 182; possibility 8, 22, 46, 58, 218, 221; scientific 73, 147–148, 153; skill 147, 150, 153, 157
transdisciplinary/ity: creativity 12
trust 63, 73, 100, 102–103, 112, 128–129, 130, 169–174, 176–177, 208, 222

unexpected 9, 184
unique: distinct 114; experiences 54, 114, 152;
unlock: unlocking research 3, 7, 9–10, 18, 22–23, 42, 46, 60, 74, 86, 92, 100, 105, 120, 143, 160, 179, 201, 215

values: pedagogy 126, 130; professional 209;
valuing 57, 60
vision 9, 13, 30, 37, 93, 134, 143–144, 172, 177, 211, 213, 221
visual art 71, 146
voice: agency 22, 46; autonomy of voice 12, 99; engaged citizens 12, 57; relationship-building 12, 33

Index

Wahl, D. C. 156
water cycle 68, 151
wellbeing 198–203
'what if' thinking 200
whole-school: approaches 20, 82
Winstanley, J. 49
wise:

Woodward, N. 182–202, 211
writing 30, 42, 49–50, 62, 68, 69, 189–190, 204, 214

Young Design programmes 39
Young, M. 147
YouTube 24

For Product Safety Concerns and Information please contact our EU representative GPSR@taylorandfrancis.com
Taylor & Francis Verlag GmbH, Kaufingerstraße 24, 80331 München, Germany